Ideology, Ethics and Policy Development in Public Service Interpreting and Translation

I0124409

TRANSLATION, INTERPRETING AND SOCIAL JUSTICE IN A GLOBALISED WORLD

Series Editor: Philipp Angermeyer, *York University, Canada* and Katrijn Maryns, *Ghent University, Belgium*

Translation, Interpreting and Social Justice in a Globalised World is an international series that welcomes authored monographs and edited collections that address translation and interpreting in settings of diversity, globalisation, migration and asylum. Books in the series will discuss how translation and interpreting practices (or their absence) may advance or hinder social justice. A key aim of the series is to encourage dialogue between scholars and professionals working in translation and interpreting studies and those working in other linguistic disciplines, such as sociolinguistics and linguistic anthropology. Books in the series will cover both translation and interpreting services provided by state and corporate entities, as well as informal, community-based translation and interpreting. We welcome proposals covering any combinations of languages (including Sign languages) and from a wide variety of geographical contexts. A guiding aim of the series is to empower those who may be disadvantaged by their lack of access to majority or official languages, and as such proposals which bridge the gap between theoretical and practical domains are particularly encouraged.

Topics which may be addressed by books in the series include (but are not limited to):

- Medical settings (including care settings and provision of public health information)
- Legal settings (law enforcement, court, prison, counselling)
- Educational settings (including community-based education)
- Asylum and migration procedures
- Access to democracy and citizenship
- Interactions with business and private-sector institutions
- The media and minority-language broadcasting and publishing
- Ethical and political considerations in translation
- Cultural translation
- Translation and language rights
- Translation and intercultural relations and conflict

Intended readership: academic and professional.

Full details of all the books in this series and of all our other publications can be found on http://www.multilingual-matters.com, or by writing to Multilingual Matters, St Nicholas House, 31-34 High Street, Bristol BS1 2AW, UK.

TRANSLATION, INTERPRETING AND SOCIAL JUSTICE IN A
GLOBALISED WORLD: 1

Ideology, Ethics and Policy Development in Public Service Interpreting and Translation

Edited by
Carmen Valero-Garcés and Rebecca Tipton

MULTILINGUAL MATTERS
Bristol • Blue Ridge Summit

Library of Congress Cataloging in Publication Data
A catalog record for this book is available from the Library of Congress.
Names: Valero Garcés, Carmen, editor. | Tipton, Rebecca, editor.
Title: Ideology, Ethics and Policy Development in Public Service Interpreting
   and Translation/Edited by Carmen Valero-Garcés and Rebecca Tipton.
Description: Bristol: Multilingual Matters, [2017] | Series:
   Translation, Interpreting and Social Justice in a Globalised World: 1 |
   Includes bibliographical references and index.
Identifiers: LCCN 2016046327| ISBN 9781783097524 (hbk) |
   ISBN 9781783097517 (pbk) | ISBN 9781783097531 (Pdf) |
   ISBN 9781783097548 (Epub) | ISBN 9781783097555 (Kindle)
Subjects: LCSH: Public service interpreting. | Translating and
   interpreting–History. | Ideology–Political aspects.
Classification: LCC P306.947 .I34 2017 | DDC 418/.02–dc23 LC record available at
   https://lccn.loc.gov/2016046327

British Library Cataloguing in Publication Data
A catalogue entry for this book is available from the British Library.

ISBN-13: 978-1-78309-752-4 (hbk)
ISBN-13: 978-1-78309-751-7 (pbk)

Multilingual Matters
UK: St Nicholas House, 31-34 High Street, Bristol BS1 2AW, UK.
USA: NBN, Blue Ridge Summit, PA, USA.

Website: www.multilingual-matters.com
Twitter: Multi_Ling_Mat
Facebook: https://www.facebook.com/multilingualmatters
Blog: www.channelviewpublications.wordpress.com

Copyright © 2017 Carmen Valero-Garcés, Rebecca Tipton and the authors of individual chapters.

All rights reserved. No part of this work may be reproduced in any form or by any means without permission in writing from the publisher.

The policy of Multilingual Matters/Channel View Publications is to use papers that are natural, renewable and recyclable products, made from wood grown in sustainable forests. In the manufacturing process of our books, and to further support our policy, preference is given to printers that have FSC and PEFC Chain of Custody certification. The FSC and/or PEFC logos will appear on those books where full certification has been granted to the printer concerned.

Typeset by Deanta Global Publishing Services Limited.

Contents

Part 2: Experiences From the Field

Tables and Figures

Abbreviations

APCI	Association of Police and Court Interpreters
CIoL	Chartered Institute of Linguists
DIT	Defining Issues Test
LIT	Legal Interpreting and Translation
NICHD	National Institute of Child Health and Human Development
NRPSI	National Register of Public Service Interpreters
PI4J	Professional Interpreters for Justice
PSIT	Public Service Interpreting and Translation
TIC	Trauma-informed Care
TII	Trauma-informed Interpreting
TIS	Trauma-informed Services
UNCRC	United Nations Convention on the Rights of the Child
VCI	Videoconference Interpreting
VT	Vicarious Trauma

Contributors

Katalin Balogh is currently coordinator of the Training for Legal Interpreters and Translators at the KU Leuven Campus, Antwerp. She is responsible for lectures on interpreting techniques within this training programme and teaches intercultural communication to MA students. She has been involved in several EU projects such as the EULITA project and TRAFUT, the three AVIDICUS projects 1, 2 and 3. She has also completed the ImPLI-project for DG Justice together with Heidi Salaets, and they were both coordinators of the Co-Minor-IN/QUEST project and the TraiLLD project.

Marjory Bancroft holds a BA and an MA in French linguistics from Laval University, Québec, and advanced language certificates from universities in Spain, Germany and Jordan. She has taught English and French as second languages and translation for two universities in Quebec and Jordan and other educational institutions. She directs the only national US training agency for community interpreting. Ms Bancroft sits on international committees and was the world project leader for an International Organisation of Standardisation (ISO) international interpreting standard. She is the lead author of several training manuals and textbooks for community interpreters.

María Brander de la Iglesia is Canadian and Spanish and has been a full-time lecturer in Interpreting at the University of Salamanca since 2006, where she teaches simultaneous interpreting from and into Spanish and English, as well as consecutive and simultaneous interpreting from French into Spanish. She has also been a freelance translator and interpreter since 2002 and has worked for the private market, international organisations and charities. Her scholarly articles focus on ethics in translation and interpreting, as well as didactics and new technologies in interpreting studies. She has taught on different undergraduate and postgraduate programmes in languages, translation and interpreting at the University of Granada, Heriot-Watt University and the University of Franche-Comté, among others. She earned her MSc in Research in Translation and Interpreting at the University of Granada and is currently writing her doctoral thesis at the University of Salamanca.

Ingrid Cáceres-Würsig, MA Translation, PhD Modern Philology, focuses on the history of translation and interpreting and on the cultural relations between Spanish- and German-speaking countries. She is a senior lecturer at the Universidad de Alcalá, where she teaches Translation and German language. She is member of the research groups FITISPos® (Universidad de Alcalá) and OLE-4 (Universidad de Oviedo).

Jérôme Devaux. After graduating with an MA in Translation and Interpreting, Jérôme worked for several years as a freelance translator and conference/public service interpreter. He is now a senior tutor in French and Translation and Interpreting Studies and a PhD candidate at the University of Salford. His research interests lie within the field of public service interpreting, and more particularly in the use of new technologies in interpreter-mediated court hearings.

Paola Gentile holds a PhD in Interpreting and Translation Studies from the University of Trieste. Her PhD research project investigated the professional status of conference and public service interpreters with two questionnaires, which obtained 1693 responses worldwide. Her research interests include the status of the interpreting profession and the professionalisation of conference and public service interpreting, the interpreter's social role, language rights and interpreting as a human right.

M. Rosario Martín Ruano (GIR Traducción, Ideología, Cultura) teaches translation at the University of Salamanca. Her research interests include legal and institutional translation, translation theory, gender studies and postcolonial critique. She has published several books, anthologies and essays on these issues, including *El (des)orden de los discursos: la traducción de lo políticamente correcto* (2003, Granada: Comares), *Translation and the Construction of Identity* (2005, Seoul: IATIS, co-edited with Juliane House and Nicole Baumgarten) and *Traducción, política(s), conflictos: legados y retos para la era del multiculturalismo* (2013, Granada: Comares, co-edited with María Carmen África Vidal Claramonte). She is also a practising translator.

Heidi Salaets currently is the head of the Interpreting Studies Research Group at the Faculty of Arts of KU Leuven, Antwerp Campus where she also trains interpreters (I-NL). She is also an assessor for the certification exams for community interpreters in Flanders. Regarding research, Heidi Salaets has completed several European DG Justice projects with Katalin

Balogh. Current fields of research are quality and assessment in interpreting (e.g. admission tests and final evaluation), LIT (Legal Interpreting and Translation), community interpreting and new technologies in interpreting.

Rebecca Tipton is a lecturer in Interpreting and Translation Studies at the University of Manchester, Centre for Translation and Intercultural Studies. Her research interests concern the history of public service interpreting in Britain and interpreting and translation policy development in the third sector. She is currently involved in a project on interpreted interviews with victims of domestic violence in the police and the third sector. She is the co-author (with Olgierda Furmanek, Wake Forest University) of *Dialogue Interpreting: A Guide to Interpreting in Public Services and the Community*, published with Routledge in 2016.

Małgorzata Tryuk is Professor of Translation and Interpreting Studies at the Institute of Applied Linguistics, University of Warsaw. She is the Head of the Department of Interpreting Studies and Audiovisual Translation and the local coordinator of the European Masters in Conference Interpreting (EMCI). She has published papers and books on conference and community interpreting, among others, *L'interprétation communautaire. Des norms et des rôles dans l'interprétation* (2004, Warszawa: Wyd. TEPIS) and *On Ethics and Interpreters* (2015, Frankfurt a/Main: Peter Lang GmbH).

Carmen Valero-Garcés is a lecturer in Translation and Interpreting as well as the Director of the postgraduate programme on Public Service Interpreting and Translation at the University of Alcalá in Madrid, Spain. She is also responsible for the Research Group FITISPos® and the online peer-reviewed journal *FITISPos International Journal*. Her main interests are training and research in public service interpreting and translation and exploring communication between languages in cultures.

Introduction

The scale of population displacement as a result of violent conflict and social instability particularly, but not exclusively, in the Middle East, Africa and Latin America at the time of writing in 2016 raises new and urgent questions about language support policy in societies directly involved in receiving displaced persons, whether on a temporary or long-term basis. At the same time, social conflict that emerges as an unintended consequence of the political ambitions of transnational entities like the European Union also raises questions with regard to the way in which individuals with limited language proficiency navigate decision-making and handle potential social breakdown after moving to a new geonational context.

These situations focus attention on the type of policy approach best suited to addressing such multifarious need, and the extent to which it is reasonable or even desirable to establish transnational principles (as distinct from standards) for the organisation and delivery of professional language support services. Efforts to establish supranational instruments, for example in the context of the European Union (e.g. EU Directive 2010/64/EU on the right to interpretation and translation in criminal proceedings), constitute an attempt to transcend national policymaking; however, substantive differences in political structures, role profiling and resources are a barrier to implementation in some cases (see Salaets & Balogh, this volume).

This collection brings together new perspectives on the struggle to establish coherent responses to ethical imperatives that inhere in relations between states and limited language proficiency speakers, regardless of their residency status. The themes of social inclusion, political participation, recognition, equality, distributive, restorative and procedural justice, health and well-being may be cited as examples of such imperatives and call into question both the capacity and willingness of public policymakers to include interpreting and translation on the policy agenda (see Sasso & Malli, 2014; Martín Ruano, this volume). A key point of departure for the collection is the acknowledgement of the limited impact to date that profession- and disciplinary-led discourses on professionalisation have had on policymakers. The assumption that such discourses would help to establish and legitimate service provision has not been realised, at least to the extent anticipated in the past two decades, prompting the need to recalibrate the terms of debate and seek new ways to engage with relevant stakeholders.

Efforts to address these issues are already in process, as seen through increasing emphasis on evidence-based policymaking. However, this highly rational, science-based approach needs to be critically appraised in relation to the wider social and political contexts in which it is embedded. Discourses on evidence-based policymaking, for instance, have been increasingly criticised for their inherent normativity and tendency to sideline values in political debate (e.g. Du Toit, 2012). Other more abstract ideological influences impact on policy and provision and therefore need to be investigated if the social basis for and consequences of policy development are to be fully understood. Even in cases where the evidence base is robust, the state and/or institutional response may still fall short in terms of quality and outcomes for service users. The fact that this is already a reality in some countries highlights the need for scholars to broaden the range of paradigms used to evaluate policy recommendations and decision-making processes.

In addition to issues of policy, the collection also provides a timely evaluation of the nature and degree of convergence between recent theorisations of interpreter and translator ethics in the academe and practice in the field. There is evidence to suggest that, despite greater emphasis on teleological over deontological frameworks in Interpreting Studies (see Baker & Maier, 2011), deontological codes continue to exert strong influence on practitioners' rationalisation processes during interaction (see Devaux, this volume). This serves as a call to educators to revisit approaches to the teaching and learning of ethics and the theoretical frameworks used to structure such approaches (see Brander de la Iglesia, this volume). Furthermore, new empirical evidence from the field also makes it possible to shed light on the relative weight given to what Rudvin (2007) describes as rules and notions of success, and relationships and well-being in settings such as detention facilities and asylum hearings (see Valero-Garcés; Tryuk, this volume, respectively).

Ideology, which is the third area of focus in this collection, has long been debated in translation studies through an emphasis on language and power relations, and on the agency of the translator in manipulating and mediating these relations (Fawcett & Munday, 2009). In interpreting studies more specifically, an emerging area of focus concerns the analysis of the product of simultaneous conference interpreting through the lens of ideology and its various discursive instantiations in studies that draw extensively on critical discourse analysis (e.g. Beaton-Thome, 2007). Research in public service interpreting and translation (PSIT) has also explored the constellations of power that impact on service provision and decision-making *in situ*, largely through an appeal to sociological theories that have yielded rich insight into the ethical and the relational in interpreted interaction. The relative neglect of ideological influences on policy formation specific to individual geonational contexts in PSIT, however, suggests that these influences are somehow less amenable to systematic analysis. By broadening the range of interdisciplinary perspectives, this collection seeks to open up scholarly investigation and challenge such perceptions.

At the same time, the collection draws attention to PSIT as sources of deep ideological tension at societal level. Overwhelmingly, the literature in interpreting studies positions both occupational activities as an ideal policy response by socially progressive societies to the complex communication needs of minority-speaking populations. However, this perspective may sometimes be perceived as limiting in relation to policy development, and highlights the potential for differentiated approaches. For instance, the interconnections between language proficiency development and interpreting and translation services are generally absent from discussions. Emerging research on the third sector provides examples of how the overlapping need for language proficiency development and interpreting and translation services plays out at the organisational level and impacts on policy development (see Tipton, this volume).

The relatively few explicit references to ideology in the collection attest to its enduring elusiveness as a concept in the humanities and social sciences (McLellan, 1995). Nevertheless, collectively, the contributions emphasise that ethical practices and the spaces in which they evolve are intimately bound up with the wider forces that infuse, enable and constrain social relations – forces which, in this case, variously take familial, juridical, monarchical, party political, pedagogical, philanthropic and psychosocial forms. By deliberately emphasising constraints and enablements, the social forces or world views that shape and are shaped by professional interactions are not limited to pejorative conceptualisations so often associated with the term 'ideology'. Furthermore, the discussions tend not to construe ideology as something that exists beyond the individual and seek to draw attention to the way in which interpreters as social actors develop a sense of the 'moral' or the 'ethical' and invite reflection on the extent to which the resulting conceptualisations are 'always-already ideological' (Freeden, 1996; Porter, 2006).

Finally, in relation to methodology, research on ethics in public service interpreting has privileged qualitative methods that permit a focus on perceptions about practice and role. Such methods are in evidence in several contributions to this collection in the form of interviews and surveys. However, in exploring interconnections between ethics and ideology, the collection includes complementary qualitative approaches based on publicly available artefacts, policy documents and case studies. Two contributions (Gentile; Salaets & Balogh, this volume) adopt cross-national comparative survey approaches, which pave the way for the systematic collection of large data sets that will be crucial to shaping both domestic (federal, national) and transnational policymaking in the future.

The collection provides a space for exploring the interconnections between the highly contested concepts of ethics and ideology and brings insights from emerging and more established researchers and practitioners in the field. It will be of interest to scholars of translation and interpreting studies, service providers and public policymakers, and aims to stimulate debate between the academe and the public, private and third sectors by permitting more nuanced understandings of language support needs and the policy contexts in which such needs are addressed.

Overview

The volume is divided into two parts; the first, titled '(Re-)defining Concepts and Policy Contexts' provides historical and contemporary perspectives on ideology in the development of interpreting at the service of state bodies and institutions. The chapters explore ideologies of recruitment, positioning, discourses of professionalisation, PSIT and the democratic process and the ethics and politics of recognition. The chapters are underpinned by theoretical frameworks that offer particular insight into political science as an increasingly important interdiscipline.

Cáceres, in 'Interpreters in History: A Reflection on the Question of Loyalty', analyses the concept of loyalty in relation to ideology, where ideology is understood as a value system. Examples from the period of the Reconquista, the discovery of the New World and other colonial endeavours, as well as from Spanish administration and diplomacy in the Early Modern period are compared with practices in the contemporary era to highlight the extent to which governments have sought and continue to seek control over interpreting activities, particularly in situations of violent conflict.

Martín Ruano in 'Developing Public Service Translation and Interpreting under the Paradigm of Recognition: Towards Diversity-Sensitive Discourses on Ethics in PSIT', explores the relevance of the concept of 'recognition' in the emerging model of PSIT, which is replacing the concept of 'equality' in the legal field and political theory. She argues for the need to conceptualise 'recognition' in a multifaceted way: as recognition of the *particularities* and *legitimate differences* of the parties involved in the translation situation, and as recognition of the *intervenient* participation of public service interpreters and translators.

Tipton in 'Interpreting-as-Conflict: PSIT in Third Sector Organisations and the Impact of Third Way Politics', investigates some of the discursive formulations that reflect the value system of the 'Third Way' politics that came to characterise the New Labour government (1997–2010), and their impact on the development of the third sector and legitimation of public service interpreting provision during this period. The findings of a survey on language support in the third sector and interviews with service providers reveal that the super-diverse local context and increasing reliance on partnership work to deliver key human services are leading organisations to adopt mixed regimes of language support that risk limiting their accountability to some service users.

Gentile in 'Political Ideology and the De-Professionalisation of Public Service Interpreting: The Netherlands and the United Kingdom as Case Studies', shows how the implementation of nationalist ideologies, including aspects such as the privatisation and outsourcing of public service interpreting, have hindered the professionalisation of public service interpreting and damaged public perception of the professions. The discussion is underpinned by examples from two multicultural and multilingual countries: the Netherlands and the United Kingdom.

Brander de la Iglesia in 'A Sea of Troubles': Ethical Dilemmas from War Zones to the Classroom', highlights the lack of attention to ethical issues in the education and training of public service interpreters and translators with reference to what she calls the 'absent curriculum'. She explores concepts and paradigms used in the disciplines of applied ethics, ethics of the professions and in the study of morality in psychology that can be applied to translation and interpreting in conflict situations, linking them to the concept of the 'ethical dilemma' as a starting point for the study of ethics in the training of translators and interpreters.

Part 2 titled 'Experiences From the Field' brings together contributions on interpreting in settings such as courtrooms, correctional facilities and in the pretrial phases of criminal investigation. It focuses on interpreter mediation with asylum seekers, refugees and trauma survivors, drawing on case studies and survey-based studies. Ethical and ideological perspectives are foregrounded through a spotlight on issues of access to justice in correctional facilities and rehabilitation for limited proficiency speakers. Interlingual communication is theorised in particular through rights-based discourses. The chapters offer new insight into different types of legal events in the European context and bring a fresh perspective on the use and training of interpreters in Europe and the United States.

The first chapter in Part 2, 'Ethical Codes and Their Impact on Prison Communication' by Valero-Garcés, focuses on the Spanish prison system and communication with members of the foreign population therein who do not share the majority language and culture. She explores issues arising from the coexistence of several professions in a single institutional site through a focus on the prison staff and the interpreters and their multiple codes of ethics. By examining overlaps between professional codes and resulting ethical conflicts, the chapter also explores how such conflicts may be resolved.

Devaux in 'Virtual Presence, Ethics and Videoconference Interpreting: Insights from Court Settings' focuses on ethical issues arising from the use of videoconference interpreting in courts in England and Wales. Using a theoretical framework informed by Camayd-Freixas (2013) and the ethical problems and inner conflicts that result from a lack of adequate guidance in ethical codes, he draws parallels with the situation in England and Wales where court interpreters are expected to abide by the National Register of Public Service Interpreters' (NRPSI) *Code of Professional Conduct*, a code that does not contain any specific guidelines on videoconference interpreting (VCI) and its use in legal proceedings.

Salaets and Balogh in 'Participants' and Interpreters' Perception of the Interpreter's Role in Interpreter-Mediated Investigative Interviews of Minors: Belgium and Italy as a Case' present a selection of findings from the Co-Minor-IN/QUEST research project (JUST/2011/JPEN/AG/2961, January 2013–December 2014). The focus is on the perception of the interpreter's role and needs by the main actors in the field of pretrial child interviewing in two countries that are selected as a comparison of practices in northern and southern Europe. The findings indicate differences in how representatives of a northern European country (Belgium) are distributed differently compared to those of a southern European country (Italy) as well as differences in the perception of the interpreter's role. The study helps to draw attention to thorny terminological issues concerning the name given to these professionals and their roles in these respective geonational contexts.

Tryuk in 'Conflict. Tension. Aggression. Ethical Issues in Interpreted Asylum Hearings at the Office for Foreigners in Warsaw', explores ethical issues in interpreter-mediated asylum hearings at the Office for Foreigners in Warsaw. She examines the views of immigration officers about the nature of community interpreting as performed by the interpreters, and presents their perceptions of the role of interpreters during refugee hearings and in relation to the recommendations of the Polish Code of Sworn Translators and Interpreters drafted by the Polish Society of Sworn and Specialised Translators (TEPIS). Her chapter also discusses officers' expectations regarding conflict situations that arise in interviews and the tensions such situations can cause between officers and interpreters.

Bancroft in 'The Voice of Compassion: Exploring Trauma-Informed Interpreting' discusses the specificities and difficulties of interpreting for trauma survivors in public service interpreting (PSI) by presenting the results from two pilot programmes for trauma-informed interpreting in the United States. Trauma-informed interpreting is considered as an emerging specialisation that requires training to address a threefold challenge for interpreters: to develop the skills and knowledge to interpret competently and professionally for survivors; to reduce or prevent their own vicarious trauma; and to balance professional ethics with humanity, which means navigating the fuzzy boundaries of the role of the interpreter with skill, delicacy and compassion.

References

Camayd-Freixas, E. (2013) Court interpreter ethics and the role of professional organizations. In C. Schäffner, K. Kredens and Y. Fowler (eds) *Interpreting in a Changing Landscape* (pp. 15–30). Amsterdam and Philadelphia: John Benjamins.
Baker, M. and Maier, C. (eds) (2011) Ethics in interpreter and translator training. *The Interpreter and Translator Trainer, Special Issue on Ethics in the Curriculum* 5 (1), 1–14.
Beaton-Thome, M. (2007) Interpreted ideologies in institutional discourse. The case of the European Parliament. *The Translator* 13 (2), 271–296.
Du Toit, A. (2012) Making sense of 'evidence': Notes on the discursive politics of research and pro-poor policy making. Plaas Working Paper 21. Institute for Poverty, Land and Agrarian Studies, University of the Western Cape.
Fawcett, P. and Munday, J. (2009) Ideology. In M. Baker and G. Saldhana (eds) *The Routledge Encyclopedia of Translation Studies* (2nd edn) (pp. 137–141). London/New York: Routledge.
Freeden, M. (1996) *Ideologies and Political Theory: A Conceptual Approach*. Oxford: Clarendon Press.
McLellan, D. (1995) *Ideology* (2nd edn). Buckingham: Open University Press.
Porter, R. (2006) *Ideology: Contemporary Social, Political and Cultural Theory*. Cardiff: University of Wales Press.
Rudvin, M. (2007) Professionalism and ethics in community interpreting: The impact of individualist versus collective group identity. *Interpreting: International Journal of Research and Practice in Interpreting* 9 (1), 47–69.
Sasso, A. and Malli, K. (2014) Trying to fit a square peg in a round hole: Is community interpreting just too big for public policy? The Canadian experience a provocation. *FITISPoS International Journal of Public Service Interpreting and Translation* 1 (1), 42–50.

Part 1

(Re-)defining Concepts and Policy Contexts

1 Interpreters in History: A Reflection on the Question of Loyalty

Ingrid Cáceres Würsig

Introduction

The 'cultural turn' emerged together with attempts in the 1990s to explore the transformation processes that result from continuous conflicts of cultural formations. This 'turn' had considerable influence in translation studies and was reflected in research that transcended linguistic aspects in order to foreground extralinguistic realities. An issue that has received particular attention concerns the analysis of the relationship between ideology and/or power and translation activity. Cronin (2002) was one of the first scholars to reflect the influence of the cultural turn in interpreting studies, asserting that the discipline needed to address questions of power and incorporate theorisations of class, gender, race and religion in the analysis of oral performance. Using examples from colonial history, he describes two systems of interpreting: *autonomous* and *heteronomous*. In the first system, colonisers train their own subjects in the language of the colonised, and in the second system, local interpreters are recruited, sometimes even by force. This approach to the recruitment of interpreters reflects a problem of control by the (colonial) authorities and, as will be argued in this chapter, helps to illuminate the political causes that influence an interpreter's change of side. Cronin's work arguably opened up new avenues for the study of ideology in interpreting studies.

According to Beaton-Thome (2015), there have been two ways to examine the relationship between ideology and interpreting. The first identifies ideology as a value system that is used as a tool by governing powers. Studies based on this approach usually deal with historical examples. The second considers ideology as a kind of world view and examines the interplay between multiple ideologies in interpreted and interpreter discourse. Relevant issues here concern interpreters' reactions to ideological stimuli and how ideology influences their scope of action.

The emergence of ideological approaches has become particularly relevant in recent years both in public service interpreting and in translation and interpreting for international institutions. The activity of interpreters in war and conflict zones has also attracted significant interest. Recent findings suggest that interpreters who intervene in intelligence and military operations are required to be ideologically aligned with the hiring institution (Inghilleri, 2010). In other words, hiring institutions seek to use an *autonomous system* in order to have more control over information and negotiation. Judicial interpreting in English-speaking countries is subject to a code of practice in recognition of the potential impact of interpreters on the judicial process. Such a code, for instance, prevents interpreters from clarifying elements in the original discourse that are deliberately ambiguous. Furthermore, in the field of interpreting with political refugees, studies reveal that interpreters have been shown to adopt certain patterns of behaviour in order to avoid empathising with the personal tragedies of the refugees (Baker & Pérez-González, 2012: 42). Thus, institutional alignment is achieved to some extent by the implementation of codes of practice, which include routinised tasks and patterns to be applied by translators and interpreters.

This chapter focuses on an understanding of ideology as a value and belief system used by state powers in order to perpetuate their interests and, in so doing, examines several cases from history. It introduces the concept of loyalty as a key element for understanding and investigating the relationship between ideology and interpreting/translation, and compares past and present frameworks that govern the activity of interpreters, especially in the fields of diplomacy and intelligence, arguing that such frameworks have remained little changed over time. It further argues that the ideological alignment shown by interpreters can be identified through expressions of loyalty found in artefacts from specific historical periods.[1]

The historical examples of translation activity presented in what follows correspond to the periods of the Reconquista, the discovery of the New World and further Spanish colonisation and, finally, European diplomacy during the Early Modern period,[2] with particular reference to interpreters in Constantinople. The geonational context of Spain made the interplay between the Christian, Arab and Jewish cultures possible. Moreover, the discovery of the New World under Spanish patronage, which brought unknown worlds into contact, is considered an extraordinary event and constitutes a fascinating example in the history of interpreting. Interpreting activity in old Constantinople, where most European diplomacy took place, represents a cultural clash between East and West and to bridge such cultural differences, dragomans were very important players in mediation and negotiation. The intensity of interpreting activity during this period makes it a suitable backdrop for the comparative analysis proposed.

In these historical periods, we can consider loyalty as obedience to a political power. Political powers, generally monarchies, were based on the defence of a value system, where religion, lineage, race and social class were fundamental aspects. Monarchies required their subjects to share the same value system, which meant accepting and defending it; in other words, being *loyal* to it. *Loyalty* and *loyal* are recurring words in the interpreters' personal files, ambassadors' reports and clerks' correspondence material which have been examined in the process of developing the history of interpreting. History also shows that the powers that employed interpreters placed greater trust in those who shared the same cultural roots, because they knew that the emotional, social and cultural bonds to their place of origin developed in childhood were very strong.

The chapter is divided into four main sections. The first section provides examples of the history of interpreting during the Reconquista, the discovery of the New World and further colonisation. It draws attention to the translation practices adopted during the era of the Reconquista, often by those who had been converted and whose children then inherited the profession. Owing to their origins, the interpreters' suitability for cooperating with the administrative bodies was endorsed both by their family tradition and by their official appointment which granted them exclusivity to the service (and consequently economic benefits). This section also charts the learning processes that shaped interpreting during the discovery of the New World when children or indigenous adults were moved to the Peninsula. Given the impossibility of removing the ethnicity of a person, these intermediaries were considered to be of low status. The second section is devoted to translators and interpreters working in European diplomacy. Linguistic services within the administration of the state were promoted while favouring families that had specialised in translation and passed it down from generation to generation so that shared religion, education and values guaranteed the same way of thinking.

The third section discusses the figure of the dragoman, who was an expert in communication between the East and the West, specifically between the Sultans and the European nations seated in Constantinople. The Spanish monarchy sought to train its own interpreters by sending young Spaniards abroad for them to learn the language and the culture. The European powers tried to develop an *autonomous* system as it guaranteed loyalty, but it required investment and long-term planning which often failed to yield the desired results. It was necessary, therefore, to combine long-term training with the recruitment of local intermediaries, who were often held in deep suspicion as they served all the European parties and their cultural backgrounds (Sephardi, orthodox) were different. The fourth section addresses the current situation of interpreters in war and their role in military conflicts. I argue that there is a trend to categorise interpreters according to their cultural roots, which suggests that governments prioritise loyalty above all other skills. Finally, a conclusion brings together the main points and offers an explanation as to why native interpreters often appear to be preferred in situations of conflict.

Interpreters in Acts of Conquest and Colonisation

The cases discussed in this section reflect the need for a political power to generate a framework of trust and security in the deployment of intercultural mediation. This framework is something that would be developed over years and supported by a language policy, which consisted of appointing translators and interpreters from among members of the same family, where this profession became a tradition. The recruitment of interpreters during the discovery of the New World, however, had to be improvised in those contexts, at least at the beginning.

During the Reconquista (711–1492), medieval Spain was a territory whose borders were subject to constant change due to the intensity of the wars between the Christians and the Moors. Jews were on both sides and numerous contacts between the three different communities took place despite their different faith-based models. Jankrift (2013) explains that each religion perceived itself as superior to the other, which resulted in a mutual disinterest in relation to learning about the faith, traditions or language of the other. Christians and Muslims believed it was their mission to impose and extend their religion to other territories; since the Crusades, these endeavours had led to both feeling threatened by the other. The distance between Christians and Muslims was affected by that mutual ignorance and also by the absence of a lingua franca. Whereas European diplomats in the 15th century used Latin as their lingua franca, Arabic was used in the East, followed by Persian and later Turkish. In order to ascend within the court – whether it was Christian or Islamic – learning the language of the enemy was not looked upon positively. Instead, it resulted in the suspicion of negotiations being conducted in secret or conversions to the other religion. Translators and interpreters began to play a part in diplomacy as a way to avoid being the object of suspicion regarding their loyalty towards the other religion (Jankrift, 2013: 138).

According to Roser Nebot (2001), those who practised linguistic mediation in Spain were designated *trujamanes*, and they played a prominent role between the 12th and the 17th centuries. Not only did they work as liaison interpreters, but they also translated and edited the correspondence between the different linguistic groups and bore witness to the content of documents for whomever they concerned. In 1294, for example, James II of Aragon issued a bill in favour of the Jew Jahudano Bonsenyor, granting him exclusive right to the city of Barcelona, as well as the legal right to write documents in Arabic (for example bills of exchange or receipts) needed to conduct commercial transactions with the Muslims, as he considered

Bonseyor's knowledge of Latin to be insufficient (Roser Nebot, 2001: 313–314).

The *trujamanes* were also responsible for the translation and editing of correspondence between the Kingdom of Aragon and the Nasrid Kingdom of Granada. The act of legalising the process of linguistic mediation is a clear indication of the desire of the Aragon Crown for control over diplomatic and commercial relations with the Arabs, which would serve as a sign of confidence. With regard to the suitability of the translator, the following is stated in the bill: 'you, Jahuda, son of Astruch Bonsenyor... are an adequate person and capable of taking charge and drawing up the exchange documents...' (Roser Nebot, 2001: 313). The reference to Jahuda's suitability could well refer to the trust placed in him, further reinforced by the act of mentioning his ancestry, while the expression 'capable of taking charge' seems to allude more to his linguistic capability.

In addition to the *trujamanes*, the role of the *alfaqueque*[3] also emerged during this period. As a result of ongoing clashes between the Moors and the Christians, prisoners were taken on both sides; with time this became a business for the captors. In the Christian towns, the name *alfaqueque* designated a person who mediated specifically for the liberation of the captives and who received a type of safe pass to be able to operate within the territories in conflict or those that had negotiated a truce. It was essential for them to have command of both Spanish and Arabic, and, over time, the post became hereditary to the point where they were recognised by King Alfonso V the Wise (Alonso-Araguás, 2012; Baigorri-Jalón, 2015). The fact that the role of interpreter was inherited was a way in which loyalty was achieved, since they would have been educated in accordance with a pro-monarchy value system.

The discovery of the New World was an important challenge for the Spanish monarchy, also in terms of linguistic mediation; there were no interpreters for the indigenous languages, which were completely unknown to Westerners. Therefore, interpreters had to be 'created'. On his first expedition to the Indies, Columbus brought with him an interpreter of Jewish origin who knew Hebrew and Arabic, but that was of little service for communicating with the indigenous peoples of the Americas (Fernández Sánchez, 2001: 18–19). In reality, Columbus had wanted to reach Japan and the conviction that he was close to that location ensured that his first encounter with the indigenous population of San Salvador Island produced numerous misunderstandings. The explorer decided to capture a group of indigenous persons so that they might learn the Spanish language during the expedition and afterwards in the Spanish court (Alonso-Araguás, 2012: 51; Valero-Garcés, 1996: 62). The most gifted of these was Diego Colón who, after being educated in the Peninsula, accompanied the explorer again in order to assist him as an interpreter.

The capture of indigenous people who could assume the task of communication was a common practice among the Spanish explorers and also among the Portuguese. This practice had its own risks in that the captives obviously tried to flee from or betray their captors. On other occasions, they served their new masters faithfully as it seems was the case with Malinche, who was under Cortés' orders. Malinche was a symbol of betrayal for Mexicans on the ground that she denied her own roots in order to help the enemy. However, she recalled feelings of admiration among Spaniards because of her flexibility and adaptation skills. Cortés also implemented the practice of indirect interpreting by using two consecutive interpreters: he addressed Jerónimo de Aguilar in Spanish (a Spaniard who had been a captive with the indigenous people for eight years and who found himself once again with the Spaniards), who then translated into Maya for Malinche, who in turn addressed the Mexicans in Náhuatl.

In accordance with Spanish religious precepts, those who were to serve as interpreters were to convert to the Catholic faith by means of a baptismal ceremony (in which they would receive a new Christian name). This was a form of annulling their 'foreign' origins, which not only served as a sign of dominance of one culture over the other, but also of psychological support as much towards the colonised as towards the colonisers. The former incorporated the 'others' into their religious model, while the latter felt protected by the new power.

Another intermediary role that appears in a process of Spanish colonisation and merits attention is that of the *capitán de amigos*, which has been the subject of research by Payás (2012) and Alonso-Araguás (2012). The role emerged on the Hispanic-Mapuche border of colonial Chile when the indigenous population who rebelled against the Spaniards (17th century) imitated their practices in the treatment of prisoners, forcing them to adopt the attire and customs of the Indians and prohibiting them from communicating in Spanish among themselves. The indigenous community used the captive Spanish soldiers as servants or slaves. When those Spaniards were freed, many of them became *capitanes de amigos* (captains of friends) due to having learned the indigenous language, which enabled them to mediate between the Mapuche society and the colonial powers. With time, the role was institutionalised and individuals were officially appointed and required to comply with certain protocols. They accompanied the indigenous groups that had been assigned to the parliaments with the colonial authorities, assisting them as interpreters. They usually lived among the indigenous community or in close proximity, given that their reintegration into Spanish society was nearly impossible, particularly in cases where their captivity had been of considerable length. In such cases, individuals were considered disowned or 'Indianised' due to their excessive acclimatisation to the indigenous culture, thus implying the practice of traditions such as cohabitation or heresy, which were utterly rejected by the Spanish colonial powers (Alonso-Araguás, 2012: 44–45). According to Payás (2012: 28), the *capitanes de amigos* were biased towards the Spanish army, but due to the circumstances in which they carried out their activities they favoured 'a bilateral approach, with the associated risk of being partial to the Mapuche side'.

As we have seen in the above examples, the systems used to recruit interpreters in acts of conquest and colonisation are born as heteronomous systems – even using enforcement measures – and they evolve into autonomous systems in order to guarantee the necessary loyalty to the relevant rulers.

Interpreters in Administration and Diplomacy in the Service of European Powers

As has already been mentioned, throughout history political powers have surrounded themselves with and served those who represented their interests. Governments understood that in order to achieve their political objectives, whether they be in the form of territorial or commercial expansion, it was imperative that all administrative, military and diplomatic personnel remain loyal to the cause in order to guarantee continuity of power. This commitment was sealed through political agreements between monarchs, aristocrats (who were also in the military) and the clergy; strata who defended the idea of empire based on the Christian religion, which was a way of understanding man and the world. The main discernible Christian features lay in the universality of their rules and authority, represented by the temporal powers (of the monarch or the Crown he represented) and by the spiritual powers (of the Pope). The temporal power remained legitimised by the divine powers.

An example of this political imperialism was identified in the practice of the Catholic kings towards the end of the 15th century; their strategy of royal marriages substantially modified the European political map and the new territories attached to the Spanish kingdom were forced to intensify their diplomatic activity. In this way, a network of embassies emerged within the main European courts, which had as their mission the negotiation and signing of treaties. This diplomatic network expanded under Charles V, who inherited a vast, multilingual and multicultural empire. Its territories included the majority of Western Europe, as well as the New World territories. Communication between the territories was carried out in written form by the diplomats themselves, displaying frequent mastery of several languages, especially Latin, French and Italian. In fact, during the 15th and 16th centuries the task of interpreting was an integral part of the diplomat's role. It was in the 18th century when translation and interpretation started to professionalise and become clearly separated from the role of a diplomat (Cáceres-Würsig, 2014a). In this period, Latin had already fallen into disuse, mostly in spoken practice, which led to French and Italian becoming the preferred languages in diplomatic encounters, although the envoys of the Holy Roman Empire continued to use Latin, just as the Polish envoys did and on occasion those from Portugal and Sweden (Schmidt-Rösler, 2014: 131). Translation and interpreting became a more technical and functional activity, leaving the task of persuasion and negotiation in the hands of the diplomats.

However, given the scale of the multicultural territories that were united under the Spanish Crown at the beginning of the 16th century, it was necessary to develop the Secretariat of the Interpretation of Languages (created in 1527), which can be considered as one of the first European models in the organisation of linguistic services (Cáceres-Würsig, 2014a). At the forefront of this service, Diego Gracián de Alderete was named a Latinist of certain renown. Gracián initiated a dynasty of translators into the service of the Spanish Crown; the responsibility of the secretariat of languages was passed from generation to generation for 200 years. This was a recurrent practice in the Spanish court. The Spanish administration used numerous secretariats of language, depending on the territory and matter, and they remained integral to the administration accompanied by a salary and status. Their capabilities went beyond mere translation; they bore witness to documents, identified possible falsifications of documents, compared other translations, and some intervened in the deciphering of documents, wrote reports or served as informants (Cáceres-Würsig, 2014a; Reiter, 2015).

Entire families could be employed in certain services in a professional capacity, whether it was in the military or as advisers to the monarch; the same was also true of translation services. As the children grew up in a court environment, it was far easier for them to learn the customs and the complex protocol of the court, which was dominated by the hierarchical power structure, than to employ people from outside. Therefore, lineage was a way of guaranteeing loyalty to the service of the Crown, which generated trust during a time when people observed one of the stipulations of the Christian religion, to serve God and the monarch with one's own descendants.

In order to prove loyalty, it was also common to serve the monarch by making one's family heritage available, in exchange for social advancements. One way to ascend in social status from within the administrative apparatus that accompanied the monarch consisted of enlisting in Orders of Knighthood. The personal files of the secretariats of language found in Spanish archives show that they also sought to elevate their status by joining said orders. In order to do so, it was necessary to pass a purity of blood test (Cáceres-Würsig, 2014a: 234–235). Witnesses who knew the candidate were called on to check that there were no 'Moors, Jews or criminals' in their ancestry. The act of listing criminals next to people of a religion other than Christianity was characteristic of the rejection that these religions generated, an animosity that was a constant in all Spanish governments until the time of Charles III. Purity of blood implied an absence of the risk of heresy, but it was also a form of controlling society. A majority of the individuals tried to erase or cover up their non-Christian origins while adopting, among other things, Hispanic names or developing Catholic rituals like attending mass, practising lent and celebrating holy days.

Reiter (2015) investigated translation activity and diplomatic relations between the courts of Madrid and Vienna (in the Modern Age), with an entire chapter dedicated to the problem of loyalty and its political connotations. For this author (Reiter, 2015: 137), loyalty is related to the trust that rulers put in translators and interpreters as they had to deal with secret tasks and also with their confessions, due to the influence of religion on political matters during this period. In both courts, there were strict and complex diplomatic ceremonials that were only accessible to those already familiarised with them, and through which the power structures were made visible. The ceremonial was central to relations between the different powers as they sought to project their dignity, supremacy as well as the hierarchical positions of the different envoys through it. Durst (2014: 106) similarly emphasises that the linguistic uses of diplomatic courtesy and court protocol played an important role since they determined the image of the envoys while they represented a monarch. Protocol required respect for and knowledge of certain regulations and traditions, such as forms of greeting and farewells. It also governed the treatment and the placement of each envoy within the space of the hearing. According to Reiter, the protocol of the Viennese court meant that it only employed interpreters in the hearings with envoys who were not familiar with the diplomatic habits and practices of Western Europe, for example the Muscovite or the Ottoman. Each embassy brought its own interpreter (an indication of their mutual mistrust) and they were placed a certain distance behind the ambassador or envoy in order to provide whispered interpretation; for the Ottoman embassy the interpreter was placed on a lower step. Reiter (2015: 141–142) tells the story of the Muscovite envoy's visit to the Viennese court in 1679. The emperor was afraid that the Muscovite interpreter would not know how to correctly address him as emperor and, for this reason, used his own interpreter (although the Russians were also allowed to use their own). Through various meetings a climate of trust was created and, by the final hearing, the Muscovite envoy accepted the Viennese interpreter as the sole interpreter.

Insight into the case of the court interpreter Adam Stylla, who served in the hearings with the Muscovite envoys, and was also documented by Reiter (2015: 142–144), highlights the importance of the tasks that were entrusted to him. Prior to the hearing with the Russian General Czeremettet, Stylla was informed of what the general would say; this was to enable him to correctly prepare the interpretation so as to inform the envoys of the details of the ceremonial. Furthermore, Stylla succeeded in being promoted to the status of Hofdolmetscher (Interpreter of the Court) by sending the court memorials that gave evidence of his loyalty, which constituted a report of his numerous services to the Crown over the years. It is also very interesting to note the case of the translator Cristóbal de Angelate who was employed by the Spanish Court in the mid-17th century. He apparently accomplished tasks of espionage for the Count of Pötting, the Austrian envoy in Madrid. The two held several meetings, with Pötting considering that Angelate was a 'good spy of ambassadors' and noting that Angelate originated from 'Iran', and therefore lacked the necessary loyalty towards the Spanish monarch (Reiter, 2015: 152). However, in Reiter's opinion, these cases of disloyalty must have been infrequent.

In summary, lineage, purity of blood and *long-term service* were the most solid evidence of loyalty that could be given to the monarchy. Furthermore, the Catholic religion served as a weapon of social discipline, as it constituted a requirement for *loyal* interpreters as well as a means to progress in administration or court.

The Interpreters in Constantinople and Culture Shock

The place where the loyalty of interpreters towards the represented Crown became a matter of great importance was, without doubt, Constantinople. Since the beginning of the Early Modern period, Constantinople was the epicentre of commercial relations between European and Oriental powers. It was home to the main European embassies, the reason being that the Levant was an extremely important commercial region that included different routes, which united the Mediterranean coast with the Middle East. All of the Western powers had a continual need of mediation with the Turkish sultans; this was channelled through the Grand Vizier who was responsible for relations with Western foreigners as well as with the other Ottoman authorities. The imperial council or divan was composed of the army, the head of chancery, the head of financial administration and the province governors (Agildere, 2009: 2–3). The practice of Ottoman hearings and courtly traditions were completely foreign to the Western powers. This made the intervention of the dragomans necessary, making them key figures in the communication and negotiation between the East and the West.

Since the beginning of the 13th century, the Ottoman Empire operated the office of the so-called *bailo*, the equivalent of an ambassador. The first power to have a recognised embassy in the Empire was the Republic of Venice, a move that reflected its awareness of the competition that the great Ottoman Porte posed to its commercial power. Attracted by business with the Orient, a migratory movement of European merchants to this region began. So-called 'factories' also emerged at this time – European businesses which traded in the Levant with the intention of securing the monopoly of the region (Masters, 2001: 70–71).

In addition to Venice, during the 16th century the Western powers represented at the Ottoman Porte (or Sublime Porte) also included France, the Netherlands and England. Subsequently in the 17th and 18th centuries, embassies were established by the Austrian monarchy, Russia, Prussia, Spain and Denmark, transforming the Ottoman capital into a melting pot of cultures. In order to contact the Ottoman authorities, they all generally used local interpreters who were nearly always Sephardic Jews or Latin Catholics (descended from Venetians, Genovese and Cypriots); in addition to the official language of Turkish, they spoke French or Italian. The Ottoman authorities created the role of the first dragoman, the interpreter of the highest status who mediated between the Grand Vizier and the foreign representatives at their hearings. They received their accreditations and translated the most important documents such as peace and alliance treaties.[4] Until the middle of the 16th century, the first dragoman in the Turkish service was a multilingual person of Christian or Jewish origin who converted to Islam. Many of them were members of the family of the so-called Phanariotes, who came from the Greek Orthodox gentry (Agildere, 2009: 4), thus giving them the monopoly over communication. It was essential that the dragomans (whether they were subjects of the sultan or a European power) had excellent language skills, legal and cultural knowledge of the Ottoman environment, knowledge of accounting, as well as an excellent aptitude for exercising mediation. They also benefited from the coveted *berat* (an exemption from taxes) and received gifts from European embassies due to the Ottoman customs that required it (Groot, 2005: 474–475).

'Trans-imperial-subjects' is the concept that Rothman (2011) uses to explain the way in which the merchants, missionaries, diplomats and interpreters acted in the Levant. It refers to members of multiple social formations that help to conform to the imperial limits through their linguistic, religious and political interactions. For Rothman (2012: 11–12), the concept has the following meaning: 'trans' alludes to the way in which a subject transfers his/her roots to another place in favour of his/her interests, scattering the family ties beyond the imperial borders. 'Imperial' refers to the universal convention sanctioned by God. The religious authorities legitimated the temporal power and cemented political affection and loyalty. Finally, 'subjects' suggests that these types of actors could not be considered as individuals in as much as they were subject to imperial authority and forced into a religion. In the case of the Spanish embassy (which was one of the last to be established in Constantinople due to a long-standing feud between the two powers), we can see the workings of Juan de Bouligny, the first Spanish ambassador in Constantinople, and an example of a trans-imperial subject as he aligns with the three defined coordinates.

Three years of negotiations (1779–1782) were necessary in order to seal a peace treaty between Spain and the Ottoman Porte, a task which was entrusted to the aforementioned Juan de Bouligny, a Spanish merchant of French origin. The Spanish envoy was acutely aware of the importance of being able to count on good interpreters and considered the dragoman as the most important employee to assist the envoy represented in Turkey. Bouligny contracted the services of foreign dragomans, non-Muslim Turks and Italians. Sephardics, however, were not hired and his correspondence made it clear that other foreign embassies had warned him against the betrayals of the Jewish community. Reports from the Arabist and secretary of oriental languages in Madrid, Miguel Casiri, also evidence that the hiring of Sephardi Jews was rejected (Cáceres-Würsig, 2012). He argued that the French *École de jeunes de langues* was created due to a lack of loyalty on the part of the Greek and Jewish interpreters. Bouligny thus tried to emulate the models of the Venetians, French and Austrians. He requested that young people who spoke other languages, were willing to train abroad and were from a good Catholic family – that generally speaking already had ties to the administration – be sent to the aforementioned school in order to serve as future interpreters, consuls and diplomats. This was the model followed by all the European powers in order to ensure the loyalty of their subordinates while determining a basis for recruitment in their own national origin, cultural roots and of course, religious roots (cfr. Agildere, 2009; Balliu, 1998; Cáceres, 2012, 2014b; Groot, 2005; Lucchetta, 1989; Petritsch, 2005; Rothman, 2012; Wolf, 2005). The difficulty with this measure concerned the length of time required in order to train a good interpreter; for this reason it was necessary to combine the training of 'their own' interpreters (autonomous system) with other 'foreigners' (heteronomous system), who also served as teachers to the budding interpreters.

Having overcome the language barrier by hiring interpreters, the foreign envoys still had to grapple with the experience of a new culture and radically different customs. Yet again, the European embassies warned Bouligny about the Ottoman culture, considering it to be corrupt and boastful. The presence of Bouligny and his family (with his sons helping as secretaries to the embassies) did nothing to alter this perception as can be seen from the reports sent to Madrid in which a negative image of the Ottoman society was portrayed. What the Bouligny family did transmit was that the Ottoman society was not a 'civilised' one. Despite the agreement that was reached between Spain and Turkey, it remained clear that both powers represented entirely different positions. From the Spanish point of view, Spain was a civilised European culture with superior precedence over the Ottoman culture. Bouligny drew attention to the opposing values such as honour ('pure' loyalty to the monarch without expecting any reward) and the materialism of the Ottoman culture, contrasting religious depth with material superficiality, promoting austerity over pretentiousness, humility over pride, simplicity over cunning and dialogue over violent character. This polarisation between the cultures, in which the other is depicted as utterly strange and worse, permits parallels to be drawn with the situation of the interpreters in war zones today; this is addressed in the following section.

The example of Constantinople's diplomacy reflects the fact that Western powers tried by all means to create their own reserve of national interpreters in order to avoid being dependent on local interpreters. Local interpreters were not trustworthy enough because of their different cultural roots or confession. On the scale of trust, interpreters with Jewish origin occupied the last position. But the creation of an autonomous system was very expensive and relatively time-consuming. Therefore, a *hybrid* system was finally put into practice, which combined native interpreters with local ones. The latter knew the languages and Ottoman customs and they often also served as Arab or Persian teachers for the future national interpreters. And national interpreters ensured the need of confidentiality for diplomatic negotiations and the flow of information. Therefore, we cannot talk in this case of a pure autonomous system.

War Interpreters Today

As a result of the recent wars in Iraq, Afghanistan and the former Yugoslavia, a line of investigation has emerged in interpreting studies concerning, in particular, the role of an interpreter in situations of military conflict (cf. Baker, 2010; Inghilleri, 2010). This new area of focus explores violent situations in which there is a significant risk to the physical and moral integrity of the interpreter. These situations primarily concern war zones and military operations; however, recent studies also exist which examine interpreters in other, particularly hostile environments in war: the concentration camps and extermination camps of the Second World War (see Wolf, 2013).

War interpreters intervene in sensitive operations and their lives are often at risk. If we take the recent war in Iraq as an example, according to the studies of Inghilleri (2010), the majority of interpreters recruited by intelligence services (in particular the American intelligence services) and journalists were local civilians who served as intermediaries and sources of information. Their tasks included the main duties of an interpreter, but also advising and influencing military decisions since they were familiar with the geography, everyday life and social mentality of the area. The interpreters put their lives at risk for various reasons: some out of political conviction as they wanted to fight for the freedom of their country; some considered themselves to be neutral, whereas others were motivated by financial needs. Some also sought the security of a professional body such as the military; however, they did not always receive the desired level of protection and acceptance due to their different roots. The existence of *ad hoc* and casual interpreters as a common practice is also documented by Baigorri-Jalón (2012) in reference to those who served in the *Brigadas Internacionales* during the Spanish Civil War (1936–1939). In another of his articles, Baigorri-Jalón (2011: 179–180) also emphasised the fact that, although the states provide trained linguists (who are especially involved during the preparatory processes of war and at the end of the hostilities) when violent conflict erupts, diplomatic and intelligence services are invariably insufficient and it is necessary to recruit locals who know the area.

The dilemma of the war interpreters can be found in the fact that there is a strong tendency to position them with the opposing parties, i.e. against each other (Baker, 2010). In this polarised situation, interpreters must choose between complying with the needs of their employer and remaining loyal to their origins, which, furthermore, makes them more vulnerable to attack from their fellow countrymen who view them as traitors. According to Inghilleri (2010: 165–166), the interpreters recruited by the Americans during the war in Iraq are classified into three categories: the first in this hierarchy are locals who are not considered as military personnel and thus do not receive protection as such. Next are the second-level interpreters, Americans with an extremely good level of English and native competency in the target language. These interpreters are involved in undercover operations. Finally, the third-level and highest-ranking interpreters are American citizens with excellent levels of English and native competency in the target language (however, this competency is not considered essential) and who are involved in high-security operations. This hierarchy is, without a doubt, directly comparable to a scale of loyalty: at the bottom are the 'untrustworthy' due to their different nationality and heritage, while the highest-level interpreters are the most loyal given their citizenship and place of origin.

Baker (2010) approaches the subject of the polarisation of interpreters in military conflict from the perspective of narrative theory. According to this theory, the interpreters are cast as victims or villains, as trustworthy allies or threats to security, contrasting the 'we' and 'they'. The 'they' is presented by the other side as a uniform group, lacking in individuality, divided and subdivided by their evil. The 'us' emerges as a contrast to the 'they' and presents itself as a superior and integrated group. The interpreter must work between these two parties with duties 'that strain their loyalties and disrupt their sense of identity' (Baker, 2010: 218). In this sense, it is interesting to highlight the example of using pseudonyms during the war: they protect an interpreter from potential attacks by making them non-identifiable; at the same time, pseudonyms help to alienate them from their origins in being considered 'other' (Baigorri, 2012: 94). Here, we find an interesting parallel with the European interpreters and diplomats from the Early Modern period, when European cultural values were compared to the Ottoman's and conclusions drawn in ways that suggested that the latter constituted an uncivilised and inferior society.

Although the military, for the most part, has a tendency to view local interpreters as a necessary evil, they are aware of their importance. And when military personnel and interpreters work in close collaboration for a certain period of time, it is possible to create an environment of trust where the local interpreters are viewed differently by the military who value them not only for their technical competency but also for their commitment.

Conclusion

History demonstrates that when a body of power has delegated its interests to linguistic intermediaries in situations of conflict or potential conflict, it has done so in an attempt to gain the highest possible control of them. States understand that the control of interpreters through ideological alignment can lead to a safer and more reliable context of negotiation. Be they *alfaqueques, capitanes de amigos, dragomans* or war interpreters, states have attempted to use intermediaries with the necessary technical competencies who would also remain loyal to their interests, this second requirement being even more important than the first. Loyalty appears between those who share the same race, culture and religion, especially when the cultural groups are more distant, for example in the case of Eastern and Western cultures. Lineage and patterns of commitment (service over a long period and economic reward) were also important signs of loyalty. In light of the difficulty of finding persons who combined all requirements (linguistic and ideological), states developed different recruitment processes.

Heteronomous systems were developed at the beginning of the contact with a new culture. Recruitment was improvised so that local interpreters were used, even by force of arms. Some time later, governments were able to train their own interpreters, who they trusted as they shared the same value system and roots. In diplomatic contexts, *hybrid systems* were developed, where local interpreters co-existed together with the national ones. The first held lower positions and were subordinated to the second.

The fact that translators and interpreters who worked for state administrations very often inherited their positions shows a way of creating networks of liaison officers trained within the family tradition of linguistic expertise, aligned with the value system of the monarchy (at least in appearance). Nowadays, we would consider this a corrupt practice, apart from the fact that democratic rules of the modern societies cannot discriminate against individuals according to their religion or values. Notwithstanding, in institutional contexts translators and interpreters are indoctrinated in codes of practice and protocols, which limit their scope of action and provide authorities with certain control over the tasks that have to be developed.

With regard to interpreters in situations of military conflict, it is possible to conclude that the authorities and society view the non-native interpreters as a possible threat since they deal with sensitive information and have the capacity to influence military and diplomatic decisions. This means an ideological position is required of them and to some extent imposed on them in that the interpreters cannot always cope due to security, ethical or financial reasons that also distort their notion of identity. We could conclude that governments are aware of this difficulty and therefore they prefer native interpreters because in cases of conflict these people might be less sensitive to ethical dilemmas.

Notes

(1) In this chapter, I draw on sources in extant literature and also on my own archival research. For the period of the Reconquista, discovery of the New World and further colonisation I rely on the research of Alonso, Baigorri, Fernández-Sánchez, Payás and Roser Nebot. For the Early Modern period in Spanish administration and diplomacy, I use my own archival research, which is complemented, among others, with the findings of Balliu, de Groot, Lucchetta, Petritsch, Reiter and Rothman.

(2) The Early Modern period extends from the discovery of the New World to the French Revolution.

(3) It is a term derived from Arabic meaning 'person who understands things' in the sense of 'capacity to perceive the true nature of things' (Roser Nebot, 2001: 311).

(4) There were other dragomans of lower rank specialised in customs and courts.

(5) These war pseudonyms were also frequently used by foreigners who enrolled in the International Brigades during the Spanish Civil War (Baigorri, 2012: 94–95).

References

Agildere, S.T. (2009) Les interprètes au carrefour des cultures: Ou les drogmans dans l'Empire ottoman (XVIe – debut du XX siècle). *Babel* 55 (1), 1–19.

Alonso-Araguás, I. (2012) Negociar en tiempos de guerra: viajes de ida y vuelta entre España y América s. XV-XVII. In G. Payàs and J.M. Zavala (eds) *Mediación Lingüístico Cultural en tiempos de Guerra. Cruce de miradas desde España y América* (pp. 37–64). Temuco: Ediciones Universidad Católica de Temuco.

Baigorri-Jalón, J. (2011) Wars, languages and the roles of interpreters. In *Les Liaisons Dangereuses: Langues, Traduction, Interpretation Collection 'Sources Cibles'*. Dirigée para Henri Awaiss et Jarjoura Hardane (pp. 173–204). Beyrouth: Université Saint-Joseph.

Baigorri-Jalón, J. (2012) La lengua como arma: intérpretes en la guerra civil española o la enmarañada madeja de la geografía y la historia. In G. Payàs and J.M. Zavala (eds) *Mediación Lingüístico Cultural en tiempos de Guerra. Cruce de miradas desde España y América* (pp. 85–108). Temuco: Ediciones Universidad Católica de Temuco.

Baigorri-Jalón, J. (2015) The history of the interpreting profession. In H. Mikkelson and R. Jourdenais (eds) *The Routledge Handbook of Interpreting* (pp. 11–28). London/New York: Routledge.

Baker, M. (2010) Interpreters and translators in the war zone. *The Translator,* special issue on *Translating Violent Conflict* 16 (2), 197–222.

Baker, M. and Pérez-González, L. (2012) Translation and interpreting. In J. Simpson (ed.) *Routledge Handbook of Applied Linguistics* (pp. 39–52). London/New York: Routledge.

Balliu, C. (1998) L'École des Enfants de Langues del siglo XVII: la primera escuela de interpretación en Francia. In M.A. Vega Cernuda and R. Martín-Gaitero (eds) *Actas de los VI Encuentros Complutenses en torno a la Traducción* (pp. 251–260). Madrid: Editorial Complutense.

Beaton-Thome, M. (2015) Ideology. In F. Pöchhacker (ed.) *Encyclopedia of Interpreting Studies.* Oxford/New York: Routledge.

Cáceres-Würsig, I. (2012) The jeunes de langues in the eighteenth century: Spain's first diplomatic interpreters on the European model. *Interpreting* 14 (2), 127–143.

Cáceres-Würsig, I. (2014a) Übersetzungstätigkeit und Sprachgebrauch am spanischen Hof der frühen Neuzeit. In J. Burckhardt and K.P. Jankrift (eds) *Sprache. Macht. Frieden* (pp. 197–219). Wissner Verlag: Augsburg.

Cáceres Würsig, I. (2014b) Im Niemandsland: Dragomane und jóvenes de lenguas in der spanischen Botschaft von Konstantinopel. *Lebende Sprachen* 59 (2), 343–357.

Cronin, M. (2002) The Empire talks back: Orality, heteronomy and the cultural turn in interpreting studies. In F. Pöchhacker and M. Shlesinger (eds) *The Interpreting Studies Reader* (pp. 387–397). London/New York: Routledge.

Durst, B. (2014) Diplomatische Sprachpraxis und Übersetzungskultur in der Frühen Neuzeit. Theorien, Methoden und Praktiken im Spiegel einer juristischen Dissertation von 1691. In J. Burckhardt and K.P. Jankrift (eds) *Sprache. Macht. Frieden* (pp. 59–107). Wissner Verlag: Augsburg.

Fernández-Sánchez, M. (2001) La práctica de la interpretación: introducción histórica. In A. Collados Aís and M.M. Fernández Sánchez (eds) *Manual de Interpretación Bilateral* (pp. 1–37). Granada: Editorial Comares.

Groot, A.H. de (2005) Die Dragomane 1700-1869. Zum Verlust ihrer interkulturellen Funktion. In M. Kurz, M. Scheutz, K. Vocelka and T. Winkelbauer (eds) *Das Osmanische Reich und die Habsburgermonarchie* (pp. 473–490). Wien/München: Oldenbourg Verlag.

Inghilleri, M. (2010) You don't make war without knowing why. *The Translator,* special issue on *Translating Violent Conflict* 16 (2), 175–196.

Jankrift, J. (2013) Missverständnisse im Haus des Krieges. In M. Espenhorst (ed.) *Unwissen und Missverständnisse um vormodernen Friedensprozess* (pp. 129–143). Göttingen: Vandenhoeck Ruprecht.

Lucchetta, F. (1989) La Scuola dei 'giovani di lingua' veneti nei secoli XVI e XVII. *Quaderni di Studi Arabi* (7), 19–40.

Masters, B. (2001) *Christians and the Jews in the Ottoman Arab World. The Roots of Sectarianism.* Cambridge: Cambridge University Press.

Payás, G. (2012) Acercamiento traductológico a la mediación lingüística en la Araucanía colonial. In G. Payás and J.M. Zavala (eds) *La Mediación Lingüístico-cultural en Tiempos de Guerra* (pp. 19–33). Temuco: Universidad Católica de Temuco.

Petritsch, E.D. (2005) Erziehung in guten Sitten, Andacht und Gehorsam. Die 1754 gegründete Orientalische Akademie in Wien. In M. Kurz, M. Scheutz, K. Vocelka and T. Winkelbauer (eds) *Das Osmanische Reich und die Habsburgermonarchie* (pp. 491–501). Wien/München: Oldenbourg Verlag.

Reiter, C. (2015) In Habsburgs sprachlichem Hofdienst. Translation in den diplomatischen Beziehungen zwischen den habsburgsichen Höfen von Madrid und Wien in der Frühen Neuzeit. PhD thesis, Karl Franzens Universität Graz.

Roser Nebot, N. (2001) Trujamán: Intérprete comunitario y traductor para fines específicos en la Baja Edad Media. In T. Martínez Romero and R. Recio (eds) *Essays on Medieval Translation in the Iberian Peninsula* (pp. 309–323). Castelló: Publicacions de la Universitat Jaume I.

Rothman, N. (2011) *Brokering Empire. Trans-Imperial Subjects between Venice and Istanbul.* Ithaca/London: Cornell University Press.

Schmidt-Rösler, A. (2014) Friedrich Carl von Mosers Abhandlung von den Europäischen Hof- und Staatssprachen (1750). In J. Burckhardt and K.P. Jankrift (eds) *Sprache. Macht. Frieden* (pp. 109–153). Wissner Verlag: Augsburg.

Valero-Garcés, C. (1996) Traductores e intérpretes en los primeros encuentros colombinos. *Hieronymus Complutensis* 3, 61–73.

Wolf, M. (2005) Diplomatenlehrbuben" oder angehende "Dragomane"? Zur Rekonstruktion des sozialen "Dometscherfeldes" in der Habsburgermonarchie. In M. Kurz, M. Scheutz, K. Vocelka and T. Winkelbauer (eds) *Das Osmanische Reich und die Habsburgermonarchie* (pp. 503–514). Wien/München: Oldenbourg Verlag.

Wolf, M. (2013) German speakers, step forward! Surviving through interpreting in Nazi concentration camps. *Translation and Interpreting Studies* 8 (1), 1–22.

2 Developing Public Service Translation and Interpreting under the Paradigm of Recognition: Towards Diversity-Sensitive Discourses on Ethics in PSIT

M. Rosario Martín Ruano

Introduction

In recent decades, calls for the professionalisation of translation and interpreting in public services have become increasingly frequent. These calls have often stressed the importance of introducing stricter control mechanisms in the profession, including codes of ethics and accreditation procedures to be complied with by language service providers (Corsellis, 2015; European Commission, 2009: 16; 2012: 4–5). In this chapter, I argue that, in spite of being useful for the consolidation of translation and interpreting vis-à-vis other external agents and stakeholders, instruments such as codes of ethics might turn out to be double-edged swords for the purpose of justice since, in some cases, they fail to keep pace with the paradigm shift currently underway in the legal field and in political theory.

It is important to bear in mind that critical approaches in these two disciplines have replaced the ideal of 'equality', central in the former redistribution model, with the concept of 'recognition' as a key pillar of social justice. In this chapter, I explore the relevance of this notion, articulated by authors such as Fraser (2002), Fraser and Honneth (2003) and Taylor (1994), for research, practice and training purposes in the field of public service translation and interpreting. In particular, I will argue for dynamic models based on the concept of 'recognition', which might take into account both the specificities of different settings and the active roles that public service translators and interpreters might adopt in their activity. In this regard, 'recognition' needs to be conceptualised in two ways: as recognition of the particularities and legitimate differences of the parties involved in the translation situation, and as recognition of the intervenient participation of public service translators and interpreters. Transforming our view of public service interpretation and translation (PSIT) as a reproduction or a search for sameness to a complex process of negotiation of diversity – a transformation in parallel to the paradigm shift experienced in legal and social theory – seems vital for the development of a profession that is to live up to the needs of our ever more diverse and also more asymmetrical societies. This may also contribute to the articulation of alternative (post-foundational, diversity-sensitive) discourses on ethics as applied to the specific field of PSIT.

Recognition: A Useful Notion for PSIT?

In recent decades, many disciplines seem to have been showing a growing interest in 'recognition', a concept which gained prominence in the field of political theory to a large extent thanks to a much quoted essay published by Charles Taylor originally in 1992. Given that our multicultural societies are characterised not only by increased diversity but also by growing economic and political disadvantages among different cultural and social groupings, a number of approaches addressing issues of social justice in various disciplines have posited recognition as a new socio-political principle for developing real democracy beyond egalitarian, difference-blind models (Fraser, 1995; Honneth, 1995; Ricoeur, 2007; Taylor, 1992). Substantial variations in the understanding of recognition separate the authors who have discussed this concept at length. Two of the most notable are Nancy Fraser and Axel Honneth (2003), who even co-authored a book discussing their perspectives. In any event, in current literature, with different nuances, the paradigm of recognition emerges as an alternative to the paradigm of redistribution, be it in opposition to it or as a necessary complement.

Authors who subscribe to the recognition model perceive that a redistribution model has dominated the articulation of the concept of justice in political philosophy. In their view, the concept of 'redistribution' informs theories seeking a fair allocation of resources and wealth in societies in which the economic structure results in and fosters inequalities among different social groups. Put in simple terms, the ultimate goal of redistributive policies would be to ensure the same rights and opportunities for all human beings. A frequent criticism in relation to prevailing redistributive policies is that, in their efforts to remedy and redress the unequal treatment of differentiated social groups, they neutralise idiosyncrasies and differences, which in fact tend to be de-emphasised, overlooked or even neglected (see Fraser, 2002: 21–22).

Whereas redistribution focuses on economic inequality and promotes as an ideal the effective and universal enjoyment of rights and advantages, proponents of recognition put their emphasis on the symbolic and cultural dimension (Lash & Featherstone, 2002: 2–3). In order to counteract the invisibilising or devaluing of distinctive features of certain social sectors or groups in egalitarian policies, they place respect for differences at the very core of their discourse. Aligned with Taylor's (1994: 26) claim that '[d]ue recognition is not a courtesy that we owe people. It is a basic human need', these theories perceive that inequalities often derive from relations of (real and symbolic) domination in and through which the specificity of certain social groups is undervalued, despised and/or stigmatised. The model of recognition enriches the vocabulary commonly used in relation to the idea of justice: 'Justice speaks the language of redistribution, recognition [speaks] the language of community. Justice is a question of morality, recognition of ethics; justice of respect, recognition of esteem' (Lash & Featherstone, 2002: 3). This new paradigm claims that recognition cannot be divorced from (social) justice. For Honneth (1995), for instance, we all need respect (to be treated like every other subject) and recognition (to be understood in our singularity); in addition to rights, 'love', 'respect' and 'esteem' become decisive elements in societies promoting the participation of different communities in public life.

For our purposes, Nancy Fraser's approach to recognition seems particularly relevant. Misrecognition, which Fraser (2002: 26) defines as 'a form of institutionalised subordination – and thus a serious violation of justice', can be identified both as the lower levels of esteem, respect and value that certain groups receive *a priori* in relation to others and as the resulting social subordination of those groups in social practices, which prevent them from both their self-realisation and their full participation in society. From the contention that differences are to be taken into account in multicultural societies where universalist formulae have proved to be problematic, recognition models seek not merely to compensate for or remedy structural socioeconomic disadvantages, but also to bring about changes at the level of the 'social patterns of representation, interpretation, and communication' where injustices are considered to be rooted (Fraser in Fraser & Honneth, 2003: 13). For Fraser (2002: 24, 29), the goal to be achieved is 'participatory parity', the possibility for every actor to act as 'a full member of society, capable of participating on a par with other members'; this purpose requires the participants to have 'independence and voice' and 'that institutionalised patterns of cultural value express equal respect for all participants and ensure equal opportunity for achieving social esteem'. In short, recognition models do not merely seek to correct the deficient performance of the system, but ultimately to revise its logic and dynamics with the insights provided by traditionally subordinated groupings and with the voice of identities which have frequently remained silent.

As an additional important remark, it is worth noting that some prominent authors have pinpointed translation as a crucial instrument for the purposes of recognition, a new ideal embraced by societies aiming to encompass the conflicting axes of equality and difference (Bielsa, 2015a; de Sousa Santos, 2002; White, 1990). In a much quoted collection of essays, de Sousa Santos (2002: 191–192) expressly argues that 'the theory of translation is the procedure that allows for mutual intelligibility' between different experiences of the world. According to this author, by translating, parties 'identify what unites and is common to entities that are separate by their reciprocal differences'. In other words, through this practice, all the parties involved ascertain their singularities and discover themselves to be different vis-à-vis the Other but do not give up on their commitment to the search for dialogical understanding. Along the same lines, in a book which equates justice with translation, James Boyd White (1990: 230) defines translation as 'an art of recognition and response, both to another person and to another language'. Legal operators and, in general, social agents are encouraged to become translators, who are carried to 'a point between languages, between people (and between peoples), where the differences between them can be more fully seen and more nearly comprehended – differences that enable us to see in a new way what each one is, or, perhaps more properly, differences in which the meaning and identity of each resides'. For White (1990: 230, xvii), translation is not only 'a model of law and justice' but also 'it can serve as a model for all ethical and political thought', since translation involves the contradictory assertion of the self and the appreciation of the particularities of the other and since 'it requires us to create a frame that includes both self and other, both familiar and strange'. More recently, in what has been called the 'cosmopolitan turn in social theories', where cosmopolitanism defined as 'the belonging to a global humanity further to one's community of origin' (Bielsa, 2015a: 367) is put forward as an advanced formula for the acknowledgement of and mutual respect for diversity in multicultural societies, certain authors have also argued that translation 'is a key factor in intercultural relations allowing for bridge-building in a cosmopolitanism where differences are not abolished, but productively confronted' (Bielsa, 2015b: 261; our translation). Even though the concept of cosmopolitanism is contested for some authors who perceive that elite and subaltern forms of cosmopolitanism, among others, continue to coexist and collide today (Prakash, 2015: 28), translation as a mindset seems to guarantee an openness to differences that increasingly hybrid, globalised societies require in their search for new avenues for the peaceful coexistence of various social, cultural and collective identities.

In this chapter, I will argue for the relevance of extrapolating to translation studies, and more precisely to PSIT, the debate on recognition, which has gained momentum in political philosophy, sociology and other disciplines. In my opinion, the concepts, analytical categories and definitions used by these approaches allow for an understanding of many of the problems faced today by PSIT as acts and/or effects of misrecognition. In this regard, whereas philosophers and sociologists envisage translation as an instrument for enhanced appreciation of differences, it might well be the case that dominant translation practices in institutional contexts and in public services frequently follow a redistributive logic, often serving ethnocentric agendas that exclude differences in the name of hegemonic ideologies, deliberately or inadvertently reified as universal. In addition to this, I will contend that, in the current search for solutions to existing problems, many efforts to consolidate PSIT seem to continue incardinated and anchored in redistribution-oriented dynamics. However, if the goal is to meet the conflictual demands and expectations that characterise multicultural societies, PSIT might find it useful to adopt and endorse the demands related to the recognition paradigm. Bhikhu Parekh (2000: 343) captured these conflictual challenges with a keen and intuitive eye.

> Multicultural societies throw up problems that have no parallel in history. They need to find ways of reconciling the legitimate demands of unity and diversity, achieving political unity without cultural uniformity, being inclusive without being assimilationist, cultivating among their citizens a common sense of belonging while respecting their legitimate cultural differences and cherishing plural cultural identities without weakening the shared and precious identity of shared citizenship (Parekh, 2002: 343).

Accordingly, translation and interpreting, and more precisely PSIT, also face this 'formidable task' that 'no multicultural society so far has succeeded in tackling' (Parekh, 2002: 343)

Misrecognition of and in PSIT as an Obstacle to the Recognition of Difference

It may be argued that a number of the problems that PSIT faces in order to cope adequately with diversity in translated and interpreted encounters are deep-seated in other instances of misrecognition, affecting translation and interpreting as a profession and related to the expectations constructed around them. If 'translation' in general is, as pointed out by Simeoni (1998) using Bourdieu's concepts, a heteronomous social field deprived of sovereignty or self-government, a field largely regulated by external authorities and social agents, this seems to be all the more true in PSIT, where there are still many (more) signs that its practitioners lack the ability to define the rules and standards according to which their performance will be evaluated. Even though in recent studies some authors distinguish positive indications of PSIT as an 'emerging community of practice' (Corsellis, 2015: 103), many others confirm the persistence of worrying signs pointing at a fragmented, unregulated and low-profile activity, especially in relation to languages of limited diffusion, where the shortage of trained professionals is more remarkable. According to a study by the European Commission (2012), these include persistent paraprofessionalism, lack of training, qualification and certification procedures and a recent decline in the already low prices paid, a situation aggravated by the prevalent outsourcing trend in increasingly privatised 'public' translation and interpreting services. What interests us here is that, from a recognition perspective, the low status of translation as a profession can be considered to be not merely a result of these factors providing a socioeconomic explanation to its precariousness, but also as an additional cause feeding into it.

Theories about recognition allow us to discern a whole power regime shaping translation and interpreting as second-rate activities in a hierarchical, cultural and socio-professional system characterised by an uneven division of labour, as well as concrete institutionalised patterns of unequal value which result in the downplaying of the nature, importance and complexity of the tasks performed by translators and interpreters. In particular, in the case of PSIT, where minority languages are habitually involved, it is worth noting that, even though in abstract terms, bilingualism or mastery of more than one language seems to be considered as an asset (and this is certainly the case of prestige languages like English or French), the different positions that languages occupy in a ladder of social value explain that proficiency in a minority language is frequently not perceived as a comparable merit, and may even be portrayed as an impediment in certain social narratives, for instance those representing it as a hindrance to social integration for second-generation communities of immigrant origin (see, e.g. Dicker, 2000: 71ff).

In any event, a more important instance of misrecognition adds up to the potential devaluing of the language skills of PSIT practitioners, namely, that translation merely involves and requires language skills. Many are the authors in the field of PSIT who have criticised that, in the widespread social perception, this activity is reduced to an automatic transmission or conversion process, a mechanical task (Angelelli, 2015; Hale, 2015). The frequent directive in PSIT to 'reproduce exactly what the text says' or to 'just translate' commented upon by Hale (2005: 20–21, 2015: 169) can be said to reveal not only the derogatory view of translation and interpreting as 'manual' rather than 'intellectual labour', to put it in Venuti's (1992: 1–2) terms, but also the prevalence of a deeply ingrained hierarchy, to use Snell-Hornby's (2006: 172) metaphor, subordinating the 'powerless transcoder providing raw material' to the '"real specialist or artist" responsible for its further processing'.

The consequences of this type of misrecognition are serious. Following Foucault, Bourdieu, Hall or Butler, theories aligned with the recognition paradigm take as a key starting point the assumption that identities (including professional identities like those of translators and interpreters) are to a great extent constituted through discursive practices which, through repetition, naturalise as legitimate certain subject positions. Inasmuch as one's self-image is to a large extent moulded by interaction with other agents, in processes of identification with subject positions affected by misrecognition the self-confidence of individuals aspiring to occupy them is likely to be undermined. In this regard, Hale (2005: 17, 20) identifies the social perception that translation and interpreting are basic, unskilled tasks which can be executed relying only on intuition and requiring no formal expertise or competence acquisition as a factor triggering what she terms the 'identity crisis' of these professionals. Moreover, a productive and not merely repressive vision of power as exercised throughout the social body helps us to understand that translators and interpreters might perpetuate the power regime within which, by necessity, they construct their identity performatively, for instance by uncritically miming the conventional behaviour attuned to dominant–subordinate relationships internalised as natural. By accommodating to dominant expectations in their quest for approval without challenging the shortcomings of long-standing practices, translators and interpreters might contribute, in the long run, to the downgrading of their professional status.

Misrecognition not only affects the self-image and praxis of translators and interpreters. It often involves being denied the status of full-partner in social (and/or professional) interaction. In PSIT, there is ample evidence that the scope of action that is expected of or allowed to professionals is often curtailed or disregarded. To the extent that expectations about their participation in the intercultural encounter are often unrealistically restrictive, translators and interpreters are likely to be seen with suspicion and distrust (see Inghilleri, 2009: 207): the prevalent translation regime constructing translators and interpreters as copyist or as non-persons easily turns them into disobedient trespassers of limits and borders, constantly sidestepping unworkable rules of communicative and (non)interpretive behaviour, into outlaws frequently exceeding their legitimate (non)space and (non)authority.

Rather than being considered as colleagues by other co-workers, translators and interpreters are often viewed with scepticism or discomfort, as out-group, untrustworthy actors. Furthermore, when the existing expectations and needs of actual performance are dissociated from the very outset, situations of conflict are bound to arise. Gómez Moreno (2014: 33–34), for example, offers a long but non-exhaustive typology of conflictual situations owing to the failure of public authorities to understand the role of interpreters and the complexities of the tasks performed by them. In any event, the manifestations of misrecognition are not only conflict and distrust. It can also show up in the form of neglect and disdain. Far from being considered to be on a par with other specialised operators, in a relation based on the expectation of reciprocal exchange of expertise and on mutual trust, both translators and interpreters and their capacities are underestimated by other stakeholders. Existing literature in the field of PSIT regrets not only that the challenging nature of this activity and its decisive importance is frequently not acknowledged but also that it is outrightly negated.

A growing complaint is that translators and interpreters are not consulted enough by their counterparts in the specialised fields (Morgan, 2011: 7), and, more generally, that the potential contribution of translation and interpreting to effective intercultural communication is commonly wasted or underutilised. This is considered to be a side effect of the restrictive model linking translation and interpreting to verbatim renditions (Mikkelson, 1998) or attributed to ignorance of the potential benefits that conceptualisations of translation and interpreting going beyond the conduit model might bring about. In a very enlightening article, Clifford (2004) establishes a direct link between the prior experience of health professionals in triadic exchanges and the degree of involvement and active participation they expect of the interpreter in achieving a successful communicative event. Seemingly, greater familiarity with these professionals enhances the social agents' awareness of differences and their perception of translators and interpreters as useful partners to discover, understand and productively negotiate them.

In relation to this latter point, for the purposes of this chapter, I am particularly interested in the importance attached (or denied) to difference and cultural specificity in widely accepted opinions about translation which to a large extent shape expectations and practices in the field of PSIT. From a recognition perspective, seemingly sacrosanct ideals that translation and interpreting are expected and often expressly required to honour, such as accuracy and fidelity – two recurrent maxims conjured up in codes of ethics – entail simplifying, depreciatory and disparaging assumptions about difference. The frequent claim for equivalence understood as an exact rendition seems to presume, or even to posit as an ideal, the congruity of cultures, the isomorphism of mentalities, representations and expressive patterns. However, in the asymmetrical dynamics of globalisation, translation practices which adhere to this normative model might in fact involuntarily take part in larger policies of cultural homogenisation, misrepresenting vulnerable users failing to assimilate to the mainstream world view and conventions or promoting their exclusion.

From the critical angle of recognition, the focus on achieving sameness to the detriment of difference can be considered to be revealing of an underlying redistribution rationality governing the widespread conceptualisation of translation and interpreting practices. Other symptoms seem to indicate the powerful grip of redistribution-inspired logics in the concrete field of PSIT, one of them being the frequent metaphorisation of translation and interpreting as remedial actions to remove the obstacles for disadvantaged communities. Thinking of translation as a solution for language diversity might ultimately entail regarding and projecting difference as a problem, as a threat to socially homogeneous and culturally integrated societies. Indeed, in statements taking this logic to the extreme, translation and interpreting may be portrayed not even as a solution, but as short-term, stopgap measures aggravating the root issue: recent criticism which had a public echo criticised translation and interpreting as having 'an adverse impact on integration' by reducing the incentive for migrant communities to learn the national language (see Beardmore, 2015). Totalising visions of language and culture and monocultural ideologies often underlie widespread opinions about translation and interpreting.

In this regard, it could be argued that, in the social narrative in which translation is construed as levelling unequal access to the institutional message of communities who do not master the language, translation seems to be construed, rather than as a universal right, as a right to the universal. The perception of inequality frequently adopts as normative a set of standards that are not questioned; the cross-cultural validity of the communicative patterns sanctioned by the institution is not disputed. In this regard, the assumption that texts and utterances to be conveyed in the institutional domain are crystal-clear, free of bias and culturally independent underlies another normative expectation in PSIT subtly activating the myth of reverse discrimination: that the goal of translation and interpreting is not to 'facilitate' or 'simplify' the messages for migrant or minority communities, but merely to place them on an equal (and perhaps an equally precarious) footing as speakers of the national language (see Mikkelson [1998] for a critical view of this expectation). The ideal of equality (among individuals) and identicalness (in translation) overshadows the existence of cultural differences that need to be bridged or negotiated and overrates the potential responsiveness of subordinate groups to misunderstanding or mistreatment. The caveat expressed by Mikkelson (2000: 45–46) in relation to the risks involved in 'provid[ing] information about a certain practice, concept, or expression when you are familiar with the subject and you want to help people communicate. There is a danger [...] that you may be perceived as favouring one side or the other by speaking for them or explaining their attitudes' reveals the prevalence of difference-blind or difference-unfriendly narratives: context-sensitive measures adopted to alleviate structural disadvantages may be seen by some actors as illegitimate support and as conferring to certain individuals extra rights which are not recognised for the mainstream population. Again, misrecognition might be seen at work in the fact that translation, essentially an intercultural activity, generates distrust and suspicion if it emphasises cultural difference.

In this panorama, translators and interpreters might feel discouraged from taking the initiative to underscore the singularities of the different participants in translated and interpreted encounters. Tymoczko (2007: 258) perceives with dissatisfaction that translators and interpreters 'often compromise cultural translation much more than they need to, vitiating their own agency and empowerment in the process. They are also often more timid in their representations than is required, undertaking less cultural transfer than they might and underestimating the ability of their audiences to tolerate, learn from, and engage with cultural difference and newness'. It might well be the case that PSIT, in order to comply with the unobtrusive behaviour expected of practitioners in this field, might regularly and inadvertently be serving domesticating agendas, opting for apparently 'fluent' renditions into the institutional idiom which, certainly, erase potential discrepancies and misunderstandings, but which also squander the opportunity for the mutual recognition of differences.

Struggling for Recognition beyond the Redistribution Model

In recent times, recommendations for advancing towards the professionalisation of translation and interpreting and for fighting against current market disorder feature as a priority issue in specialised literature in translation studies in general and, more specifically, in PSIT. Repeated proposals include creating or strengthening specialised training programmes in different subfields, clearly defined certification and accreditation procedures, reliable registers of expert professionals and enforceable professional codes of conduct (European Commission, 2009, 2012). The latter merit special attention, as these are seen as vital tools in ensuring quality by providing binding norms and standards for professionals who could be subject to disciplinary procedures in case of breach of their principles. The argument I will put forward is that, even though codes of conduct may prove helpful to build public trust and to stimulate reflection on the standards to be met by practitioners, it is also true that they might contribute to the fossilisation of the profession if they uncritically reify restrictive, limiting or obsolete visions of translation and interpreting as a profession and as a social activity. In this regard, from a recognition perspective, the requirements expressed in certain codes of ethics could be seen as attuned to redistribution-oriented or redistribution-inspired models.

The insistence on the preservation of the source message except for changes in the syntactic or semantic dimension, the explicit call for the unobtrusive performance of practitioners and the restraining and proscriptive nature of many of the rules referring to translators' or interpreters' demeanour in recent codes (EULITA, 2013) can be seen in this light: they can be considered to set a frame within which translation is called to operate as unnoticeably and smoothly as possible between purportedly 'equal' partners, identical in their beliefs and expectations and not separated by cultural or power divides. However, in light of the demographic make-up of current societies, these well-intended assumptions could turn out to be either naïvely or restrictively blind to diversity and, in the long run, prove to be unable to meet the challenges of identitarian and cultural pluralism.

For this reason, in addition or even in parallel to investing extra efforts to further regulate an activity traditionally overregulated by impracticable expectations and simplistic preconceptions, promoting recognition of what translation and interpreting really imply remains an urgent and pending task. Instead of further limiting the scope and room for manoeuvre of translators and interpreters, it is vital to explain its complexities, challenges and potentialities. For Taylor (1994), recognition requires re-cognition, 'knowing again', changing our mental habits, transforming our previous visions, thinking otherwise. In relation to misrecognised identities affected by negative stereotypes and distorted views, recognition implies 'revising the inherited social meaning of their identities, [...] constructing positive life scripts where there once were primarily negative ones' (Gutmann, 1994: xi). Much remains to be done in terms of making society in general and other experts in particular aware of the cognitively intricate, culturally challenging and interpersonally demanding nature of translating and interpreting activities and of the positive effects that closer synergies with these professionals who do far more than mechanically swapping words from one language to another could have for institutional actors and users in intercultural situations. If, according to Fraser (1995), transforming the social patterns of representation, interpretation and communication which routinely create subordinate status is vital for enhanced recognition, codes of conduct could be seen as a privileged text-type where operating this transformation from within could begin. Critical perspectives have claimed that codes of conduct merely invoke abstract values offering no solutions in situations of conflict (Baker & Maier, 2011: 4) or that they overlook rather than tackle actual problems (Koskinen, 2000: 82). To counter the shortcomings of current instruments, codes of conduct could adopt a more explanatory function, and overtly recognise and address the dilemmas of contemporary societies. In this regard, if given the opportunity to establish the principles guiding translator and interpreter behaviour and decisions in a vast array of situations, the translation community may not merely claim recognition for what is already expected of them, i.e. for the limited role legal translators and interpreters have been forced to play. Translators could fight to enlarge understanding and appreciation for what they really do and may need to do in practice: transforming texts or speeches into another language and for a difference target audience, mediating between different cultural and institutional systems, incommensurable conceptual universes and diverging behavioural expectations and making dialogue possible through complex acts and decisions requiring discretionary expertise. Ultimately, translators could even fight for recognition for what they could do at the service of society if their full capacities were exploited. In this regard, Koskinen (2008: 64–67, 146–155) and Stecconi and Hermans (2002: n.p.) make a call to institutions to capitalise on the strengths and training of translators, and make a parallel call to translators to be 'proactive' in showcasing their values and potential.

Highly representative and symbolic as codes of conduct are due to their binding nature – despite the fact that a number of authors have also called into question their allegedly regulatory function (Koskinen, 2000: 82; Wolf, 2010: 37) and have pointed out the significant variations in the vague principles recurrently invoked by them (Ko, 2006; McDonough, 2011) – these texts are but the tip of the iceberg of a complex network of discursive practices constituting translation and interpreting as socially regulated activities towards which transformative efforts could also be geared. Other current and potential initiatives to enhance recognition by institutions and social stakeholders of the complexities, challenges and possibilities of translation and interpreting in our contemporary societies include explanatory workshops and publications directed to the institutional players using translation and interpreting services in order to raise their awareness about the intricacies of translation and interpreting in general and about the specific challenges that translators and interpreters face in certain institutional settings, for instance courts or health services.

The 'Guidelines for magistrates and judges on working with interpreters in court' included in Hale (2015) are one enlightening example in this regard. These guidelines can be read as an enlightening recognition-building exercise in relation to interpreting as a profession. In these recommendations (Hale, 2015), normative expectations are coupled with practical advice revealing the strategy in which they need to take concrete form ('Explain their role: "To interpret everything faithfully and impartially in the first/second grammatical person"') and subsequently qualified in order to remedy misconceptions ('Remember that interpreting faithfully does not mean interpreting "literally" – word-for-word translations normally produce nonsensical renditions'); negative scripts about interpreters are challenged and reversed ('Tell the interpreter to feel free to seek clarification when needed, seek leave to consult a dictionary or to ask for repetitions. N.B. It is a sign of a good interpreter to take such actions when needed, to ensure accuracy of interpretation'). The traditional representation of the interpreter as a non-person, the origin of undue distrust or disappointment, is replaced by a more realistic image generating feelings of understanding and empathy, a necessary basis for any collaborative relation ('Ask the interpreter when s/he would like to take her breaks'; 'Instruct lawyers and witnesses to speak clearly and at a reasonable pace'; 'If there is anything to be read out, provide the interpreter with a copy of it so s/he can follow').

Another relevant example can be found in a guide for interpreted–mediated medical consultations (Bischoff et al., 2009) which provides practical clues for establishing a collaborative relation with interpreters and which, additionally, is inspirational in its promotion of an enhanced recognition of diversity. Cultural difference is portrayed as an asset for all the interlocutors involved; interpreters are praised as privileged agents granting the other parties the unique and enriching opportunity of accessing and getting acquainted with cultures different from their own (Bischoff et al., 2009: 19). This guide can be considered to be actively fostering 'social relations of symmetrical esteem' which, according to Honneth (1995: 129) represent a prerequisite for solidarity: 'to esteem one another symmetrically means to view one another in light of values that allow the abilities and traits of the other to appear significant for shared praxis. Relationships of this sort can be said to be cases of "solidarity", because they inspire not just passive tolerance but felt concern for what is individual and particular about the other person'. Among those particularities, the vulnerable position of patients, who might feel intimidated by the presence of two professionals, is stressed as a potentially differential factor that needs to be taken into account (Bischoff et al., 2009: 18).

As a third and last example, vulnerability, linguistic and cultural differences and diminished abilities on the part of the victims to express themselves clearly in relation to facts and issues that have been a source of suffering are listed as distinctive features often characterising interpreter-mediated encounters dealing with gender-based violence situations. Based on the acknowledgement of the recurrent specificities identified in these contexts, a number of guides have recently been published to help translators and interpreters to adequately address them, by integrating additional requirements derived from the recognition of salient context-bound particularities (for instance, avoidance of judgemental vocabulary or gestures, psychological strength to deal with the distressing effects of these situations, unprejudiced treatment of explicit terms in relation to sexual violence, empathy, etc.) into the professional demands to be met: '[a]s with all interpreting situations, interpreters must remain professional while taking into account the sensitivity of the situation' (Glasgow Violence Against Women Partnership, 2011: 5). Perceiving that many differential traits potentially causing misunderstanding, oppression or domination might be interconnected in these situations related to gender-based violence, Lucero

(2015) argues for an 'intersectional approach' allowing the interpreter to define a contextually appropriate strategy which, within the boundaries of professional behaviour, might effectively respond to the combination of axes overlapping in each situation. Recognising difference(s) as a factor to be addressed entails recognising enhanced decision-making responsibilities for translators and interpreters, acknowledging their active and intervenient role in the interpretation and construction of meanings and avowing their participation as fully fledged agents negotiating intelligibilities for other parties, including for those traditionally excluded or subordinated in social practices. Recognition thus emerges as a potential basis for the 'participatory parity' called for by Fraser (2002: 24, 29).

Conclusion

In any event, and in order to conclude, it must be stressed that recognition is not only dependent on being understood by others; it also requires self-recognition. It is both an external and internal process by which individuals or groups discover new self-definitions. In addition to the need for enhancing recognition by societal stakeholders of the challenges that translation and interpreting face today, raising further awareness among translators and interpreters in relation to the challenges posed by an increasingly culturally diverse future which calls for a stronger commitment to difference in their professional praxis is of utmost importance. Taking into account their significance as 'the main socialising factor for the agents' future community practice' (Wolf, 2010: 42), training institutions appear to be privileged sites to actively revise the definition and value of translation and interpreting in public services. From the perspective that translation and interpreting are activities in a constant state of evolution, and which need to change if they are to meet the challenges of the changing societies within which they operate, the function of training programmes cannot be reduced to teaching students to fulfil norms, but need to be envisaged also as fostering their critical capacities. Both future practitioners and the profession may thus discover and overcome the limitations of existing models.

In this regard, Martín Ruano (2015) discusses transformative didactic approaches in relation to deontological requirements. In particular, given the low status of the profession, training institutions face the challenge of helping students to build a more positive self-image and to develop stronger self-confidence for exploring further possibilities for enhancing reciprocal recognition among interlocutors. Introducing the demands of recognition in the training process might help students to discover and resist the ethnocentric bias and the limitations of utilitarian and proceduralist models of translation which, in their quest for equality, negate or postpone existing differences. It may also encourage them to take more initiative in acting as peers, as full partners, in social interactions and in promoting participatory parity for all parties involved in translated or interpreted encounters by allowing for the appreciation of their particularist identities. Recognition theories help to approach norms not merely in a restrictive manner, but rather as a starting point for agency.

As Lash and Featherstone (2002: 9) remind us with Bauman in their introduction to a reference book on the recognition paradigm, '[p]ower no longer resides in the frame of the master and the slave but rather in the hands of the "frame-breakers".' Translators and interpreters have the power to break existing frames in PSIT currently contributing to the invisibilising of diversity and to the cancelling out of differences, or acting as accomplices of ideologised representations of minority groups as exotic, as radically Other, as incommensurably alien. In this regard, for instance, Alkhalifa (1999) and Martin and Taibi (2010) argue for alternatives to dominant literalist practices which, in their opinion, generate distorted visions, humorous surprise or intercultural suspicion vis-à-vis alterity. Translators and interpreters have the possibility to move forward from the dominant 'ethics of representation' (Clifford, 2004) in order to explore new avenues for encompassing the demands of diversity. Recognition of their potential to influence the shaping of tomorrow's society is a crucial step in advancing towards the recognition of differences.

Acknowledgements

This chapter is part of the research carried out by the GIR 'Traducción, Ideología, Cultura' in the projects financed by the Spanish Ministerio de Economía y Competitividad FFI2012-35000 and FFI2015-66516-P/MINECO/FEDER, UE.

References

Alkhalifa, W.S. (1999) El tortuoso camino de la traducción: la traducción jurídica del árabe. In M. Hernando de Larramendi, J.P. Arias and M. Arkoun (eds) *Traducción, emigración y culturas* (pp. 231–240). Cuenca: Universidad de Castilla-La Mancha.

Angelelli, C. (2015) Justice for all? Issues faced by linguistic minorities and border patrol agents during interpreted arraignment interviews. *MonTI*, special issue on *Legal Interpreting at a Turning Point* 7, 181–205.

Baker, M. and Maier, C. (2011) Ethics in interpreter and translator training. The *Interpreter and Translator Trainer* 5 (1), 1–14.

Beardmore, E. (2015) Sheffield Council blasted for spending £700,000 on translation. *The Star*, 18 February. See http://www.thestar.co.uk/news/sheffield-council-blasted-for-spending-700-000-on-translation-1-7111386 (accessed 16 June 2015).

Bhikhu, C.P. (2000) *Rethinking Multiculturalism: Cultural Diversity and Political Theory*. London: McMillan.

Bielsa, E. (2015a) Apertura cosmopolita al otro. Una aproximación al papel de la traducción en la teoría social del cosmopolitismo. *Papers. Revista de Sociologia* 100 (3), 365–382.

Bielsa, E. (2015b) Cosmopolitismo, alteridad, traducción. *Papers. Revista de Sociologia* 100 (3), 261–264.

Bischoff, A., Loutan, L. and García Beyaert, S. (2009) *En otras palabras. Guía para la consulta médica intercultural.* Geneva: Universal Doctor Project.

Clifford, A. (2004) Is fidelity ethical? The social role of the healthcare interpreter. *TTR* XVII (2), 89–114.

Corsellis, A. (2015) Strategies for progress: Looking for firm ground. *MonTI*, Special Issue on *Legal Interpreting at a Turning Point* 7, 101–114.

de Sousa Santos, B. (2002) Nuestra America: Reinventing a subaltern paradigm of recognition and redistribution. In S. Lash and M. Featherstone (eds) *Recognition and Difference: Politics, Identity, Multiculture* (pp. 191–192). London: Sage.

Dicker, S.J. (2000) *Languages in America: A Pluralist View.* Clevedon: Multilingual Matters.

EULITA (2013) Code of Professional Ethics. See http://www.eulita.eu/sites/default/files/EULITA-code-London-e.pdf (accessed 16 June 2015).

European Commission (2009) *Reflection Forum on Multilingualism and Interpreter Training. Final Report.* Luxembourg: European Commission. See http://ec.europa.eu/dgs/scic/docs/finall_reflection_forum_report_en.pdf (accessed 16 June 2015).

European Commission (2012) *The Status of the Translation Profession in the European Union.* Luxembourg: European Commission. See http://ec.europa.eu/dgs/translation/publications/studies/translation_profession_en.pdf (accessed 16 June 2015).

Fraser, N. (1995) From redistribution to recognition? Dilemmas of justice in a 'postsocialist' age. *New Left Review* 212 (July/August), 68–93.

Fraser, N. (2002) Recognition without ethics. In S. Lash and M. Featherstone (eds) *Recognition and Difference: Politics, Identity, Multiculture* (pp. 20–42). London: Sage.

Fraser, N. and Honneth, A. (2003) *Redistribution or Recognition: A Political-Philosophical Exchange* (J. Golb, J. Ingram and C. Wilke, trans.). London: Verso.

Glasgow Violence Against Women Partnership (2011) Good practice guidance on interpreting for women who have experienced gender based violence. See http://www.womenssupportproject.co.uk/userfiles/file/GVAWP%20Good%20Practice%20Guide%202011%20Final%20Nov.pdf (accessed 15 June 2015).

Gómez Moreno, P. (2014) Situaciones de conflicto en el ámbito de la interpretación en los tribunales de justicia españoles: análisis descriptivo y estrategias de prevención. In C. Valero-Garcés (ed.) *(Re)considerando ética e ideología en situaciones de conflicto/(Re)considering Ethics and Ideology in Situations of Conflict* (pp. 33–37). Alcalá: Universidad de Alcalá.

Gutmann, A. (1994) Preface (1994). In A. Gutmann (ed.) *Multiculturalism and the Politics of Recognition.* Princeton: Princeton University Press, ix–xii.

Hale, S. (2005) The interpreter's identity crisis. In J. House, R. Martín Ruano and N. Baumgarten (eds) *Translation and the Construction of Identity* (pp. 14–29). Seoul: IATIS.

Hale, S. (2015) Approaching the bench: Teaching magistrates and judges how to work effectively with interpreters. *MonTI*, special issue on *Legal Interpreting at a Turning Point* 7, 163–180.

Honneth, A. (1995) *The Struggle for Recognition. The Moral Grammar of Social Conflicts* (J. Anderson, trans.). Cambridge: Polity Press.

Inghilleri, M. (2009) Translation in war zones: Ethics under fire in Iraq. In E. Bielsa and C. Hughes (eds) *Globalisation, Political Violence and Translation* (pp. 207–221). Houndsmills: Palgrave Macmillan.

Ko, L. (2006) Fine-tuning the code of ethics for interpreters and translators. *Translation Watch Quarterly* 2 (3), 45–96.

Koskinen, K. (2000) *Beyond ambivalence. Postmodernity and the ethics of translation.* Academic dissertation, University of Tampere.

Koskinen, K. (2008) *Translating Institutions*. Manchester: St. Jerome.

Lash, S. and Featherstone, M. (2002) Recognition and difference. In S. Lash and M. Featherstone (eds) *Recognition and Difference: Politics, Identity,* Multiculture (pp. 1–19). London: Sage.

Lucero, M. (2015) Interseccionalidad y Feminist-Relational Approach: nuevos enfoques para la formación y actuación de intérpretes en contextos de violencia de género. *Asparkía 26,* 91–104.

Martin, A. and Taibi, M. (2010) Translating and interpreting for the police in politicised contexts: The case of Tayseer Allouny. In J. Boéri and C. Maier (eds) *Compromiso Social y Traducción/Interpretación* (pp. 38–40, 214–226). Granada: ECOS.

Martín Ruano, M.R. (2015) (Trans)formative theorising in legal translation and/or interpreting: A critical approach to deontological principles. *The Interpreter and Translator Trainer 9* (2), 141–155.

McDonough, J. (2011) Moral ambiguity: Some shortcomings of professional codes of ethics for translators. *JoSTrans* 15, 28–49.

Mikkelson, H. (1998) Towards a redefinition of the role of the court interpreter [originally published in *Interpreting* 3(1)]. See http://www.acebo.com/pages/towards-a-redefinition-of-the-role-of-the-court-interpreter (accessed 16 June 2015).

Mikkelson, H. (2000) *Introduction to Court Interpreting*. Manchester: St Jerome.

Morgan, C. (2011) The new European directive on the rights to interpretation and translation in criminal proceedings. In S. Brau and J.L. Taylor (eds) *Videoconference and Remote Interpreting in Criminal Proceedings* (pp. 5–10). Guildford: University of Surrey.

Parekh, B. (2002) *Rethinking Multiculturalism: Cultural Diversity and Political Theory*. Cambridge, MA: Harvard University Press.

Prakash, G. (2015) Whose cosmopolitanism? Multiple, globally enmeshed and subaltern. In N.G. Schiller and A. Irving (eds) *Whose Cosmopolitanism? Critical Perspectives, Relationalities and Discontents* (pp. 27–28). New York/Oxford: Berghahn.

Ricoeur, P. (2007) *Reflections on the Just* (D. Pellauer, trans.). Chicago, IL: The University of Chicago Press.

Simeoni, D. (1998) The pivotal status of the translator's habitus. *Target* 10 (1), 1–40.

Snell-Hornby, M. (2006) *The Turns of Translation Studies*. Amsterdam: John Benjamins.

Stecconi, U. and Hermans, T. (2002) Translators as Hostages of History, lecture, DGT Brussels and Luxembourg. See http://web.letras.up.pt/mtt/tt/Hermans.pdf (accessed 16 June 2015).

Taylor, C. (1994) The politics of recognition. In A. Gutmann (ed.) *Multiculturalism and the Politics of Recognition* (pp. 25–73). Princeton, NJ: Princeton University Press.

Tymoczko, M. (2007) *Enlarging Translation, Empowering Translators*. Manchester: St Jerome.

Venuti, L. (1992) Introduction. In L. Venuti (ed.) *Rethinking Translation: Discourse, Subjectivity, Ideology* (pp. 1–17). London/New York: Routledge.

White, J.B. (1990) *Justice as Translation: An Essay in Cultural and Legal Criticism*. Chicago, IL: University of Chicago Press.

Wolf, M. (2010) Translation 'going social'? Challenges to the (ivory) tower of Babel. *MonTI 2,* 29–46.

3 Interpreting-as-Conflict: PSIT in Third Sector Organisations and the Impact of Third Way Politics

Rebecca Tipton

Introduction

Greater reliance on the non-profit, voluntary and charities sector (commonly described as the third sector) in the delivery of human services in Britain over the past two decades reflects ideological shifts in the political landscape and raises questions as to the way in which the sector handles an increasingly linguistic and culturally diverse service user base. Such shifts also invite a reassessment of what constitute public services and challenge dichotomised approaches to the statutory and voluntary sectors that have been prevalent in interpreting studies to date. As a consequence, new understandings of how interpreting services achieve legitimation are made possible, where legitimation is understood, following Gaus (2011: 4), as 'acts or processes through which views about the worthiness of an order are established'.

Fears that a mixed economy of welfare, that is, one based on various forms of partnership work between government, private enterprise and third sector organisations, is likely to undermine legitimation due to the increased use of unpaid volunteer interpreters (whether trained or untrained) merits particular attention in Britain where the third sector is characterised by changing organisational forms, increased professionalisation and different approaches to stakeholder accountability. This chapter aims to shed light on language support policy and practice in the third sector against the backdrop of third way politics under New Labour. In particular, it explores the extent to which professionalisation of the sector during the period in question extended to interpreting and translation provision, and the impact of language support policy on organisational operations and mission.

The chapter firstly discusses recent theorisations of the legitimation of interpreting and translation in public services. It highlights the scope for more contextual-historicist approaches in exploring issues of legitimation, which in this case take the form of a particular political party's term of office as a unit of analysis. This is followed by an examination of some of the ideological elements of third way politics in which problems of reflexivity and emancipation are foregrounded. Drawing on the work of Fairclough (2000a, 2000b) and Squire (2005) on selected discursive formulations characteristic of New Labour rhetoric, conceptualisations of reciprocity in interpreting and translation services are discussed in relation to the new social contract promoted during the period. The final sections examine the impact of third way politics on the development of the third sector and issues of accountability for limited proficiency speaking service users. The discussions are supported by a study of language support regimes in a selection of third sector organisations in England between 2009 and 2015.

Public Service Interpreting and the Crisis of Legitimation

The emphatic electoral victory of New Labour in 1997 was followed by a marked rise in immigration, a buoyant employment market, higher numbers of foreign students, the accession of new Member States to the European Union and the Human Rights Act (Finch & Goodhart, 2010). The rise in asylum cases in particular prompted demand for suitably qualified interpreters to support status determination processes and access to public services, but support was also required for migrants with other residency statuses in domains where the technical demands of institutional interaction far exceeded proficiency levels.

Although the professionalisation of interpreting and translation for public services in Britain had progressed significantly in the 1990s through accreditation and certification schemes, the process was strengthened by the incorporation into UK law of the European Convention on Human Rights. Article 6, for example, stipulated the right to a fair trial and the right to the free assistance of an interpreter. Support also came in the form of Lord Justice Auld's Review of the Criminal Courts of England and Wales (2001) and a National Agreement on Arrangements for the Use of Interpreters, Translators and Language Service Professionals in Investigations and Proceedings within the Criminal Justice System, which had been in place since 1998 and revised in 2007, and which set out best practice. It is important to note, however, that sections of the Agreement were disapplied on the entry into force of the Ministry of Justice's Framework Agreement through which some criminal justice organisations undertook contracts with a single contract holder from 2011.

In services outside of the judiciary, language support for limited proficiency speakers was couched in much broader terms. General statutory authorities were required, for example, through the Race Relations (Amendment) Act 2000 to have due regard to the need to eliminate unlawful discrimination and promote equality of opportunity. Translation and interpreting were understood as potential means for achieving these ends; however, despite being subject to formal procurement processes during the period in question, the level of support for commissioning and monitoring quality interpreting and translation services appeared minimal. For example, the 2002 DH Circular LAC (Department of Health, 2002) outlined a national eligibility framework designed to achieve consistency in the assessment and allocation of care services. Point 29 of the circular set out the need for councils to promote the development of services to supply interpreters and translators, and advocate their use. However, it contained no detailed guidance on commissioning professional services or on what service users could expect. Although this might not be surprising given the circular's overarching aims, the lack of available supporting information meant that the nature of the contract between state and service user remained opaque.

In many respects, despite the gaps and inconsistencies, the early part of the New Labour era was characterised by considerable political sponsorship for interpreting and translation services, supported by the need to comply with national and supranational legal instruments, and by the wider human rights agenda. The Human Rights Act (2000) marked, in principle at least, a significant cultural change in the delivery of public services by creating a new ethical basis for relations between state and citizens; however, the extent of its subsequent implementation has received considerable criticism (see, for example, Donald *et al.*, 2009). Whether it explicitly served to support the legitimation of public service interpreting and translation across sectors and domains of activity is open to question. Even in cases where it appeared to have a positive impact, it tended to conceal broader issues of accountability, to which I return later.

In interpreting studies more generally speaking, the problem of legitimation has been theorised in ways that draw on global political theory, sociology and moral and political philosophy. Cronin (2006), for example, explores legitimation through the lens of what might be termed subaltern cosmopolitanism in order to chart the development of 'intrinsic' translation, as exemplified by recent Irish and German experiences of migration. He promotes a differentiated approach to cosmopolitanism as a more useful theoretical vantage point than multiculturalism, communitarianism and pluralism, which tend to predicate entitlement to certain rights and services on the individual's membership of a particular community. Since the cosmopolitan perspective permits multiple affiliations, it raises the possibility of individual choice, and in so doing echoes other approaches that explore membership or belonging 'as a matter of degrees' (Erel, 2011: 2053, see also Yuval-Davis, 2006) and in relation to new sociolinguistic landscapes (Blommaert, 2013). For Cronin (2006: 20), the unwillingness of cosmopolitan theory 'to be wholly subject to any fixed, permanent, all-encompassing notion of belonging or being' is important in defending public service interpreting and translation against their critics.

In other approaches, the problem of legitimation has been framed for example in terms of occupational vulnerability and theorised through the Bourdieusian concepts of field, capital and habitus (Inghilleri, 2003, 2005a, 2005b). In addressing the seemingly incommensurable position of interpreting as a radically liminal activity that takes place in zones of uncertainty (i.e. the spaces between fields), Inghilleri (2005a: 70) draws on Bernstein's (1990) concept of 'pedagogic discourse' to articulate the means by which such zones are 'endowed with the potential to create new forms of legitimate social practice'. However, the ability to realise this potential depends on relevant agents understanding hierarchical field relations and their accompanying habitus, which means that the question of 'whose normative practices prevail' (Inghilleri, 2005a: 73) is posited as integral to the problem of legitimation (see also Martín Ruano; Valero-Garcés this volume).

Inghilleri's approach is less concerned with the sociohistorical influences on the legitimation of interpreting in public services, and instead foregrounds the problem of competition over capital between agents and the wider structures of power in which interpreting activity is located. Interpreting as a legitimate and legitimising social practice is emphasised as a result. Furthermore, while both Cronin's and Inghilleri's approaches are considered in relation to specific geonational contexts, there is arguably scope to extend contextual-historicist approaches in the analysis of legitimation in order to more fully understand how the political landscape shapes attitudes, policy and life experiences across time. In Britain, such evaluations need to take account of changes to service delivery to migrant and ethnic minority populations and the surrounding sociohistorical context.

In this regard, the period in question saw a move away from multicultural policy approaches that were deemed to have largely failed the populations they were designed to serve, to an emphasis on policies that purportedly promoted social inclusion and cohesion (e.g. Erel, 2011; Phillimore, 2011; Phillimore & Goodson, 2010). Although it might be argued that service delivery began to take account of diversity and the needs of 'super-diverse' populations that emerged under New Labour, it is striking that in early policy documents changes to population mobility, family structures and the aging population were emphasised to the relative neglect of issues of cultural and linguistic diversity.

'Super-diversity' is a summary term introduced by Vertovec (2007) to draw attention to the variables that shape understandings of diversity in modern Britain, based on the assertion that public discourse and policy have relied – at least until recently – on a conceptualisation of diversity that has its roots almost exclusively in the colonial migration of the post-war period. Connectivity and scalarity (i.e. how individuals move between different interaction events and meaning-making processes – see Van Dijk, 2011) in super-diverse societies is predicated to some extent on language acquisition processes that obtain from interactions with institutions and organisations across sectors and time. In other words, interactions and, by extension, connectivity can be theorised in terms of 'truncated multilingualism' (Blommaert et al., 2005: 199), which is illustrative of the lack of full language proficiency commonly experienced by new arrivals. Any judgements about language competence and proficiency must therefore be 'situation-based and sensitive to scale' (Blommaert et al., 2005: 200), hence the need to de-pathologise what is meant by language support when evaluating the accountability of organisations to service users with limited language proficiency. The way in which organisations, and particularly those in the third sector, handle (perceived) language competence is integral to understanding responses to extreme linguistic diversity. It is important, however, for translation and interpreting not to be viewed simply as a response to super-diversity, since its roots lie in forms of migration that predate the phenomenon; its intensification under New Labour, nevertheless, has implications for the way in which the legitimation of translation and interpreting services are understood and investigated.

Third Way Politics, Discursive Formulations and Language Support Services

The type of politics espoused by New Labour, especially in its first term of office (1997–2001), marked an attempt to forge a renewed form of social democracy and create a 'new ideological space outside of the traditional antagonism' of left and right (Bastow & Martin, 2003: 21). It emerged, broadly speaking, as a result of the disjuncture brought about by globalisation and the need to respond to the realities of what has been termed 'reflexive modernisation' (Giddens, 1994, 1998; Mouzelis, 2001), realities that encompass a broad range of human experience (e.g. employment related, biological and environmental), and risks that earlier generations have not had to face (Giddens, 1991). It also promotes a vision of the individual in late modernity as someone who needs to empower the self in ways that permit successful reflexive navigation of (and emancipation from) the vagaries of globalisation, the post-industrial economy and the information age.

The third way has been criticised variously for its vagueness (e.g. Pollack, 2000), and its inconsistencies and flaws, of which an overly homogenised approach to the concept of community in conceptions of multiculturalism (e.g. Black *et al.*, 2002) is one example. Working in the sociological tradition, Loyal (2003: 128) critically examines Giddens' conception of reflexivity, which is essential to the emancipatory strand of the third way, and asserts that it fails to acknowledge individuals as socially embedded within 'determinate contexts of social/material interests'. As a result, shifts in human behaviour cannot be accounted for in relation to reflexivity as something that is 'hierarchically distributed and ideologically loaded' (Loyal, 2003: 127–128). The processes of social participation, inclusion and voice therefore appear insufficiently problematised, especially in relation to those facing multiple barriers to social participation.

The brutal disjuncture and concomitant social (hierarchical) and material constraints typically brought about by migration, and forced migration in particular, are critical to understanding the ways in which individuals with limited or no language proficiency confront the realities of reflexive modernity and pursue emancipation from physical and psychological abuse, torture, poverty, discrimination and fear at the initial point of contact with the new geonational context. Individuals face the multiple challenges of re-establishing the stability and normality of everyday life, and also of confronting the conditions of late modernity to which the indigenous population is also exposed. This multi-stage process involves more than 'integration'; it encompasses broader processes of coming to terms with a new life and the psychosocial and material demands this implies. The stages may overlap and intersect and, as a result, language needs will evolve over time. The nature of this evolution, that is, how individuals move beyond 'truncated multilingualism' is an aspect that studies of legitimation in public service interpreting have not comprehensively addressed to date.

This is not to suggest, however, that interpreting services are or should be positioned at the service of reflexive modernisation and as part of the long-term biographical project of the self. In part, this is because it would reductively construe the individual's relations with the world as being in radical isolation from the other networks and memberships of social groups that are able to support this project. However, in order to understand the development and positioning of interpreting and translation services under New Labour, it is important to ascertain the extent to which the discourses of the third way approach enabled a coherent and sustainable approach to service access for limited English language proficient speakers. The question may be rephrased in terms of whether the language policy generated during the period encouraged migrants to invest in the subject-position of intercultural contact (in itself a reflexive process), which Cronin (2006) argues, is likely to be more effective if professional translation and interpreting services are provided than if they are not.

In this respect, the problem of intercultural contact, inclusion and exclusion can be usefully evaluated in relation to the series of carefully crafted, but problematic discursive formulations that promoted the transcendence of themes traditionally considered irreconcilable such as patriotism/internationalism, and rights/responsibilities, and that were central to the third way (see Blair, 1994). These formulations underpinned what could be described as the new form of social contract, or 'deal' promoted during the period. Cammack (2004) for example, questions the stated aim of the third way to create a new social democratic agenda by analysing the rhetorical structures used in key policy pronouncements of the period. He concludes that the structures appear to 'legitimise neo-liberal policies by clothing them in the vocabulary of social democracy' (Cammack, 2004: 154), as opposed to offering a social democratic alternative to neo-liberalism, due to the fact that they subvert the very discourses they appear to promote.

Fairclough's (2000a) critical discourse analysis of the 1998 Green Paper, *New Ambitions for Our Country: A New Contract for Welfare*, also explores the rhetoric of New Labour in relation to rights and responsibilities, and focuses on the particular discursive formulation: 'work for those who can, security for those who cannot'. This is evaluated in relation to the 'but also' relation (as in 'work for those who can but security for those who cannot'), which purports to emphasise the ethical and moral aspects of welfare reform. Fairclough (2000a: 49) draws attention to the equal weight that appears to be given to both elements, asserting that in practice this is unlikely to be realised. The contractual and stakeholder approach to social life expressed in this and other similar formulations suggests a tendency to over-idealise individual capacity, motivation and opportunity, and the conditions under which social inclusion is made possible. Fairclough's analysis shows that individuals can and do regularly confront asymmetry, particularly with regard to those on the margins of full societal participation, which resonates with the experience of some limited proficiency speakers. It therefore raises the question of how they are to navigate their social position in practical terms, where navigation is understood as an example of reflexivity.

Mention needs to be made, if only briefly, of Fairclough's initial highly normative position through which he establishes a high degree of suspicion towards agents of ideology and expresses an overtly negative position towards New Labour's approach. Engelbert (2012: 57), for example, observes that Fairclough is interested in both the durability and salience of language in the social practice of government, highlighting that it is its salience that results 'in the postulation and acceptance of a version of the social world that [Fairclough] deems problematic and hazardous'. In other words, it is clear that Fairclough construes the discursive formulations as a form of 'rhetorical coercion', which Engelbert seeks to counter by adopting a less normative approach.

If applied to language provision for limited English proficient migrant populations, albeit hypothetically, the 'but also' relation can be used to conceptualise a contractual relation between the state and a limited proficiency speaker expressed as 'the duty to learn English but also the right to interpretation and translation'. It captures a reciprocal relation in ways that may make language support services more acceptable to critics, but which is unreflective of the often highly asymmetric situations in which such support is commonly provided. In criminal justice proceedings, for instance, such asymmetry is largely unproblematic since there is no requirement for the service user to make a commitment to acquire language proficiency on receipt of state-provided interpreting services; provision is seen as short term and highly circumscribed. However, asymmetry is also a feature of the relation between service providers and service users who may have suffered high levels of personal trauma (affecting learning capacity), and who may also lack access to English language provision (English for speakers of other languages [ESOL]). In this regard, the premise of 'something for something' that underpinned the new social contract under New Labour dissolves. In part, this is because the lack of broader societal support on which New Labour depended for the realisation of the new social contract is not characteristic of super-diverse societies; however, other structural reasons have to be considered, such as limited ESOL provision (see Tipton, forthcoming).

The rhetorical construction of social inclusion under New Labour is also discussed by Squire (2005) in relation to the formulation 'integration with diversity'. The analysis draws on the Home Office (2002) White Paper *Secure Borders, Safe Haven: Integration with Diversity in Modern Britain* and the 2000 *Integration Strategy*. Squire asserts that despite promoting an overtly progressive approach to multiculturalism through the Integration Strategy (e.g. through the provision of funds for refugees to access accommodation and healthcare), the White Paper limits those who qualify for such services. She argues that this was compounded by the introduction of citizenship tests in 2005 under the Nationality, Immigration and Asylum Act 2002 for those seeking indefinite leave to remain or become a naturalised British citizen, since they can be interpreted as 'limiting integration in terms of its application to those who are deemed easily assimilable' (Squire, 2005: 69). Furthermore, Squire (2005: 69) asserts that the formulation conceals an essentialist conception of the nation, through which integration policy moves away from an explicitly multiculturalist approach 'toward a monoculturalist one through articulating diversity in non-diverse terms'. A paradox emerges according to which 'the identity of the nation can only be maintained in relation to "diversity" if the latter is conservatively absorbed' (Squire, 2005: 70).

Translation and interpreting would appear therefore to run counter to the one nation project if they are considered to promote diversity over integration, as is often the case, especially in a context like Britain where the primacy of the 'monolingual norm' is asserted (following Canagarajah, 2007). Such a norm is present in situations where multilingualism occurs but where interaction (and hence integration) is promoted exclusively on the basis of monolingualism, constituting an example of the conservative absorption of diversity mentioned above. However, this perspective omits to take account of the nature of inter- and intra-lingual communication within and between established and new immigrant and migrant populations for whom plurilingualism may be a strategic resource in social life. As a consequence, any discussion of the influence of interpreting and translation services on diversity and integration needs to more comprehensively reflect the lived experiences of such populations.

In summary, this brief examination of third way politics under New Labour reveals a key shift in the ethical relation between government and individuals through the introduction of the Human Rights Act. However, the analysis of certain discursive formulations suggests an over-idealised capacity for and opportunity for individuals, especially limited proficiency speakers, to engage with what might be termed the new social contract in the manner anticipated. In many respects, the politics of the third way were unable to keep pace with the super-diverse society that emerged over the period, which led to confused policy pronouncements in relation to translation and interpreting provision, and inconsistency in their application.

Development of the Third Sector

Increased reliance on the private non-profit and voluntary sector for the delivery of public services has emerged in many countries, which has placed a greater burden on organisations without adequate funding being provided (Bloom & Kilgore, 2003). This is due, in part, to governments leveraging their investment, knowing that they can trust that the organisations will deliver despite inadequate funding (Bryce, 2012). Public sector reform under New Labour focused on widening choice and personalising services, supported by the third sector and its expanded role 'in shaping, commissioning and delivering public services' (Kelly, 2007: 1003); such services encompass welfare benefits, social care, education, crime reduction and healthcare. The reform was supported by a series of compacts following the recommendations of the Deakin Commission's Report on the Future of the Voluntary Sector (Independent Commission, 1996). Although policy changes led to increased partnership work, what constitutes partnership work and the forms it takes are open to interpretation. Crucially, the reforms led some organisations in the sector to adopt practices and language more likely to be found in the business sector in order to bid for funding (cf. Denhardt & Denhardt, 2000). This explains to some extent why such a large number of paid roles were created in the sector during the period in question (Hardill & Baines, 2011).

The change in approach impacted on the traditional role of the volunteer, as expert input was needed to support complex bidding and service delivery processes. At the same time, there appeared some reluctance on the part of government to accept that management practices associated with commercial organisations and large public service bureaucracies 'might not be appropriate to the range of organisations operating in fields like community care' (Taylor, 1996: 18). As a result, the period was also characterised by efforts within the sector to maintain its distinctiveness through the promotion of features such as its values base, closeness to beneficiaries, user and community involvement and flexibility.

Billis and Glennerster (1998: 94) explore the comparative advantage of the voluntary and for-profit sectors in delivering human services, and draw attention to the fact that groups and individuals who are described as societally disadvantaged and stigmatised are 'unattractive customers for public sector agencies', which is why they 'are to be found almost exclusively in the voluntary sector'. They also argue that there are certain structural characteristics of organisations in the voluntary sector that 'predispose them to respond more or less sensitively to different states of "disadvantage"' experienced by their users (Billis & Glennerster, 1998: 79). However, they assert that any comparative advantage of voluntary sector organisations needs to take account of the 'characteristics of the clients and their interaction with the supply characteristics of different agencies' (Billis & Glennerster, 1998). On one hand, the level of flexibility and closeness to beneficiaries that characterise much voluntary sector activity suggests that limited proficiency speakers would be better served by them in some cases than by the for-profit sector; however, the nature of language support available in both sectors is likely to play a determining factor in the quality of service and level of accountability to such groups of service users.

An important additional category of organisation to emerge during the period in question concerns refugee community organisations (RCOS) and migrant and refugee community organisations (MRCOs), which are created by asylum seeking or refugee communities for the benefit of those communities. Lukes (2009) describes how such organisations usually start by offering befriending services, cultural activities, emergency support and assistance, translation and interpreting services and later might evolve to provide advice and advocacy services (usually with some funding support); they may even become a partner in providing housing and care services. These organisations are salient for their potential in supporting human services provision in ways that meet the specific needs of migrant populations; however, they have been described as having limited effectiveness. Phillimore and Goodson (2010: 181) for instance identify the supporting role they play for newcomers and draw attention to the limitations in terms of their ability to work with institutions 'to transform systems and ensure that welfare provision is adapted for diverse needs'. Of the many reasons cited as to why limitations exist, the disempowerment of these organisations through restrictionalist approaches that 'present migration as a problem for the UK and thus RCOS as part of that problem rather than the solution' are cited (Phillimore & Goodson, 2010: 184).

In terms of public service interpreting and translation, migrant and refugee organisations are of interest in the wider context of the super-diverse society, as the linguistic and cultural makeup of staff and service users creates a fluid structure in which members provide language support as an integral part of the organisation's activities. In some cases, as the organisation grows, language services might be offered on a commercial basis. To some extent, these organisations bring a new perspective to understanding 'intrinsic translation' discussed earlier, which was predicated on incoming service needs being largely met by the receiving country. The concept of reaching out to otherness and defending difference takes on a new perspective when translation is initiated by the incoming other in what could be termed a form of diasporic solidarity.

In addition to issues arising from the practical reasons of expertise, coordination and voice, these organisations face limitations in providing language support to service users in cases where they take on more formal roles of advocacy and care services. In short, as relatively small units with limited resources, organisations face challenges in relation to up-skilling due to issues such as poor literacy and limited prior educational opportunities among some members, and the associated issues of status and legitimacy that affect the translation and interpreting services offered. There is evidence that former asylum seekers and refugees engage in professional language service training (e.g. Lai & Mulayim, 2010) but there is no research that investigates the range of contexts in which such up-skilling occurs.

In summary, over the period in question, formal partnership arrangements between the third sector and government gained prominence. As this section has shown, organisational hybridity became a characteristic of the period and the rise of dedicated refugee and migrant community groups contributed to the mixed economy of welfare service providers. These in turn created operational issues for service delivery to limited proficiency speakers that require new understandings of what is understood by accountability in the sector and how it is to be achieved in practical terms.

Accountability and the Third Sector

Partnership work has led organisations to grapple with the contractual nature of their activities and make adjustments to internal structures and practices to accommodate new requirements and obligations to a range of stakeholders. Consequently, there is a need to understand the nature of accountability in these and other organisational forms (e.g. those that operate independently from the state). This section examines some of the available literature on accountability from both the business world and the third sector. Particular attention is given to the concept of 'relational accountability' (following Painter-Morland, 2006) and how this might be applied in investigations of language support services.

Lloyd *et al.* (2007: 11) define accountability as 'the processes through which an organisation makes a commitment to respond to and balance the needs of stakeholders in its decision making processes and activities and delivers against this commitment'. Investigating such processes entails understanding what organisations are accountable for (e.g. finance, governance, performance and mission) and to whom ('agential accountability'), issues that have shaped much of the scholarship in this field. Ebhrahim's (2009, 2010) work on non-profit organisations, for example, identifies two main forms of 'agential accountability' that also apply to other organisational forms: upwards accountability to funders or patrons (that usually concerns issues of funding), and downwards accountability to clients (that usually concerns relations with groups who receive services). These categories are useful for structuring analysis but the actual nature of accountability in each is unclear.

Painter-Morland's (2006) evaluation of accountability takes account of traditional approaches to business ethics and promotes a relational approach, in contrast to more mechanistic approaches that are characteristic of older management models. In such models, businesses are viewed as sharing characteristics that make it possible to hold an agent morally accountable, based on an understanding of moral agents as inherently rational agents. The problem with such a perspective is that it fails to sufficiently problematise decision-making and presents the rational moral agent as 'someone who is unencumbered in his/her moral determinations by personal biases and social pressures' (Painter-Morland, 2006: 90).

A relational approach places special emphasis on the tacit knowledge and understanding that emerges between co-workers, making it possible to acknowledge the fact that 'an individual's professional inclinations and an organisation's moral priorities develop relationally in the course of interpersonal interaction between agents' (Painter-Moreland, 2006: 94). Drawing on Foucault's (1994) concept of the 'geneaological unpacking' of the dynamics of power and knowledge that informs the self, Painter-Morland (2006; see also Painter-Morland, 2007) explores how the 'social dynamics of power and knowledge creation plays into how an individual understands him/herself as well as the relationships and responsibilities to others'. Such unpacking has important applications to practices beyond the business sector, precisely because of the greater fluidity of roles and decision-making that is characteristic of many organisations in the third sector.

'Downwards accountability' to limited proficiency speakers rests to a large extent on choices made with regard to language support regimes at the organisational level and the way these are implemented and supported over time. In some organisations, a mixed economy of language support operates which combines paid professional interpreters, unpaid volunteers (professionals and/or non-professionals) and bilingual staff (paid and volunteer). In many cases, it appears that these language support regimes are not the result of a formal policy approach to migrant groups with limited language proficiency, but instead arise organically as a response to changes in local demographics and need. In such circumstances, it is not unreasonable to assume that moral responsibilities develop relationally, but it also suggests that they risk developing inconsistently, which has implications for both staff and service user experience and outcomes.

This situation suggests that decisions about language proficiency and the choice of approach to communication are made on the basis of resource availability rather than as a result of a planned approach to super-diversity. Some might argue that organisational accountability to limited proficiency speakers can only be fully actualised by using paid professional services, regardless of the organisation's status. This raises the question as to whether organisations that operate on the basis of volunteer interpreting (whether unpaid professionals or non-professionals) are any less accountable to service users than those who draw on paid professional provision only. In this regard, generalisations are unhelpful; there is a clear difference, for example, between an organisation that only uses volunteer interpreters but that operates a selective recruitment process and provides regular training, support, feedback and monitoring, to one that provides no training and that draws on a pool of interpreters who are professionally trained but lack exposure and expertise in a particular domain or sector. Professional interpreters who have achieved a high-level qualification in legal interpreting for instance have found that their, often 'hyperformal', approach is deemed less suitable for interactions in the third sector that focus on counselling and helping service users come to terms with their situation, especially in terms of rapport-building processes between the service user and primary service provider (see Tipton, 2012).

Some providers argue that investment in unpaid volunteers generates loyalty and support for organisational goals among interpreters in ways that are less likely among interpreters employed from outside on a paid basis. There is, however, also evidence to suggest that to retain the best interpreters for complex human service encounters in the third sector, paid professional provision is preferred for the same reasons. This is the case in the charitable organisation Freedom from Torture where interpreters are recruited on the basis of their alignment with organisational goals and commitment to the development of its services through attendance at regular training and development events with core staff (see Tipton & Furmanek, 2016).

The discussions suggest that the link between the choice of language support regime and accountability to limited proficiency service users is not as linear or as straightforward as simply advocating professionalised provision. The study presented in the following section was designed to investigate approaches in the field and illuminate some of the structural and perceptual issues that shape approaches to language support policy.

PSIT Provision in the Third Sector: Investigating Language Support Regimes

This section reports on language support regimes in a selection of organisations in the third sector in England that were surveyed between 2009 and 2015 through a combination of publicly available information online and semi-structured interviews. Of note is the fact that this period encompasses the end of New Labour's term of office and the term of office of the coalition government, which was characterised by a downturn in the global financial climate. A total of 30 organisations representing different service areas from housing to health, social care and education were surveyed using publicly available data online. The organisations were selected on the basis of their location within a specific geographical area (although some were local branches of organisations with national coverage) and the sample included a range of funding regimes (e.g. independent/part-state funded) and different target service user populations.

The desk survey of publicly available information provided some evidence of mixed economies of language support, but yielded little, if any, insight into how the organisations concerned navigated this mixed economy in practice, or how the moral obligations to service users are articulated and operationalised through practices that evidence accountability. This is why semi-structured interviews with employees from a selection of the organisations surveyed were also conducted. Table 3.1 provides an indication of the publicly available information for the organisations approached for the semi-structured interviews.

Interviews were held with staff from four organisations (11 interviews in total), subject to relevant institutional ethical approval processes. As the

Table 3.1 Extract from a desk survey of publicly available information on language support in a selection of third sector organisations

Organisation type/status	Activities	Permanent staff	Language support regime	Funding	Support for interpreters and staff training on working with interpreters	Statement of language support policy in publicly available documentation
Faith-based organisation (1)	Support for asylum seekers (advocacy/housing/ counselling/social programmes)	Accredited immigration advisors; qualified social workers; fundraiser manager administrator	Paid professional interpreters; bilingual staff; non-professional former service users (unpaid)	Supported by church, donations and fundraising activities	None	None
Homeless advice drop-in centre (2) (Registered Charity)	Support for homeless through advice and activities (social, educational, employment related)	Volunteer coordinator; case workers	Nonprofessional volunteers (unpaid)	Regular grant funding (restricted and unrestricted) including local government funding; donations; fund-raising activities	None	None
Post-conflict trauma care (Registered Charity) (3)	Psychological support services for refugees and asylum seekers; campaigning	Qualified counsellors and therapists	Paid professionals bilingual staff	Independent donations	In-house training, monitoring	Extensive
Domestic violence (Registered Charity) (4)	Support (psycho-social and material) for victims of domestic violence	Service manager; qualified social workers and case workers	Paid professionals bilingual staff (face-to-face and remote)	Independent donations; some local government funding; fund-raising activities	None	None

number of permanent staff in the organisations is typically quite small, the interviews can be said to be broadly representative of the organisation's approach to policy development and implementation. Interviews were recorded where permitted, transcribed and analysed using a 'framework' analysis, following Ritchie and Spencer (1994), selected as an approach to qualitative research commonly used in applied social policy research. This permits a focus on four key types of information: contextual, diagnostic, evaluative and strategic, and privileges themes that are important to the respondents in question.

Interview findings

In Organisation 1, three of the six permanent staff members were interviewed. The interview data show that the organisation was well informed about professional interpreting and the risks associated with using non-professionals. Financial constraints meant that discernment had to be used increasingly with regard to the amount of paid professional services staff could call upon and, reluctantly non-professional services were used to support service provision. The fact that over 80% of service users had limited language proficiency highlights the pressure that the service was under at the time of the interviews, pressure that had been exacerbated by financial cuts in local statutory social services leading more service users to seek support from this organisation. Respondents reported relying on bilingual volunteers and staff, and former service users-cum-volunteer interpreters for less critical and complex interventions. This was felt to be in keeping with the ethos of mutual support characteristic of the sector; however, the lack of training available for former service users and the ethical issues involved in using their services were highlighted as problematic:

> Because we are a charity and we don't have the funds for [interpreting and translation] here...we are looking for what is the cheapest thing or even volunteers now.
> We don't know how to recruit the volunteers and we are also looking at boundaries because there are quite a lot of service users who would like to interpret and become volunteers and with the voluntary sector - a lot of the work is about user-led services and helping each other - whereas in the statutory sector it would be like 'well no, there are confidentiality issues'.

Fears over the lack of access or inconsistent access to interpreters (whether professional or non-professional) also impacted on some service delivery:

> We are using people who are not trained interpreters... I went on an appointment... and someone came in who wasn't a trained interpreter... the appointment lasted very long and I was basically trying to get as much information off the service user as possible because I wasn't sure if this [interpreter] was available again...and I didn't know if we could get another interpreter...I packed into the appointment what I'd do over two appointments... even the girl summarizing it said 'I felt like you were really pushing her on about [welfare] benefits and she really didn't want to talk about it', and I could sense that but I thought 'if I don't see her again, I'm not going to get this picture and I need to move on ...'.

The interview data also challenged perceptions of some behaviours associated with professional interpreters by drawing attention to the importance of interpreting services fitting with the organisation's needs and aims. For instance, it was reported that some professional behaviours did not necessarily transfer well to the third sector or suit the nature of the organisation's (largely therapeutic) work; this was generally described in terms of the interpreter being too 'business-like' and remote during interaction. Furthermore, as service user language proficiency developed, interaction with staff was conducted increasingly in English; however, on some occasions this was the only option available and was felt to jeopardise service goals and limit the service's accountability to its service users:

> ...actually we can get a lot done still and the person says that they like it because they are using their English as well and, but they are on more basic level appointments that we can use and do that and that is good, but when it is more complex information and you are talking about and trying to explain things, then you need an [professional] interpreter.

The opportunity to practice English was recognised as an important part of the therapeutic process (confidence and resilience building), but the complexity of casework led to some concerns that time was not being used as efficiently as it needed to be. Respondents felt that a more reliable long-term support mechanism would be to train a group of former service users as volunteers; however, the lack of capacity building through access to appropriate training was reported as a limitation.

In Organisation 2, interviews were held with two representatives (the service manager and volunteer manager/caseworker, two of only five permanent staff members). The organisation, which provides support services for the homeless, had recently started to recruit volunteer interpreters (interpreting students from a local university scheme) with the support of a dedicated volunteer manager to support the activities of a drop-in centre that provided social space and advice several times a week. The centre had experienced a sudden rise in the number of non-English-speaking homeless individuals (in this case from other Member States of the European Union) who were unable to join in with the activities of the centre or derive benefit from the signposting by advice workers to other support services:

> I feel that what we are able to offer for some of the men is very limited. I mean, they can enjoy the warmth and the buzz of being around others in the drop-in sessions in the café... but they are very isolated and it is hard for them to have confidence to join in the other social activities we offer.

The limited opening hours and small space of the centre meant that volunteer interpreters were recruited with an explicit multi-role remit: language support provision was expected to take place alongside work with other volunteers and activities (e.g. serving in the café). Language support needed to encompass general conversation and interactions, and not only interlingual communication. The emphasis on social contact was aimed at improving a sense of belonging and facilitating awareness of resources, options and participation in activities that help to build confidence (e.g. gardening, arts and crafts). The interpreters were recruited on the basis of their willingness to serve as a more integral part of the organisation than just as an interpreter. They were not expected, however, to serve as advocates for service users.

The organisation's response to the increased diversity of the service user base was reflected in its increased attention to planning and accommodating new service user needs. Staff were aware of the need to employ professional interpreter services for formal interactions with other service structures where very specific service user goals needed to be achieved (including understanding of legal positions and consequences of decision-making); however, a very challenging funding environment meant that this was not always possible. The partnership with the local university and the creation of a volunteer interpreter scheme had brought a number of benefits to the organisation in helping individuals make informed decisions about whether to stay or return to their country of origin, but the scheme could not address the full linguistic diversity of the service user base and support was not guaranteed during the university vacation period. This limited efforts in relation to downward accountability.

Organisation 3 provides support for survivors of conflict and one interview was conducted with a staff member who had been instrumental in shaping the language regime put in place over the 30 years that the service had been in operation independently from government funding. The interview cannot therefore be considered as representative of the organisation in question, but it provides a rich description of the service's ethos and development over time, and yields some insight into how accountability is addressed.

The organisation had moved from employing volunteers to using paid professional interpreters only, and had developed a very comprehensive language policy which was shared with all members. Interpreters were also paid to attend development and training sessions, as it was recognised that there was a lack of specialised training for interpreters working in complex therapeutic settings where the need to create a safe environment is crucial. These sessions are designed not only to improve accountability to service users by enhancing the quality of service provided, but also to generate loyalty to an organisation for whom the continuity of contact between service user, provider and interpreter is deemed central to the success of the therapeutic process. Some bilingual staff in the organisation worked as therapists; however, more often than not they had completed their training in England and so did not have the vocabulary to deliver services directly to service users from a similar background. As a result they worked with service users of different ethnic backgrounds and often required interpreter mediation. Overall, the interview data reveal a very strong sense of upwards and downwards accountability.

Organisation 4 provides support services for victims of domestic violence and combines input from bilingual workers with paid professionals and unpaid and untrained volunteers. The complex nature of assessing risk for new referrals meant that paid professionals and experienced bilingual staff would only be involved in this type of work, with unpaid bilingual volunteers being used in the more supporting activities designed to build confidence and resilience among service users. The involvement of former service users was deemed mutually beneficial in social and emotional terms, and enhanced the organisation's ability to demonstrate (upwards) accountability to funders by ensuring better engagement by service users in relevant activities and in achieving better outcomes. Among such outcomes, demonstrating awareness of relevant legal processes and the consequences of personal decisions (e.g. to the court system) were salient.

The five staff interviewed showed evidence of having to manage limited funds for interpreting services; however, special attention was given by all interviewees in terms of accountability to the development of service user language competence in helping prepare them for independent living. This meant that while interpreting services (professional and volunteer) were deemed to play an important role in service delivery, they needed to be carefully managed to avoid over-dependence and slowing down the process of moving on:

A couple of weeks ago a woman came into the office where her support worker was and automatically started speaking to another staff member in the room who happened to speak her language. The staff member said to her directly 'no, you need to speak to [x, the refuge worker] because it will help you with your English and because it is not my job to help you.'

Sometimes they try it on with you, but a lot of it is to do with how they are feeling in themselves. If they have lost confidence and been made to feel they are not good enough, then we understand why they might want to communicate in the language they feel most comfortable with. Last week a client said to me 'can you contact [the commercial interpreting service provider]?' and I said 'but you can speak English… let's try first'…and in fact, it was fine.

Discussion

In relation to issues of accountability, in only one of the publicly available documents in relation to the organisations surveyed was there mention of limited proficiency speaking service users. This is understandable in the sense that an organisation is unlikely to want to privilege one group of service users over another. However, the absence of references, especially in areas where the service user base is known to be particularly diverse, suggests that language support is not commonly considered in formal terms at operational or managerial level or by wider governance structures, although it might be recognised as important by those on the front line of service delivery, as the interviews showed.

In many respects, the desk survey and interviews reflect the increasingly professionalised approaches to service organisation in the third sector, confirming the need for specialist input into bidding processes and fund raising, for instance. They also yield important insight into the tension between attempts to incorporate professional language support services and the reality on the ground, which is invariably shaped by financial concerns. For instance, organisations may include a budget for professional interpreting services when putting together a bid for funding and starting up, but not necessarily incorporate it into later bids, resulting in a change of regime or the use of a mixed regime, as was the case with the faith-based organisation that provides support services for asylum seekers and refugees. Furthermore, mixed regimes can emerge at a point where the organisation has become a recognised source of support for a particular community and demand is high, thereby soon becoming normalised and unchallenged by management.

It is clear that a mixed language regime poses risks for service users if their language competence is not adequately assessed. Staff might develop a feel for when it is possible to 'get by' using simplified language to communicate and when professional support is needed; however, this seems to support a highly organic and *ad hoc* approach to language support and suggests that the higher echelons of organisations are unaware of experiences on the ground or the nature of accountability to certain categories of service users. The domestic violence charity interviews suggest how it may even be important to consider limiting access to interpreting services, for example, to build resilience and connectivity with the community as service users move on; however, this was viewed as a strategic decision concerned with life planning, and not one to be imposed through budgetary constraint.

Although volunteer interpreting services are considered as an important, though not always ideal part of service delivery, the role of the former service user as a volunteer interpreter can help to support organisational goals (e.g. greater interpersonal trust can be gained if the interpreter can empathise with the service user, leading to greater commitment to the programmes of support on offer). The management of volunteer services, however, can be problematic and not only due to a lack of training as reported above. Volunteers may come forward to offer support and can find that their proficiency in more than one language can be unduly relied upon. Some of the interviews revealed that volunteers can feel resentful of requests to support communication as *ad hoc* interpreters because they would rather develop skills in other areas. This raises an important issue of how interpreting and translation are valourised within and by organisations, and how transition to professional careers can be promoted.

Conclusion

This chapter has examined aspects of language support provision in Britain through the lens of ideological change under New Labour and its impact on human service delivery and the development of the third sector. It has argued that the super-diversity that has come to characterise certain areas of Britain in the modern age intensified during the New Labour era and brought challenges for the new social contract and the nature of reciprocity that it espoused, particularly for limited proficiency speakers.

There is some evidence to suggest that the professionalisation of the third sector has impacted on language provision. However, the apparently widespread use of mixed support regimes in the geographical area selected for the study reflects the limited attention given to the issue in some cases, and the impact of poor planning and financial constraints in others. Regardless of whether third sector organisations work in partnership to deliver specific projects that draw on public funding or operate independently, there is an argument to suggest that accountability to stakeholders (taxpayers and service users) needs to rest on a more robust and consistent approach to provision, not least because of the sometimes high-stakes nature of the human services provided. The risk to service users as a result of poor communication (including issues of safeguarding) is integral to organisational accountability, and needs to be factored into the commissioning process of public service and translation services more consistently than appears to be the case at the moment, at least in Britain.

A key issue in relation to the legitimation of professional provision in the sector concerns the fact that a number of the areas of human need covered by the third sector are areas that are less likely to receive support from the diaspora, which can be weaker in super-diverse societies. The stigmas associated with domestic violence and HIV/AIDS, for example, are examples of where local solidarities are often weak or ineffective, and where professional translation and interpreting emerge as an important source of independent and impartial support. At the same time, the ethos of mutual support promoted by the charities sector in particular means that the potential role played by former service users cannot be neglected in relation to service planning and outcomes.

The interviews with service providers provide some evidence of relational accountability in action. Difficult choices in relation to communication are negotiated daily, highlighting the extent to which an organisation's moral and strategic priorities evolve as a result of interpersonal interaction among staff and between staff and service users. There is arguably scope at the macro-organisational level to recognise super-diversity as a normal and normalised feature of the service landscape across and within sectors, and for the vagaries of the mixed economy of language provision to be addressed more formally by senior management teams. The interviews with front-line staff in most cases provided rich insight into interactions with service users, but the lack of senior management representatives across the sample prevented the establishment of a more comprehensive picture of the nature of organisational planning. The insights from this study will hopefully pave the way for larger-scale studies in the field. Longitudinal studies would be especially useful in gauging how organisations weather the storms of demographic and political change, the financial climate and developments in volunteer management and training.

Acknowledgements

The author gratefully acknowledges the support from ESRC IAA grant R118571, which has helped to fund part of the study discussed in this chapter.

References

Auld, R.E. (2001) *Review of the Criminal Courts of England and Wales*. London: HMSO.
Bastow, S. and Martin, J. (2003) *Third Way Discourse: European Ideologies in the Twentieth Century*. Edinburgh: Edinburgh University Press.
Bernstein, B. (1990) *The Structuring of Pedagogic Discourse: Class, Codes and Control, Vol. 4*. London: Routledge.

Billis, D. and Glennerster, H. (1998) Human services and the voluntary sector: Towards a theory of comparative advantage. *Journal of Social Policy* 27, 79–98.

Black, L., Keith, M., Kalbir, S. and Solomos, J. (2002) New Labour's white heart: Politics, multiculturalism and the return of assimilation. *The Political Quarterly* 73(4), 445–454.

Blair, T. (1994) *Socialism.* Pamphlet 565. London: The Fabian Society.

Blommaert, J. (2013) *Ethnography, Superdiversity and Linguistic Landscapes: Chronicles of Complexity.* Bristol: Multilingual Matters.

Blommaert, J., Collins, J. and Slembrouck, S. (2005) Spaces of multilingualism. *Language and Communication* 25 (3), 197–216.

Bloom, L. and Kilgore, D. (2003) The volunteer citizen after welfare reform in the United States: An ethnographic study of volunteerism in action. *Voluntas: International Journal of Voluntary and Nonprofit Organizations* 14 (4), 431–454.

Bryce, H.J. (2012) *Players in the Public Policy Process. Nonprofits as Social Capital and Agents.* (2nd edn). New York: Palgrave Macmillan.

Cammack, P. (2004) Giddens' way with words. In S. Hale, W. Leggett and L. Martel (eds) *The Third Way and Beyond: Criticisms, Futures and Alternatives* (pp. 151–166). Manchester: Manchester University Press.

Canagarajah, S. (2007) Lingua franca English, multilingual communities and language acquisition. *The Modern Language Journal* 91 (Focus Issue), 923–939.

Cronin, M. (2006) *Translation and Identity.* London/New York: Routledge.

Denhardt, R.B. and Denhardt, J.V. (2000) The new public service: Serving rather than steering. *Public Administration Review* 60 (6), 549–555.

Department of Health (2002) Fair access to care services: Guidance on eligibility criteria for adult social care. Local Authority Circular (2002) 13. London: Department of Health.

Donald, A., Watson, J. and McClean, N. (2009) *Human Rights in Britain since the Human Rights Act 1998: A Critical Review.* Manchester: Equality and Human Rights Commission.

Ebhrahim, A. (2009) Placing the normative logics of accountability in 'thick' perspective. *American Behavioral Scientist* 52 (6), 885–904.

Ebhrahim, A. (2010) The Many Faces of Nonprofit Accountability. Working Paper (10-069) Harvard Business School. See http://www.hbs.edu/faculty/Publication%20Files/10-069.pdf (Accessed 5 July 2015).

Engelbert, J. (2012) From cause to concern: Critical discourse analysis and extra-discursive interests. *Critical Approaches to Discourse Analysis across Disciplines* 5 (2), 54–71.

Erel, U. (2011) Complex belongings: Racialization and migration in a small English city. *Ethnic and Racial Studies* 34 (12), 2048–2068.

Fairclough, N. (2000a) *New Labour, New Language?* London: Routledge

Fairclough, N. (2000b) Discourse, social theory, and social research. The discourse of welfare reform. *Journal of Sociolinguistics* 4 (2), 163–195.

Finch, T. and Goodhart, D. (2010) Introduction. In *Immigration Under Labour.* London: Institute for Public Policy Research.

Foucault, M. (1994) *Ethics: Subjectivity and Truth.* In P. Rabinow (ed.) *Essential Works of Foucault 1954–1984, Volume 1* (R. Hurley and Others, trans). London: Penguin Books.

Gaus, D. (2011) The dynamics of legitimation: Why the study of political legitimacy needs more realism. ARENA Working Paper, Centre for European Studies: University of Oslo.

Giddens, A. (1991) *Modernity and Self-Identity: Self and Society in the Late Modern Age.* Cambridge: Polity Press.

Giddens, A. (1994) *Beyond Left and Right: The Future of Radical Politics.*, Cambridge: Polity Press.

Giddens, A. (1998) *The Third Way: The Renewal of Social Democracy*. Cambridge: Polity Press.

Hardill, I. and Baines, S. (2011) *Enterprising Care? Unpaid Voluntary Action in the 21st Century*. Bristol: The Policy Press.

Home Office (2002) *Secure Borders, Safe Haven: Integration with Diversity in Modern Britain*. London: HMSO.

Independent Commission on the Future of the Voluntary Sector in England (1996) *Meeting the Challenge of Change* (the Deakin Commission Report). London: National Council for Voluntary Organizations.

Inghilleri, M. (2003) Habitus, field and discourse: Interpreting as a socially-situated activity. *Target* 15 (2), 243–268.

Inghilleri, M. (2005a) Mediating zones of uncertainty: Interpreter agency, the interpreting habitus and political asylum adjudication. *The Translator* 11 (1), 69–85.

Inghilleri, M. (2005b) The sociology of Bourdieu and the construction of the 'Object' in translation and interpreting studies. *The Translator*, special issue on *Bourdieu and the Sociology of Translating and Interpreting* 11 (2), 125–146.

Kelly, J. (2007) Reforming public services in the UK: Bringing in the third sector. *Public Administration* 85 (4), 1003–1022.

Lai, M. and Mulayim, S. (2010) Training refugees to become interpreters for refugees. *International Journal for Translation and Interpreting Research* 2 (1), 48–60.

Lloyd, R., Oatham, J. and Hammer, M. (2007) *2007 Global Accountability Report*. London: One World Trust.

Loyal, S. (2003) *The Sociology of Anthony Giddens*. London/Sterling, VA: Pluto Press.

Lukes, S. (2009) The potential of migrant and refugee groups to influence policy. See https://www.jrf.org.uk/report/potential-migrant-and-refugee-community-organisations-influence-policy (accessed 5 July 2015).

Mouzelis, N. (2001) Reflexive modernization and the third way: The impasses of Giddens' social democratic politics. *The Sociological Review* 49 (3), 436–456.

Painter-Morland, M. (2006) Redefining accountability as relational responsiveness. *Journal of Business Ethics* 66 (1), 89–98.

Painter-Morland, M. (2007) Defining accountability in a network society. *Business Ethics Quarterly* 17 (3), 515–534.

Phillimore, J. (2011) Approaches to health provision in the age of superdiversity: Accessing the NHS in Britain's most diverse city. *Critical Social Policy* 31 (1), 5–29.

Phillimore, J. and Goodson, L. (2010) Failing to adapt: Institutional barriers to RCOs engagement in transformation of social welfare. *Social Policy and Society* 9 (2), 181–192.

Pollack, M.A. (2000) Blairism in Brussels: The 'Third Way' in Europe since Amsterdam. In M. Green Cowles and M. Smith (eds) *The State of the European Union: Risks, Reform, Resistance and Revival* (pp. 266–291). Oxford: Oxford University Press.

Ritchie, J. and Spencer, L. (1994) Qualitative data analysis for applied policy research. In A. Bryman and R.G. Burgess (eds) *Analyzing Qualitative Data* (pp. 173–194). London: Routledge.

Squire, V. (2005) Integration with diversity in Modern Britain: New Labour on nationality, immigration and asylum. *Journal of Political Ideologies* 10 (1), 51–74.

Taylor, M. (1996) What are the key influences in the work of voluntary agencies. In D. Billis and M. Harris (eds) *Voluntary Agencies: Challenges of Organizational Management* (pp. 13–28). Basingstoke: Macmillan.

Tipton, R. (2012) A socio-theoretical account of interpreter-mediated activity with specific reference to the social service context: reflection and reflexivity. Unpublished PhD thesis, University of Salford.

Tipton, R. (forthcoming, 2017) Contracts and capabilities: Public service interpreting and third sector domestic violence services. *The Translator*, special issue on *Translation, Ethics and Social Responsibility*.

Tipton, R. and Furmanek, O. (2016) *Dialogue Interpreting: A Guide to Interpreting in Public Services and the Community*. London/New York: Routledge.

Van Dijk, R. (2011) Cities and the social construction of hot spots: Rescaling, Ghanaian migrants, and the fragmentation of urban spaces. In N. Glick Schiller and A. Çağlar (eds) *Locating Migration: Rescaling Cities and Migrants* (pp. 104–122). Ithaca, NY: Cornell University Press.

Vertovec, S. (2007) Super-diversity and its implications. *Ethnic and Racial Studies* 30 (6), 1024–1054.

Yuval-Davis, N. (2006) Belonging and the politics of belonging. *Patterns of Prejudice* 40 (3), 196–213.

4 Political Ideology and the De-Professionalisation of Public Service Interpreting: The Netherlands and the United Kingdom as Case Studies

Paola Gentile

Introduction

Public service interpreting[1] (PSI) is a young occupation, which is still undergoing professionalisation. Since it is deeply rooted in society (Valero-Garcés, 2014), it is highly vulnerable to external factors, such as 'changes in immigration policy and demographic shifts' (Laster & Taylor, 1994: 17), which can all represent an obstacle to the achievement of full professionalisation. Over the last few years, the economic downturn and increasing migration flows have led to the implementation of austerity policies in the EU. The enforcement of such policies has impacted on national approaches to immigration, and governments have begun either to outsource PSI or to cut funding for interpreting services altogether. In turn, private companies, whose primary interest is profit, have taken advantage of this situation, often hiring non-qualified interpreters at very low rates (Del Pozo Triviño & Blasco Mayor, 2015). Southern European countries such as Spain (Valero-Garcés, 2014) are frequently regarded as a case in point, but recently even in the Netherlands and the UK, two countries in which PSI is (at least formally) a recognised profession thanks to the establishment of national registers, cuts and privatisation have reduced fees below the minimum standard, leading to an exodus of qualified interpreters from the profession. Even though economic concerns have always been high on the EU political agenda and cuts to social welfare have been implemented to a larger or lesser extent in all EU Member States, the rationalisation of services for allochtonous people in these two countries derives not so much from financial issues but rather from a political ideology, which dismisses the challenges faced by newcomers as the immigrants' problem and responsibility. Despite the large number of studies showing that immigrants understand the importance of learning the language of the host country to better integrate (Schweiger, 2014), politicians are often unaware that these people may also have the need to communicate with public services *before* they are able to master the new language. If they fall ill or become victims of violence, they have the right to make themselves understood by the doctors who will treat them and by the solicitors who will legally assist them. As interpreters enable foreign people to express themselves in their own language in hospitals, police stations, courts and other public institutions, translation and interpreting could be described as human rights professions that can make a genuine difference between freedom or captivity, between life or death (Bancroft, 2015; Gentile, 2014; SIGTIPS Final Report, 2011).

Nevertheless, the economic downturn – which has led to rising unemployment and social inequalities – has contributed to the creation of a fertile ground for populist political ideology in certain EU Member States, according to which cuts to human services for allochtonous people are deemed necessary, based on the rationale 'European citizens come first'. Among these services we find PSI, where outsourcing to external agencies has had (and continues to have) negative consequences. In turn, the lack of professional and qualified interpreters results in misdiagnoses (PatientVeilig. nl, 2013), miscarriages of justice (Bowcott, 2013; Slaney, 2012) and other social injustices, which is why some of the policies implemented at national level have led to the infringement of human rights in Europe. As Viezzi argues:

> If inadequate or unavailable language assistance leads to inadequate or unavailable services, if those who do not know the local language(s) are dealt with less justly, or are treated less effectively or are not provided with what they are entitled to, the situation may be described as being characterised by discrimination on the ground of language, hence by a violation of the Charter of Fundamental Rights. Since the violation is not limited to just a few cases, but is spread all over the EU territory, one might be led to conclude that the European Union is characterised by a democratic deficit. (Viezzi, 2015: 512)

This chapter therefore attempts to show empirically how and to what extent the political measures taken at national level are contributing to the de-professionalisation of PSI in the Netherlands and in the UK, where cuts to interpreting services are not only hampering the professionalisation process (with a decrease in remuneration and status), but also reflect the low esteem of the social value of interpreting in society. The chapter is based on quantitative and qualitative data of a questionnaire completed by 114 interpreters in these two countries, designed to provide further insight into the interpreters' perspective on this issue, with special focus on the decrease in remuneration and in status. The methodological framework draws inspiration from the theories formulated by Inghilleri (2004, 2007), who analyses the way in which the macro-level of social reality (in this case, of governmental policies) influences the micro dimension of the interpreters' world (self-perception of status).

'They Should Just Learn Our Language': The Collapse of Public Service Interpreting in the Netherlands and the UK

The consequences of the recent economic crisis have had a negative impact not only at a financial, but also at a political and social level. According to the British newspaper *The Guardian* (2015), a worrying xenophobia is the common denominator of several political parties, which is a matter of serious concern especially at a time when general elections are being held in many EU countries. At a social level, populist political ideology and cuts to welfare services have contributed to the violation of social rights[2] particularly those of the most vulnerable and marginalised persons. Referring to the media coverage of public expenditure on interpreting services, García-Beyaert (2015: 53) underlines that in the UK, 'the argument that the burden of language acquisition and adaptation to the national language falls on the foreign individual is pervasively expressed in one way or the other. The "other should learn our language" is the rationale'. When it comes to dealing with immigration issues, populist right-wing parties adopt a twofold approach. On the one hand, they appeal to people's gut feelings by portraying the phenomenon of immigration as a social threat. For example, during a party meeting in The Hague in 2014, Geert Wilders, the leader of the Party for Freedom, asked the crowd: 'Do you want, in this city and in the Netherlands, more or fewer Moroccans?' When the crowd shouted 'fewer, fewer', Wilders answered: 'We'll fix it' (De Volkskrant online, 2014). On the other, they label PSI as a useless service, which the foreign person does not have the right to be provided with. The sociologist Jackson (2012) argues that, generally, the most widespread political attitudes towards immigrants are rejection and acculturation (or cultural assimilation). Aside from the first option, the objectives of which are quite clear, the second stance concerns the acquisition of the host society's language. In their comparison of the provision of interpreting services in Ireland, Scotland and Spain, O'Rourke and Castillo (2009: 45) also mention the link between populist ideology and political choices; in 2008, after hearing about the costs of interpreting services, the justice spokesman for Fine Gael called for allochtonous defendants to pay the costs of interpreters themselves. The authors observe that the underlying message in this remark was that 'a person's need for an interpreter is also linked to laziness and lack of effort on the part of the ethnic minority language speaker to learn and gain competence in the host language'. Even though recent studies (Hendricks, 2011: 210) reveal that today's immigrants are integrating faster than their predecessors, populist slogans such as 'they should just learn our language' subtly show that the sharp reductions in language services for new immigrants is indeed an ideological choice, as the cases reported below will illustrate.

The situation of healthcare interpreting in the Netherlands

In a hospital in the Netherlands a woman wearing a hijab goes to a medical consultation because she shows signs of a serious allergy: the conversation is held in Dutch, as the woman appears to speak and understand it. After finding out that the woman is allergic to lactose, the doctor tells her that she must not eat dairy products (*zuivel*) and asks her whether she has understood the diagnosis or not. The woman says that she has understood everything perfectly, so she is discharged from the hospital and goes back home. A few days later, during a dinner with friends, a friend of her asks her whether she prefers milk or sugar with tea. She replies that she cannot eat sugar (*zuiker*) and pours milk into her tea.

This is the short story of a video released by the Dutch non-profit organisation *Wij Zijn Sprakeloos* (2012, We Are Speechless) as a sign of protest. After having provided budgetary support for interpreting services in healthcare settings for 35 years, at the end of May 2011, the former Dutch Health Minister, Edith Schippers, announced that the government would no longer pay for language services. The underlying reason behind this is that if patients do not have a good command of Dutch, they should pay for interpreters themselves.[3] Before the implementation of this measure, healthcare providers could make use of interpreter services for free, because the interpreting services provided by an 'Interpreter and Translator Service' (called *Tolk- en Vertaalcentrum Nederland – TVCN*) were paid by the Ministry of Health, Social Welfare and Sport (VWS). In the most significant passage of the decision, the former minister reports that:

> patients/clients (or their representatives) are responsible for their own command of the Dutch language. Government subsidies for interpretation and translation services in health are incompatible with this principle and we are therefore discontinuing these from 1st January 2012. A patient/client may bring someone with them so that they and

the caregiver understand each other better (...). If desired, patients/ clients can hire a professional interpreter or translator at their own expense. When a caregiver has insufficient confidence that they and the patient/client understand each other, the caretaker can, with the agreement of the patient, make their own arrangements for a translator or interpreter. (Mighealthnet, 2011)

In the same statement, the former minister maintains that 'there is no evidence that the quality of healthcare services is negatively influenced by the fact that the provision of interpreters is no longer paid for by the central government. The IGZ (the Healthcare Inspectorate) has not received any reports or declarations of incidents related to language problems in healthcare' (*Ministerie van Volksgezondheid, Welzijn en Sport*, 2013: 1, my translation). At the end of the report, the minister underlined, with a touch of pride, that the adoption of this measure had already led to a reduction by three quarters of the number of professional interpreters used, and that this gap was filled by foreign language speakers, which is why the provision of an external professional interpreter was 'no longer necessary' (*Ministerie van Volksgezondheid, Welzijn en Sport*, 2013: 2).

These remarks caused dismay and outrage among professional interpreters, who protested with letters and petitions and even succeeded in presenting a motion in the Dutch parliament in December 2011, which was defeated by a narrow margin, as 74 voted against the cuts, 76 in favour (Hof, 2013). The petition against Minister Schippers (2011) highlighted that 'the cost of certified interpreters and translators are estimated [...] to stand at about 14 million euros, 1 million of which [...] are exempted from this measure [...]. Moreover, a large share of the remaining 13 million euros goes back to the State through taxes' (my translation). As de Boe (2015) writes, in 2006 the healthcare inspectorate drew up some field norms concerning the provision of interpreters in healthcare settings and strongly discouraged the use of informal interpreters. Since 2012, these provisions have continued to exist but they no longer insist on the use of professional interpreters. On the contrary, 'they recommend that care providers follow a step-by-step plan in case of communication problems with patients in order to find out whether the use of an interpreter is necessary in the first place and, secondly, whether this interpreter should be a professional or an informal interpreter' (De Boe, 2015: 176). According to Dr Mariette Hoogsteder, former senior adviser at Mikado,[4] 'some big hospitals and mental healthcare organizations have decided to start paying for professional interpreters themselves, but most haven't. Hardly anybody talks about rights; everybody talks about budgets and cuts' (Hof, 2013). Other hospitals decided to devote part of their budget to professional interpreting services: according to Jolanda van Luipen, MD, 'it is an illusion to think that patients can learn Dutch so well that they could understand what a doctor says. Sometimes it is difficult even for us. Generally, these people have no money to pay for a professional interpreter […] The Utrecht Hospital decided to take responsibility and pays interpreting and translation services out of its pocket' (UMC Utrecht, 2012, my translation).

In September 2015, the Dutch Institute for Healthcare Research launched a survey investigating the views of healthcare service providers as regards the use of professional interpreters, which shows that the debate is still ongoing in the Netherlands[5] (*Nederlandse Instituut voor Onderzoek van de Gezondheidszorg- Nivel* 2015). Nevertheless, for those hospitals and healthcare personnel that have not yet made alternative arrangements for dealing with foreign patients, there are only two possible alternatives: improvisation and, in extreme cases, body language, in the hope of guessing, with a little bit of luck, the right diagnoses and treatments.

Lost in privatisation: Court interpreting in the UK

In the UK, a similar situation is developing both at a political and a social level. Eight hundred years after the signing of the *Magna Charta Libertatum*, on 23 March 2015 at the Royal Institution of Chartered Surveyors, the then Home Secretary Theresa May gave a speech entitled *A Stronger Britain, Built on Our Values*, in which she outlined ways in which the UK might effectively tackle the threat posed by Islamic terrorism. In order to build a stronger civil society, May (2015) argued that 'Government alone cannot defeat extremism, so we also need to do everything we can to build up the capacity of civil society to identify, confront and defeat extremism wherever we find it'. But when she proposed one of the possible ways in which this could be done, she maintained that:

> We will plan a step change in the way we help people to learn the English language. There will be new incentives and penalties, *a sharp reduction in funding for translation services*, and a significant increase in the funding available for English language training. (May, 2015; my emphasis)

However, Theresa May is not the only politician in the UK who believes that interpreting and translation services are not necessary. As MP Eric Pickles once remarked, translation services have an 'unintentional, adverse impact on integration by reducing the incentive for some migrant communities to learn English and are wasteful where many members of these communities already speak or understand English'. Therefore, they are regarded as 'a very expensive and poor use of taxpayers' money' (Hope, 2013). Nevertheless, evidence has recently been produced about the extra costs of unqualified interpreters to the justice system. As Bowcott (2013) observes in *The Guardian*: 'There has been an extra cost both to the courts and to prisons caused by the postponement of judicial proceedings. In the future, the ministry must undertake comprehensive cost and benefit analysis of its new policies'.

Indeed, for some years now, court proceedings have not taken place or have been postponed in the UK due to a lack of an interpreter or to the presence of an unqualified one: in a burglary case in east London, a retrial was ordered when it came out that the interpreter had mixed up the words 'beaten' and 'bitten'. In Winchester, a murder trial was brought to a halt when the court interpreter confessed that he was an unqualified stand-in for his wife, who was busy that day. In Shrewsbury, an Italian man spent two nights in jail for failing to give a breath test because there was no interpreter to explain to him what to do (Drury, 2014). These are just a few examples which give an idea of the current situation of how the provision of court interpreting is managed in the UK, where such episodes have become commonplace.

Until 2011, professional legal interpreters were selected from the National Register of Public Service Interpreters (NRPSI), the UK's independent voluntary regulator for the interpreting profession set up in 1994. However, in 2012 'the provision of interpreting services for justice courts and tribunals was progressively assigned nationwide to Applied Language Services, soon to be absorbed by Capita, a for-profit company' (García-Beyaert, 2015: 52). Since then, Capita has downgraded fees for interpreters, which has caused many professionals to leave the profession. A survey carried out by Involvis (2013: 30) showed that, in 2013, 74% of the interpreters interviewed declared that they were not registered with Capita TI, a sign that the majority of qualified interpreters are not willing to work under the conditions laid down by the Framework Agreement. Recently, Geoffrey Bowden (2015), General Secretary of the Association of Translation Companies, remarked that the problem 'is not only about ensuring fair access to services for all people living in the UK but one of cost to the taxpayer. The problems that we saw on a large scale with the failure of the Ministry of Justice contract in 2011 led to serious delays and costs throughout the justice system that took years to recover'. According to an article published by *The Guardian* (2015), there is 'serious concern about the increase in ineffective trials as a result of non-attendance of interpreters, particularly in magistrates courts'.

Against this background, interpreters have also tried to raise awareness of this topic by increasing their visibility on the internet and social media. Several online platforms such as *Linguist Lounge* have been created to express concern about the fact that inadequate communication harms primarily the institutions themselves, with higher financial costs in the long term coming from wrongful convictions or misdiagnoses. These actions appear to be, at least for the time being, only a drop in the ocean, although Capita was recently fined £46,319 by the Ministry of Justice for its poor performance between May 2012 and November 2013 (BBC News online, 2014; Kaszyca 2013). As Maniar (2014) remarks, 'under the pretext of value for money and savings, with a legal system increasingly geared towards those who can afford it, the real victim in the UK is the justice system, which is up for sale'.

The Consequences of Privatisation for the Interpreting Profession and for Society

The above-mentioned situations demonstrate that there is a close connection between the simplistic and divisive anti-immigration rhetoric, the disruption of PSI and the violation of language rights. As recent studies on the status of interpreters reveal (Dam & Zethsen, 2013; Gentile, 2013), professional status is measured according to socioeconomic parameters (education and remuneration) and indicates the skills enabling a professional to offer a service to society. On the other hand, prestige is determined by the value that society assigns to the work of a professional. Generally, high prestige derives from high socioeconomic status (as for instance in the medical profession), but sometimes these two clash, as in the case of politicians (who are often highly remunerated but are often attributed low moral esteem). As the second case demonstrates, although remuneration does not always provide an idea of the level of esteem enjoyed by a profession, in the case of semi-professions[6] such as PSI, economic factors could largely contribute to enhancing their level of autonomy (Drudy et al., 2005). Hence, a decrease in standard fees undermines the professionalisation of PSI because it causes professional interpreters to leave the profession, especially in the UK, as previously underlined by the Involvis report (2013).

As far as the social value of interpreting is concerned, research has shown that the profession is generally misunderstood and that the interpreter's role is still unacknowledged (Valero-Garcés & Martin, 2008). The PSI scenarios from the Netherlands and the UK mentioned earlier demonstrate that myths and misconceptions over PSI still abound even at the highest decision-making levels. Expressions such as 'they should just learn our language', 'family members can do it' and 'it's not the government's responsibility', underestimate the fundamental social role that professional interpreters play in society. In his study about the social value of the profession, Clifford (2004: 104) argues that most interpreters interviewed 'complained that the value of their work was not generally recognized [...] many of the healthcare practitioners they worked with seemed to believe that anyone with knowledge of two languages could do the job, even those with little general education or specific training'.

When the value of a service is not understood by society in general, policymakers thoughtlessly implement cuts (like, for example, in the Netherlands) because they believe that the presence or absence of an interpreter is just a contingent communication problem that concerns only the single doctor, police officer or lawyer. On the contrary, it should be seen as an issue affecting society at large. Recent research carried out in the United States (Lindhom et al., 2012) has shown that patients with limited English proficiency who did not receive professional interpretation had an increase in their length of stay in hospital of between 0.75 and 1.47 days compared to those who had a professional interpreter. Therefore, if foreign patients are released from the hospital early because of communication problems, the consequences for society at large may vary depending on whether the patient has a mere allergy to lactose or a serious infectious disease. Moreover, the lack of quality interpretation compounds the work of service providers, who cannot adequately perform their professional tasks. As Bonnie Heath (AVLIC, 2014) remarks, interpreters are allies, not just for foreign speakers but also for 'the public servants who work with these clients. The lawyers, doctors, nurses and others in the public sector rely on us to be ethical and professional in our work so that they can succeed in theirs'. As the above-mentioned examples have shown, the same leaders who enhance the values of 'equality' and 'social justice' are doing their best to stifle the only professional category able not only to facilitate dialogue and integration, but also to guarantee social safety. To that end, in order to gain insights about the current situation in the Netherlands and the UK, the voice must be given back to the interpreters themselves.

Methodology and Model of Analysis

The theoretical framework of this chapter draws inspiration from the theories formulated by Moira Inghilleri (2004, 2007), whose research methodology conceptualises the complex interconnections between the global and the local, with the societal (macro) and the personal (micro) level of sociological analysis. According to Inghilleri (2007), descriptions of what happens at micro-interactional level give insights into the complexity of the interpreter's role, but they shed no light on the social and political realities of interpreters' places of work or on how the interpreting profession should be situated. To that end, she recommends carrying out analysis that combines a focus on the political context and interpreters' subjective perspectives. In order to investigate the effect of political ideology on the interpreting profession, quantitative data have been gathered through an online questionnaire, which is part of a doctoral project investigating conference and public service interpreters' perceptions of their professional status. After carrying out a pilot study, the questionnaire was distributed in November 2014 and was closed in mid-January 2015. It consisted of 37 close-ended questions with a space for comments placed at the end of the survey. The questionnaire includes the following sections:

(1) Demographics (sex, age, country of residence).
(2) Professional identity (years of experience, professional associations, freelance or staff, interpreting as a full-time profession).
(3) Opinions on conference interpreting.
(4) Education and opinions on research in interpreting.

(5) Remuneration.
(6) Exposure of the interpreting profession in the media.
(7) Self-perception of status.
(8) The social value of interpreting.
(9) Self-perception of role.
(10) Considerations on the future of the interpreting profession.
(11) Opinions on the European Directive 2010/64/EU and other similar measures.

Although the total number of respondents was 888, this chapter will focus exclusively on responses obtained by the two countries under scrutiny (the Netherlands and the UK), which account for 114 respondents. The sample population was chosen on the basis of interpreters' qualifications: in the UK, the questionnaire was sent to the Chartered Institute of Linguists (CIoL), to the National Register of Public Service Interpreting (NRPSI) and to the Association of Police and Court Interpreters (APCI). In the Netherlands, the NGTV (*Nederlands Genootschap van Vertalers and Tolken* – the Dutch Association for Translators and Interpreters) was contacted. In addition, the associations Wij zijn Sprakeloos (2012), Mikado (2013) and Pharos (2014) contributed by providing valuable information on the situation of PSI in the Netherlands. With regard to data analysis, the parameters taken into account were remuneration, perception of status and the social value of interpreting in society.

Remuneration

The first, most evident consequence of privatisation and outsourcing in every public sector is the decrease in remuneration. Although public service interpreters' rates have always been (and still are) low in many EU Member States, they have fallen as a consequence of the austerity measures implemented in the Netherlands and of the outsourcing in the UK. In the first case, as interpreting services in healthcare are no longer being paid for by the government, fewer professional interpreters are likely to be hired compared to the last few years: even though official reports on the situation of healthcare interpreting have not yet been compiled, it is estimated that in 2008 and in psychiatric hospitals alone, more than four million euros were spent on professional interpreting services. A report published by Van Osenbruggen *et al.* (2009: 10) before the implementation of cuts revealed that 'Differences were found in the frequency of use of professional or ad-hoc interpreters between GPs and psychiatrists. Data suggest that the majority of psychiatrists avail themselves of professional interpreters always or very often, whereas they rarely or never resort to informal interpreters' (my translation). It would be interesting to replicate this study now to see whether healthcare providers still choose to use professional interpreters.

With regard to the UK, the Involvis questionnaire (2013) included a comparison of rates of pay to court interpreters under the National Agreement and the company Applied Language Solutions (which was subsequently bought by Capita). For an interpreter travelling from North West London to Westminster Magistrates' Court (half a day, three hours+two hours travel time) the gross income per hour, which was £23.39 under the National Agreement (and was considered to be low by the majority of interpreters), decreased to £4.44 for one hour of work. If the interpreter works, for instance, from 10am to 1pm, the income per hour is £9.86. These are the hourly rates of interpreters working in courts in the UK, who, as freelancers, have no pension, holiday, sick pay or job security. As one respondent remarked, 'there are very few of us who can afford to work full-time as a public service interpreter with the possibility of only earning £13.32 in a day (before tax)'. As the article published on *Linguist Lounge* (Slaney, 2012) highlights, 'outsourcing has proven to be detrimental to the sustainability and development of the public service profession, to the supply of qualified interpreters and translators, and to the delivery of justice'. Data gathered from the questionnaire on the status of interpreters confirm the trends illustrated above. When asked whether they think that PSI remuneration is adequate or not, the answers were as follows (Figure 4.1).

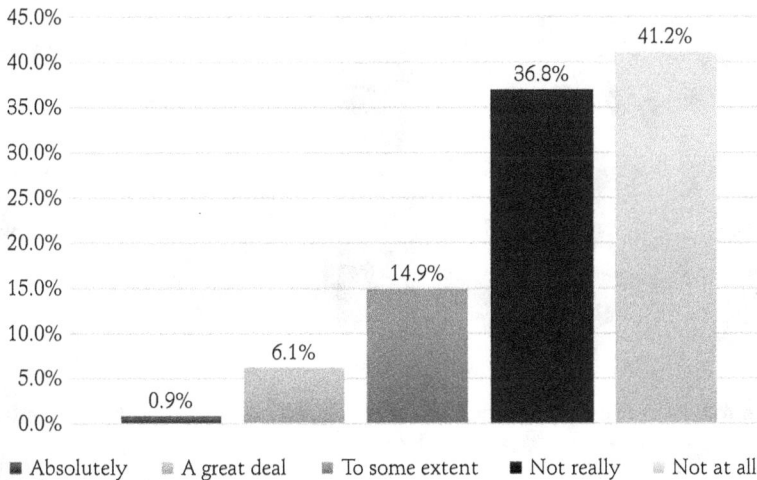

Figure 4.1 Remuneration of public service interpreters in the Netherlands and the UK

Out of 114 respondents, 36.8% (*n*=42) believe that the rates offered to public service interpreters are 'not really' adequate for the type of work expected of them and 41.2% (*n*=47) answered that their fees were 'not at all' adequate. In total, 78% of professional interpreters who responded believe that PSI is undervalued from a financial point of view. Among the most noteworthy comments we find: 'In the UK PSI has been de-professionalized through outsourcing. Unqualified, inexperienced foreigners are used as interpreters by agencies and paid the minimum rate and this is becoming standard. Myself and many colleagues are leaving the profession' (UK). Another respondent pointed out that 'we are paid far below the minimum rate. I am a certified and trained interpreter with more than 25 years of experience and yet I have to do 3–4 jobs to make ends meet. Is this the way a "professional" is supposed to live in my country?' (the Netherlands). These data confirm that, unless remedial action is taken soon, many professional interpreters will probably leave the profession, and the quality of the services will no longer be maintained.

Low professional status

As one of the main determinants of professional status is remuneration, the logical consequence is that when remuneration is low, status will always be low (Armer & Marsh 1982). When asked to evaluate their external perception of status (how society sees them), interpreters answered as follows (Figure 4.2).[7]

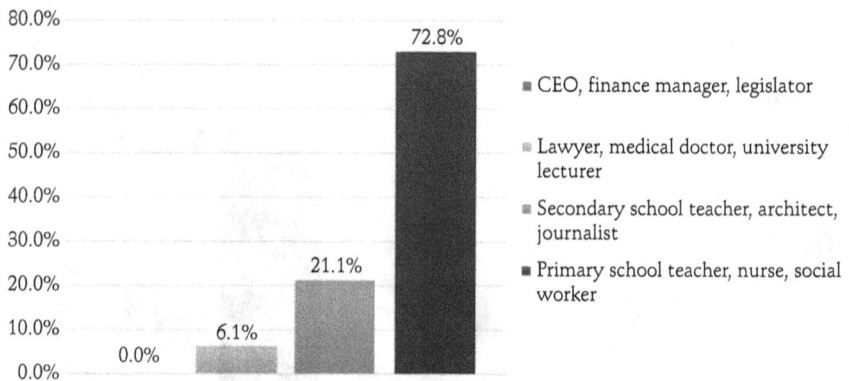

Figure 4.2 Perception of the status of public service interpreters in the Netherlands and the UK

As many as 83 respondents out of 114 (72%, $n=83$) believe that their status is comparable to that of a primary school teacher, nurse or social worker, against a smaller percentage of those who believe that they enjoy the same status as secondary school teachers, architects and journalists (21%, $n=24$) and an even smaller percentage of participants (6.1%, $n=7$) who believe that PSI are regarded in the same way as lawyers, medical doctors and university lecturers. Although a longitudinal study would have proved more efficient in order to corroborate the data with a diachronic analysis (before and after the cuts to interpreting services), the interpreters' open comments clearly suggest that the situation has considerably worsened in the last few years due to financial cuts. Among these comments we find:

- The profession of a court interpreter in the UK has been virtually destroyed since rates were slashed under the new framework agreement and a lot of poorly qualified people have entered the profession. It is only going to get worse with the introduction of video link technology (UK).
- In the UK, we had a national register of interpreters appropriately qualified since 2000; however, in 2012 the government outsourced legal interpreting to an exploitative agency. The profession has been completely destroyed and professional interpreters are now leaving the profession *en masse*. There is no future for PSI in the UK, soon there will only be amateur bilinguals working as interpreters, the professionals are going (UK).
- In the UK, in theory, the profession is already regulated; a National Register has already been established (NRPSI), it is highly respected and very efficient; interpreters must be properly qualified (DPSI, level 6); the European Directive 2010/64/EU, apparently, has not yet been implemented. The real problem lies somewhere else: the power of the agencies and their influence on the government (UK).
- There is no future for interpreters in the UK. Many professionals have left the profession. Since the new laws were implemented, the conditions and treatment became unacceptable for qualified interpreters. With all due respect, cleaners are better off than interpreters. There seems to be no future, at least in this country. We feel sorry for the ones who are starting. Also there is no request of quality, anybody can become an interpreter. Courts have got used to low quality and performance. Judges do not complain anymore, it is a fait accompli unfortunately (UK).
- We are underrated, under paid, receive bad press, are made out that we are paid fortunes and we are not really needed 'as they should learn to speak English' (UK).
- PSI is undermined by the current UK government who see it as an easy cost-cutting target and because of the general immigration debate at present (UK).
- Unfortunately, the powers that be are not in the least concerned about enhancing the status of public service interpreters. Cost-cutting is the name of the game (the Netherlands).
- Nobody cares about what we do, nobody values our profession. Since 2012 and the new laws on healthcare interpreting we are considered to be less than nothing. The powers that be don't know that they are playing with people's lives (the Netherlands).

- In the Netherlands we have a register, which is controlled by the government: it pulls all the strings and uses them to its own benefit. Outsourcing PSI and translation assignments has further devalued our profession. It encourages people to think the work is easy: if paid so little, it can't be much (the Netherlands).
- In the Netherlands, the government should work with the existing register of qualified interpreters and translators. Unfortunately, there are translating agencies that will hire interpreters that are not in that register, because it's much cheaper. The government does nothing against this (the Netherlands).

Although several studies have shown that the perceived status of PSI has never been high (Ricoy *et al.*, 2009; Valero-Garcés & Martin, 2008), these quantitative and qualitative data clearly demonstrate that the pursuit of full professionalisation of PSI in the UK and the Netherlands has become a longer and more discouraging venture as a result of the measures adopted by national governments in the last few years, which means that much needs to be done to raise awareness about the linguistic and, above all, the social role played by interpreters.

The social value of interpreting

The prestige of a profession is mainly determined by the value that society attributes to it. Drawing on the works of Bourdieu, Brown and Szeman (2000: 208) observe that social acknowledgement, which corresponds to symbolic capital, is 'systematically misrecognised and economically disinterested'. In the case of a semi-profession such as PSI, societal acknowledgement cannot exist without a form of official state recognition. Just as states need professionals to ensure that certain human rights are protected, professionals need the legitimacy of the state in order to conduct their professional practice. According to Marks (2012), there is a principle of double dependency in this respect, defined as *professional dependence claim* and *state dependence claim*. By way of example, every state has the need to provide medical care to the sick, but this obligation cannot be completely satisfied without the assistance of physicians and other health professionals; likewise, states cannot make sure that foreign people fully understand their diagnosis unless there are professional interpreters who facilitate communication.

The social value of interpreting has to be understood as the social contract that interpreters (in this case, professional interpreters) have made with society (see also Tipton, this volume). This concept, which originated during the Age of Enlightenment, constitutes the basis of professionalism, as it defines the reciprocal rights and obligations of professionals in society. For example, the social contract states that, for the medical profession to remain relevant and valid, 'individuals must realize the real and meaningful benefits to health attributable to the profession of medicine' (Mitchell & Ream, 2014: 43). In the specific case of medicine, all members of the public intuitively understand and trust doctors as the only category of professionals that can provide a solution to a problem of society (i.e. illness). In the light of these premises, *trust* could be said to be the basic element of the social contract. As Harteis *et al.* (2014: 32) underline, 'lay people have to place their trust in professional workers and these professionals must acquire confidential knowledge. Professionalism, therefore, requires these working as professionals to be worthy of that trust [...]. In return for that, professionals are rewarded with authority, privileged rewards and high status'. However, when asked to evaluate the degree of appreciation of public service interpreters in their country of residence, responses were as follows (Figure 4.3).

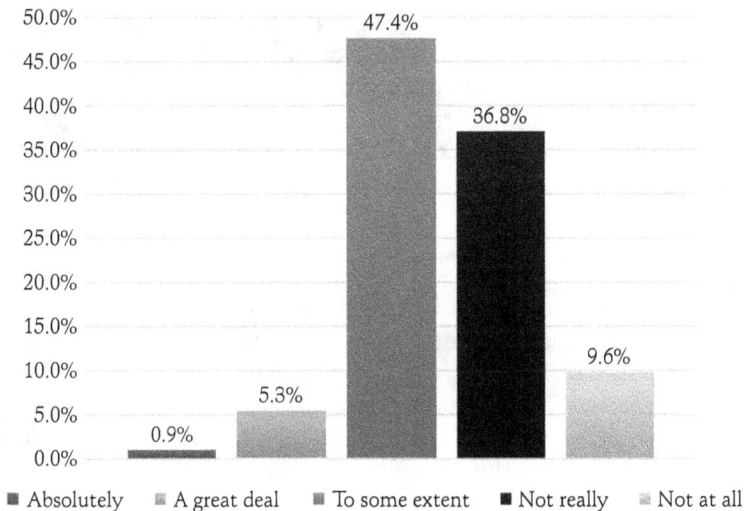

Figure 4.3 The social value of interpreting in the Netherlands and the UK

    More than 47% of interpreters (*n*=54) believe that society considers interpreting to be important only 'to some extent', whereas the remaining 46.4% (*n*=53) believes that PSI is deemed to be 'not really' or 'not at all' socially valuable. A chi-square test showed that 49.7% of British respondents chose the two lowest options compared to 41% of responses gathered from the Netherlands, thus revealing that British interpreters are slightly more pessimistic than their Dutch colleagues. Among the most noteworthy comments, we find 'No one seems to appreciate the work the interpreters do' (UK), 'the British public hates interpreters' (UK),

'I really don't understand why our profession is so underestimated' (the Netherlands). Remarkably, one respondent wrote that 'the outsourcing of interpreting services to Capita has made judges lose their trust in our work, a trust we interpreters of the NRPSI have fought so hard to gain' (UK). This statement further underlines the link between professionalisation and the bond of trust connecting professionals and members of society. In order to achieve full professionalisation and public recognition, PSI has to gain and maintain the trust of the general public, as enshrined in the above-mentioned rules of the social contract.

Nevertheless, the outsourcing of and cuts to interpreting services implemented by national governments in the EU are not only transforming PSI into a commodity, but are creating a situation in which the winner is (and will always be) not a quality service, but a cheap one. Recently, a similar trend towards de-professionalisation has been found in other professions, such as nursing and teaching, which appears to be caused by neo-liberal policies. According to Groenke and Hatch (2009: 20) 'the de-professionalization of teaching has been, and continues to be, a central dimension of a larger right-wing effort to do away with any serious type of teaching education'. Given that quality and cheapness are two incompatible and contradictory concepts, the result is that the capitalist logic wins by trampling on the rights of the most vulnerable segments of society (cf. Buchli, 2004).

Conclusion

This chapter provides insight into the current situation of PSI in the Netherlands and the UK. The two case studies were chosen to challenge the progressive dismantling of the provision of interpreting services, which is causing serious human consequences especially in two key areas: the healthcare sector in the Netherlands and the legal field in the UK. Without ignoring the problems of professionalisation faced by other European countries, financial cuts to translation and interpreting services, privatisation and outsourcing to external agencies in the countries discussed here appear to be destroying two systems where service providers were once encouraged to use registered and state-certified interpreters. Drawing on the theoretical conceptualisations about the impact of the external world on the micro level of self-perception (Inghilleri, 2004, 2007), this chapter aims to highlight the link between the policies implemented at national level and their impact on professionalisation processes and interpreters' perception of their status. To that end, quantitative and qualitative data extracted from a world survey on the professional status of public service interpreters provide insights into interpreters' opinions and comments of 114 respondents on three questionnaire parameters: remuneration, perception of status and the social value of interpreting.

Despite the discouraging results, a positive aspect that emerges from the survey is that many interpreters continue to work in this setting because they consider it to be a moral imperative, a sign of justice towards the most vulnerable. As one interpreter remarked: 'despite all odds, I still practice the profession. Helping those who are in need is an ethical and civil duty' (the Netherlands). This attitude suggests that the 'ethical interpreter' is not only called upon to interpret 'well and faithfully', but also to follow the principles of social justice in order to tackle the 'democratic deficit'. Therefore, interpreters' codes of ethics should arguably pay attention to the link between PSI and social justice, by specifying that interpreters are actively involved in addressing discrimination in hospitals, in courts and all the other settings where their services are required. This method is proving useful in enhancing the professionalisation of nursing; Cohen and Ezer (2013) have recently introduced the concept of human rights in patient care, which aims to provide 'a powerful language to articulate and mobilize around justice concerns, and to engage in advocacy through the media and political negotiation'.

A few steps forward were recently taken in March 2015 (PI4J, 2015), with the Manifesto launched by Professional Interpreters for Justice, an umbrella group representing over 2000 interpreters in the UK. The requests submitted by the Manifesto include: the use of qualified interpreters, full consultation with the interpreting profession and the full regulation of the NRPSI, which should not be managed by private providers. On 2 June 2015 in Nieuwegein, the Netherlands, the *Nationale Tolkendag* (The National Interpreter's Day) was organised with professionals and local authorities in order to take stock of the current situation of PSI in the country (NGTV, 2015).

One possible solution to enhance the professionalisation process could be a study of the financial costs of outsourcing and privatisation in PSI to show that incorrect diagnoses and miscarriages of justice can result in much higher costs than an interpreter's daily rate. Therefore, dialogue with the institutions and service providers could prove fruitful to raise awareness on these topics, which can also lead them to actively denounce language rights violations, wherever and whenever they might take place. In a Europe in which welfare states are progressively being dismantled, gaps between the rich and the poor are increasing, migrants are ghettoised and discriminated against, there is a strong need to listen to the opinions, fears and struggles of interpreters who, despite all odds, work responsibly to make sure that human rights are respected, an ethical duty which many national governments seem to have forgotten.

Notes

(1)   Throughout the chapter, 'PSI' is used, since it includes interpreting in the legal settings and represents 'a reflection of the more usual practices in the UK and in parts of the European Union' (Corsellis, 2005: 153).

(2)   Article 21 of the Charter of Fundamental Rights of the European Union (European Commission, 2001) states that 'any discrimination based on any ground such as sex, race, colour, ethnic or social origin, genetic features, language, religion or

belief, political or any other opinion, membership of a national minority [...] shall be prohibited'.

(3)   It should be pointed out, however, that the Dutch government has always supported the provision of PSI, although a certain level of quality is guaranteed only in certain settings (i.e. courts, police), which is why court interpreting and all other interpreting services for refugees have been so far left untouched by these measures (Bot, 2013; De Boe, 2015).

(4)   The National Centre of Expertise on Intercultural Healthcare in the Netherlands.

(5)   The results were published in mid-2016 at the following link (in Dutch): http://www.nivel.nl/.

(6)   A 'semi-profession' is defined as an occupation which has already achieved a few features of professions but does not possess sufficient autonomy to be sociologically classified as such (Saha & Dworkin, 2009). Sela-Sheffy and Shlesinger (2011: 3) refer to translators and interpreters as 'an extreme example of an understudied semiprofessional occupation'.

(7)   These parameters are classified according to the International Labour Organization (2008).

References

Armer, J.M. and Marsh, R.M. (1982) *Comparative Sociological Research in the 1960s and 1970s*. Leiden: BRILL.

Association of Police and Court Interpreters (APCI) News page. See http://www.apciinterpreters.org.uk/apci_interpreters_news.aspx (accessed on 5 May 2015).

AVLIC (2014) Interpreters and Human Rights. See http://www.criticallink.org/cliblog/2014/10/20/avlic-2014-interpreters-and-human-rights (accessed on 16 May 2015).

Bancroft, M. (2015) Community interpreting. A profession rooted in social justice. In H. Mikkelson and R. Jourdenais (eds) *The Routledge Handbook of Interpreting* (pp. 217–235). London: Routledge.

BBC News online (2014) Court Interpreting Firm Capita Fined Thousands, newspaper article. See http://www.bbc.com/news/uk-25824907 (accessed 6 January 2016).

Bot, H. (2013) *Taalbarrieres in de Zorg. Over Tolkenbeleid en Tolken met Beleid*. Assen: Van Gorcum.

Bowcott, O. (2013) Trials Collapsing Thanks to Shambolic Privatisation of Translation Services, editorial. See http://www.theguardian.com/law/2013/feb/06/court-interpreting-services-privatisation-shambolic (accessed 7 April 2015).

Bowden, G. (2015) Government Putting Fair Access to Language Services at Risk, news. See http://www.atc.org.uk/es/hot-newsflash/item/646-government-putting-fair-access-to-language-services-at-risk (accessed 23 October 2015).

Brown, N. and Szeman, I. (2000) *Pierre Bourdieu: Fieldwork in Culture*. New York: Rowman & Littlefield.

Buchli, V. (2004) *Material Culture: Critical Concepts in the Social Sciences*. London/New York: Taylor and Francis.

Chartered Institute of Linguists, organization profile. See http://www.ciol.org.uk/index.php?option=com_content&view=featured&Itemid=435 (accessed 13 May 2015).

Clifford, A. (2004) Is fidelity ethical? The social role of the healthcare interpreter. *TTR: Traduction, Terminologie, Rédaction* 17 (2), 89–114.

Cohen, J. and Ezer, T. (2013) Human rights in patient care: A theoretical and practical framework. *Health and Human Rights* 15 (2). See http://www.hhrjournal.org/2013/12/human-rights-in-patient-care-a-theoretical-and-practical-framework/ (accessed 8 January 2016).

Corsellis, A. (2005) Training interpreters to work in the public services. In M. Tennent (ed.) *Training for the New Millennium: Pedagogies for Translation and Interpreting* (pp. 153–176). Amsterdam/Philadelphia, PA: John Benjamins Publishing.

Dam, H.V. and Zethsen K.K. (2013) Conference interpreters – The stars of the translation profession? *Interpreting* 15 (2), 229–259.

De Boe, E. (2015) Overview of the professionalization and certification of community interpreters in the Netherlands. *Translation and Interpreting* 3, 166–185.

De Volkskrant online (2014) *Wilders laat publiek scanderen: 'Wij willen minder Marokkanen'*, newspaper article. See http://www.volkskrant.nl/politiek/-wilders-laat-publiek-scanderen-wij-willen-minder-marokkanen~a3618750/ (accessed 5 January 2016).

Del Pozo Triviño, M. and Blasco Mayor, M.J. (2015) Legal interpreting at a turning point. *MonTI 7*, 41–71.

Drury, I. (2014) Court translator costs double in a year: Taxpayers' bill now more than £15million after service was outsourced in move branded as 'shambolic' by MPs, newspaper article. See http://www.dailymail.co.uk/news/article-2634484/Court-translator-costs-double-year-Taxpayers-bill-15million-service-outsourced-branded-shambolic-MPs.html (accessed 20 March 2015).

Drudy, S., Martin, M., Woods, M. and O'Flynn, J. (2005) *Men and the Classroom: Gender Imbalances in Teaching*. London: Routledge.

European Commission (2000) Charter of Fundamental Rights of the European Union. *Official Journal of the European Communities*, website. See http://www.europarl.europa.eu/charter/pdf/text_en.pdf (accessed 15 May 2015).

García-Beyaert, S. (2015) Key external players in the development of the interpreting profession. In H. Mikkelson and R. Jourdenais (eds) *The Routledge Handbook of Interpreting* (pp. 45–61). London: Routledge.

Gentile, P. (2013) The status of conference interpreters: A global survey into the interpreting profession. *RITT – International Journal of Translation* 15, 63–82.

Gentile, P. (2014) Interpreting democracy. Interpreters as drivers of democratization. *VAKKI Publications* 3, 86–98.

Groenke, S.L. and Hatch, J.A. (eds) (2009) *Critical Pedagogy and Teacher Education in the Neoliberal Era: Small Openings*. Berlin: Springer.

Harteis, C., Billett, S. and Gruber, H. (2014) *International Handbook of Research in Professional and Practice-Based Learning*. Heidelberg: Springer.

Hendricks, T. (2011) Who will report the next chapter of America's immigration story? In M.M. Suárez Orozco, V. Louie and R. Suro (eds) *Writing Immigration: Scholars and Journalists in Dialogue* (pp. 204–217). Berkeley, CA/Los Angeles, CA: University of California Press.

Hof, M.R. (2013) The Death of Healthcare Interpreting in The Netherlands, AIIC blog. See http://aiic.net/page/6612/the-death-of-healthcare-interpreting-in-the-netherlands/lang/1 (accessed 23 October 2015).

Hope, C. (2013) Stop wasting millions translating leaflets into foreign languages, Eric Pickles tells councils, newspaper article. See http://www.telegraph.co.uk/news/politics/9924577/Stop-wasting-millions-translating-leaflets-into-foreign-languages-Eric-Pickles-tells-councils.html (accessed 19 March 2015).

Inghilleri M. (2004) Aligning macro-and-micro dimensions in interpreting research. In C. Schäffner (ed.) *Translation, Research and Interpreting Research* (pp. 71–76). Clevedon: Multilingual Matters.

Inghilleri, M. (2007) National sovereignty versus universal rights: Interpreting justice in a global context. *Social Semiotics* 17 (2), 195–212.

International Labour Organization (2008) Classification of Occupations. See http://www.ilo.org/public/english/bureau/stat/isco/ (accessed 20 May 2015).

Involvis (2013) *Quality and the Need for Regulation. The Fifth Interpreters' Survey*, report. See http://www.iti.org.uk/attachments/article/544/Quality%20and%20the%20need%20 for%20regulation%20%28independent%20survey%20of%20interpreters%29%20 16~.pdf (accessed 6 May 2015).

Jackson, J. (2012) *The Routledge Handbook of Language and Intercultural Communication*. London: Routledge.

Kaszyca, K. (2013) *The ALS/Capita case: How much longer?* blog. See //aiic.net/page/6293 (accessed 3 March 2015).

Laster, K. and Taylor, V. (1994) *Interpreters and the Legal System*. Sydney: The Federation Press.

Lindhom, M., Hargraves, J.L., Ferguson, W.J. and Reed, G. (2012) Professional language interpretation and inpatient length of stay and readmission rates. *Journal of General Internal Medicine* 27 (2), 1294–1299.

Maniar, A. (2014) Lost in privatisation: Capita, court interpreting services and fair trial rights, blog. See http://www.irr.org.uk/news/lost-in-privatisation-capita-court-interpreting-services-and-fair-trial-rights/ (accessed 15 April 2015).

Marks, J.H. (2012) Towards a unified theory of professional ethics and human rights. *Michigan Journal of International Law* 33 (2), 215–263.

May, T. (2015) A Stronger Britain, Built On Our Values, speech. See https://www.gov. uk/government/speeches/a-stronger-britain-built-on-our-values (accessed 22 April 2015).

Mighealthnet (2011) *Informatienetwerk over 'good practice' in de gezondheidszorg voor migranten en minderheden* in Europa, Wikipedia. See http://mighealth.net/nl/index.php/Passage (accessed 12 April 2015).

Mikado (2013) *Interculturele zorg*, blog. See http://www.mikadonet.nl/artikel.php?artikel_ id=1654 (accessed 12 March 2015).

Ministerie van Volksgezondheid, Welzijn en Sport (2013) *Kamerbrief over Inzet Tolken*, ministerial document. See https://www.rijksoverheid.nl/documenten/ kamerstukken/2013/05/28/kamerbrief-over-inzet-tolken (accessed 9 January 2016).

Mitchell, D.E. and Ream, R.K. (2014) *Professional Responsibility: The Fundamental Issue in Education and Health Care Reform*. Berlin: Springer.

National Register of Public Service Interpreters, news page. See http://www.nrpsi.org. uk/news-and-links.html (accessed 12 May 2015).

Nederlandse Instituut voor Onderzoek van de Gezondheidszorg (2015) *Enquête: tolken in de Zorg*. See https://www.nivel.nl/nieuws/enqu%C3%AAte-tolken-in-de-zorg (accessed 11 October 2015).

NGTV (2015) *Nationale Tolkendag. 5 jaar WBTV: Beoogde doelen, bereikte resultaten*, website. See https://ngtv.nl/agenda/de-algemene-agenda/nationale-tolkendag-5-jaar-wbtv-beoogde-doelen-bereikte-resultaten (accessed 16 May 2015).

O'Rourke, B. and Castillo, P. (2009) 'Top down' or 'bottom up'? Language policies in public service interpreting in the Republic of Ireland, Scotland and Spain. In R. De Pedro Ricoy, I. Perez and C. Wilson (eds) *Interpreting and Translating in Public Service Settings: Policy, Practice, Pedagogy* (pp. 33–51). London: Routledge.

PatientVeilig.nl (2013) *Veilig Zorgen zonder Tolk, Kan Dat?*, blog. See http://www. patientveilig.nl/verhaal/tolken-zonder-tolk/ (accessed 21 April 2015).

Petitie aan Minister Schippers van Volksgezondheid, Welzijn en Sport (2011), online document. See http://www.mikadonet.nl/downloads/petitietegenbezuinigenopcen-tralevergoedingtolken.pdf (accessed 27 September 2015).

Pharos (2014) *Tolken in de Zorg*, blog. See http://www.pharos.nl/nl/kenniscentrum/ tolken-in-de-zorg (accessed 5 April 2015).

PI4J (2015) Manifesto. See http://b.3cdn.net/unitevol/479d44c183a5393fb9_jbm6ibft6. pdf (accessed 15 May 2015).

Ricoy, R.D.P., Perez, I. and Wilson, C. (2009) *Interpreting and Translating in Public Service Settings: Policy, Practice, Pedagogy.* London: Routledge.

Saha, L.J. and Dworkin, A.G. (2009) *International Handbook of Research on Teachers and Teaching.* New York: Springer.

Schweiger, C. (2014) *The EU and the Global Financial Crisis.* Cheltenham: Edward Elgar.

Sela-Sheffy, R. and Shlesinger, M. (2011) *Identity and Status in the Translational Professions.* Amsterdam/Philadelphia, PA: John Benjamins.

SIGTIPS Final Report (2011) *Special Interest Group for Translation and Interpreting for Public Services Final Report.* The Directorate General for Interpretation, European Commission, online report. See http://ec.europa.eu/dgs/scic/news/2011_sigtips_en.htm (accessed 31 March 2015).

Slaney, K. (2012) De-professionalisation of public service interpreting in the UK. Linguist Lounge, blog. See http://www.linguistlounge.org/all-articles/analysis-and-comment/580-de-professionalisation-of-public-service-interpreting-in-the-uk (accessed 27 September 2015).

The Guardian (2015) *The Guardian view of Europe's populists: left or right, they are united by a worrying xenophobia,* editorial. See http://www.theguard ian.com/commentisfree/2015/feb/01/guardian-view-europe-populists-left-right-united-worrying-xenophobia (accessed 12 May 2015).

UMC Utrecht (2012) *UMC Utrecht gaat tolken zelf betalen,* online newsletter. See http://www.umcutrecht.nl/nl/Over-ons/Nieuws/2012/UMC-Utrecht-gaat-tolken-zelf-betalen (accessed 19 April 2015).

Valero-Garcés, C. (2014) *Health, Communication and Multicultural Communities: Topics on Intercultural Communication for Healthcare Professionals.* Newcastle Upon Tyne: Cambridge Scholars Publishing.

Valero-Garcés, C. and Martin, A. (eds) (2008) *Crossing Borders in Community Interpreting. Definitions and Dilemmas.* Amsterdam/Philadelphia, PA: John Benjamins.

Van Osenbruggen, A., Boersma, N. and Bont, P.F.H. (2009) *Kosten en Batenanalyse van Tolkdiensten. Eindrapport.* Regioplan. See http://www.regioplan.nl/publicaties/rapporten/kosten_en_batenanalyse_van_tolkdiensten (accessed 1 April 2015).

Viezzi, M. (2015) Linguistic pluralism, multilingualism and plurilingualism in the EU. *Annuario di Diritto Comparato e di Studi Legislativi,* 503–520.

Wij zijn sprakeloos (2012), blog. See http://www.wijzijnsprakeloos.nl/ (accessed 12 March 2015).

5 'A Sea of Troubles': Ethical Dilemmas from War Zones to the Classroom

María Brander de la Iglesia

Introduction

'Vita brevis,
ars longa,
occasio praeceps,
experimentum periculosum,
iudicium difficile'.[1]

In 1947, 23 doctors and medical administrators were tried in Nuremberg, in what were known as the Medical Trials, for crimes of war and against humanity, including medical experimentation on patients. The defendants put forward evidence and arguments in order to justify their actions during war; they argued that there was no such thing as standard universal research ethics, that they had not broken any laws, that the US also used prison inmates as guinea pigs and that the war was to blame for the conditions of the experiments.

Both the Nazi defence and American prosecutors used the Hippocratic Oath to their advantage: the argument on the Nazi side was that human experimentation is not covered by the oath and, what is more, they did not consider the oath appropriate for National Socialism because it is a pagan, or aristocratic, document. The Nazi defence argued that Hippocrates, in the letters attributed to him, stated that he would not heal barbarians. To them, this meant that in a war situation a doctor is not obliged to help the other side. The Nazi doctors who were on trial believed that they had always abided by the Hippocratic Oath and that they had always stood by *their* patients.[2]

Students often ask me, as I did my lecturer when I first learnt about the working conditions of public service interpreters in Spain, why, if doctors abide by a single code of conduct, do translators and interpreters not create a single ethical code. Instead of settling for the answer I received as a student ('because that would be prescriptive'), I ask them the following questions: 'Does patient confidentiality extend to the family of patients with inherited diseases who could be putting the lives of their children at risk?' 'Are euthanasia, or abortion, morally accepted exceptions to the Hippocratic Oath in your country?' 'Is the Hippocratic Oath applicable in modern times and situations, and in every culture?' This usually provokes a discussion on whether prescriptive rules, such as laws, or regulations, are necessary for the well-being of a community, and the extent to which they are right or wrong at a given time. At what point and on what basis should laws and rules be revised and improved in order to help citizens or, indeed, professionals, in their day-to-day tasks?

In this chapter, I first explore the notion of moral development and the ethics of war by drawing on findings in other fields of study such as psychology, philosophy or applied ethics[3] and a variety of professions, including medicine, law and education. I will then apply these insights to theorising what constitutes an 'ethical dilemma' as a starting point for the study of ethics in the interpreting classroom. This will serve as a basis for exploring the meta-ethical[4] consequences of what could be called the 'absent curriculum' in translation and interpreting.

Throughout the chapter, I refer to and, when necessary, briefly explain key concepts and paradigms used in the disciplines of applied ethics, ethics of the professions, the study of morality in psychology, among other philosophical concepts that can be applied to translation and interpreting in conflict situations. I will do so by adopting a constructivist approach to knowledge; the discussion is not presented according to different paradigms or schools of thought, but will proceed from the more straightforward to the more complex notions with examples that will allow the reader to understand why certain ideas are pertinent and applicable to translation and interpreting in situations of conflict.

Moral Development and the Ethics of War

As is the case in a number of disciplines, including translation and interpreting studies (Pöchhacker, 2006), the field of applied ethics is constituted by a wide variety of paradigms and approaches, all of which contribute not only to enriching philosophical and practical debates on a variety of world views, sub-disciplines and professional practices, but also to advancing moral thought and to proving or disproving age-old patterns of beliefs.

In this section, I discuss connections between cognitive-developmental approaches and the basic definitions of concepts in applied ethics, as a necessary first step in developing a clear language through which to discuss ethical issues in a given profession. I also draw on some of the most important approaches in the study of ethics as a basis for discussing modern virtue ethics in conflict situations. Using a constructivist approach to knowledge, I will develop a conceptual basis on which arguments about ethics in translation and interpreting can be built; by studying ethics in violent conflict, lessons can be learned for interpreters in public services in more general terms.

A foundational model that is empirical in nature is Lawrence Kohlberg's (1973) cognitive-developmental approach, according to which there are six stages of moral development. The model changed the way that psychologists viewed socialisation: instead of assuming that society determines what is right or wrong, Kohlberg realised it was the individual who decides this. 'The individual interprets situations, derives psychological and moral meaning from social events, and makes moral judgments' (Rest, 1994: 2).

Kohlberg argued that conformity to social rules can at times be morally wrong in the same way that non-conformity can sometimes be morally right (Rest, 1994: 2), and defined six stages or basic problem-solving strategies that 'comprise a developmental sequence' in which 'each new stage is an elaboration of the previous one' (Rest, 1994: 5). Kohlberg's six stages can be summarised in the following manner:

- Stage 1. The morality of obedience and punishment.
- Stage 2. Self-interest and simple exchange.
- Stage 3. Interpersonal accord and conformity.
- Stage 4. Authority and social-order maintaining orientation (the law).
- Stage 5. Social contract (consensus) and individual rights.
- Stage 6. Universal ethical principles (non-arbitrary social cooperation).

These stages can be measured by means of tests that Kohlberg published throughout his career in which he used ethical dilemmas and asked the subjects of his research to reason what they would do in a given situation (see, for example, Kohlberg *et al.*, 1987/2011). Children move from one stage to the next as they grow up, and not all individuals reach the upper stages, as we can see in the following example:

The tragedy of Richard Nixon, as Harry Truman said long ago, was that he never understood the Constitution, a Stage 5 document. No public word of Nixon ever rose above stage 4, the law-and-order stage. His last comments in the White House were of wonderment that the Republican Congress could turn on him after so many Stage 2 exchanges of favors in getting them elected. The level of reasoning in much of the White House transcripts was similar, including the discussion of laundering money. While the tragedy of Richard Nixon was that he never understood the Constitution, the triumph of America is that the Constitution understood Richard Nixon. It is not free citizens who are bound in 'the chains of the Constitution' (Jefferson's phrase) but men who attain power without Stage 5 understanding or acceptance of the justice, rights and principles enshrined in the Declaration. (Kohlberg, 1976: 11)

Politicians, who are responsible for starting wars in the first place, as well as for passing laws or creating the policies and protocols that professionals working in a war zone must abide by, could also benefit from improved ethical training. Understanding the distinction between the three levels: Deontology, Ethics and Meta-ethics (see Note 3) is necessary in order to discuss ethical issues in any profession (e.g. Brander de la Iglesia, 2012). Similarly, being aware of the fact that acquiring problem-solving strategies is a learned skill that can be measured in stages is essential when talking about improving ethical training for public servants, the military, teachers or translators and interpreters.

Psychologists such as Kohlberg, among others, for many decades, have undertaken studies on the acquisition of moral thought, as have experts in philosophy and ethics, as well as other professionals from a variety of fields dealing with work ethics. From a critical perspective, the fact that research on ethics in interpreting has been undertaken for the most part by practitioners unaware of how other researchers map the field of applied ethics provides us with the opportunity to analyse the existing literature by looking at it through a different prism, or indeed through many others.

Let us take, for example, Darwall's (2003) classification[5]: Is the choice of moral principles in, say, a given case study in interpreting, self-interested or is it grounded in a moral idea of reciprocity, reasonableness or fairness? Are other practitioners' approaches to research in applied ethics more akin to consequentialism, or perhaps even to Aristotle's virtue theory?

Chan (2012) advocates for an approach anchored in modern virtue ethics,[6] specifically in conflict situations:

> The simplicity of the decision-making process proposed by utilitarians and deontologists may fail to take into account morally salient facts and to recognize the moral complexities of hard choices. Thus, determinacy may be purchased at too high a price. The ethics of war is concerned with many complex dilemmas and it may be to the advantage of virtue ethics that it does not oversimplify the choices that are faced in wartime. In fact my criticisms of just war theory as a rights-based deontological ethics include the problem that the conditions providing a leader or a soldier with the right to do certain things in war do not give sufficient consideration to the intolerable harms that result when these things are done. (Chan, 2012: 65)

According to this viewpoint, utilitarianism does allow for harm to be built into the equation, but it is nevertheless too easy for utilitarians to 'offset the harms' (Chan, 2012). He believes that the best way to look at conflict situations is through the prism of modern virtue ethics (as opposed to utilitarianism or deontological approaches, which have been standard approaches in workplace ethics in the past few decades).

Beauchamp's (2003) paper is perhaps one of the most enlightening and useful for scholars of other areas seeking to understand how philosophers view ethics in the workplace. According to this author, on the one hand, moral quandaries can be studied from a top-down approach to ethical studies in a given discipline, where general norms are applied to specific situations, a 'perspective that emphasizes general norms and ethical theory' (Beauchamp, 2003: 7). On the other hand, moral quandaries can be studied from a 'bottom-up approach' (Beauchamp, 2003, 8–10), that is, research on the ethics of interpreting can be undertaken by providing examples, or case studies, in order to explore how practical decisions are made. The author may draw conclusions from an example of an ethical quandary, whether fictitious or taken from a real-life situation.

Beauchamp's various classifications are useful as an introduction to the language of applied ethics, and his 2003 paper is seen by many philosophers as a successful attempt at organising the existing literature on work ethics and as a way of conceptualising what scholars in other disciplines might not be able to discern when exploring ethics from their own profession. Beauchamp (2003) provides us with a method, an instrument with which to start exploring applied ethics as academics.

As seen in Darwall's classification above, there are countless ways to approach both general ethical principles and specific case studies; some theories may exclude others and, depending on the circumstances, one or more might be considered applicable (or perhaps more practical) for dealing with the type of ethical dilemmas facing interpreters in war zones. Indeed, the different actors involved in a single case study may follow not only a different set of laws or deontological rules each, but also conflicting world views and thus, different ethical principles altogether, as we will see in the example below.

Genuine Moral Dilemmas and the Law in War

In July 2008, Erik Camayd-Freixas was summoned to interpret at the hearings of 306 illegal immigrant workers who had been arrested while working in a meatpacking plant. They had been accused of falsifying social security documents. Although they were individual cases, they were treated collectively; if they pleaded guilty they would be in prison for a month but, if they pleaded not guilty, they would remain in custody for more than a year pending trial, surrounded by criminals and unable to provide for their families.

Camayd-Freixas saw numerous irregularities during the trial: the prisoners had been chained, as if they were dangerous criminals, and they did not know which papers they were accused of having forged, as it was probably the traffickers who had provided them each with a social security card and number. But Camayd-Freixas' contract as an interpreter and the deontological code of professionals in his area forbade him from speaking to anyone about what he had seen, heard and interpreted. In addition, if he had spoken up at the time, the trials would have taken longer and the immigrants would not have been able to return home to Postville (Iowa) immediately, where their family members were still in hiding, most probably lacking enough resources and unprotected until the heads of the family returned to town.

Presented with this moral dilemma, Camayd-Freixas reached what can be termed a hybrid solution: he waited until the end of the trial and then revealed everything in an essay that reached the local press, causing a stir in the interpreting community and much debate among legal interpreters on 'whether it was appropriate for a translator to speak publicly about conversations with criminal defendants who were covered by legal confidentiality' (Preston, 2008).

In various essays, Camayd-Freixas treats this case study from an internalist perspective, which can be very useful when starting to discuss moral issues with younger generations of interpreters. He knew the rules and the probable outcomes of taking the different decisions available to him at the time; what is more, he foresaw the consequences and acted accordingly. In the end, he broke the rule of confidentiality, but only once the immigrants were safely back home. He *did* provoke the outrage of part of the interpreting community, but also the applause of those who understand that laws and codes are meant to protect people and their freedom, not curtail it, and of those who value human lives and dignity above all else. Camayd-Freixas brought the interpreting community's attention to the fact that, at times, pre-existing general norms may not apply to all situations. In fact, following existing norms may at times result in unfairness.

In his article, Camayd-Freixas (2008) makes reference to common sense and justice, which may also provide proof of his having reached the sixth stage of moral judgment through what Kohlberg (1976), and Piaget (1932) before him, called 'cognitive disequilibrium'; the situation he experienced provoked growth and movement to higher stages of moral development, leading also to growth in moral judgment.

As Beauchamp observes, research based on principles or theories (top-down approaches), on the one hand, and on cases or particular judgments (bottom-up approaches), on the other, are nowadays regarded as insufficient resources for applied ethics in themselves, as 'neither general principles nor particular circumstances have sufficient power to generate conclusions with the needed reliability. Principles need to be made specific for cases, and analysis needs illumination from general principles' (Beauchamp, 2003: 10).

That is why specialists in applied ethics are now widely supportive of a third approach called 'reflective equilibrium', or coherence theory (Beauchamp, 2003).

A practical example of this third approach is found in a case study on interpreting in conflict zones by Riega Arrieta (2015). The study involved the analysis of an authentic interpreting encounter in Afghanistan in which an *ad hoc* interpreter was considered to have failed to fulfil his role as a mediator. It is likely in this case that the interpreter's perceived failure was due to having had little formal training in interpreting and in ethics, and because he was trying to follow orders as a soldier, which included adherence to the deontological code of the US military. In this case, the question arises as to where accountability lies for the interpreter's actions: the interpreter or his institutional employer? Arrieta's analysis strongly suggests that certain rules, however useful in other interpreting circumstances, may not necessarily apply in life-or-death conflict situations where mediation is needed. Indeed, it is precisely in life-or-death situations that the most challenging moral dilemmas are found:

> To call something a moral dilemma — as opposed to a purely practical problem or a (possibly idiosyncratic or merely) personal quandary — is to emphasize that the choice confronting the agent is one that essentially involves issues of moral significance [...] To call it a dilemma — as opposed to a problem that is fiendishly difficult, yet still possible, to solve — is to suggest that the interpretation of the situation as confronting the agent with the forced choice between two, mutually exclusive, equally attractive (or equally repugnant) options, is correct. (Davis, 2003: 488)

Interpreters, like other professionals who work in war zones, may find themselves in situations where they may disagree with either, or both, of the following: the rules of war (*jus in bello*[7]) – however humanitarian these may or may not turn out to be – or the reasons why the conflict itself is taking place (*jus ad bellum*[8]). The professional translator/interpreter may be a freelancer or work for a government or institution participating in the conflict from a biased viewpoint, and he or she may not have been informed of the ethical stakes concerning the assignment. This is why the ethical quandaries that ensue from the acceptance of an assignment are likely to vary in terms of the obligations and responsibilities (see, for example, Inghilleri, 2010), and thus in the perceived justice, neutrality and/ or ethical awareness of the actors involved.

As Chan (2012) observes, 'conflicts of duty are facts of human life. In war-time, the moral certainties that guide choices are threatened by traumatic life-and-death struggles experienced by those who serve in the military'. Professionals in a war zone may not know the reasons why they are fighting, but they do know that their lives depend on the decisions they make in a split second, which, in turn, depend on their training (or lack thereof) and their ability to trust and carry out the orders they are given.

> They [soldiers] have only a narrow view of what they are doing and are under tremendous stress. When they think they might be doing something wrong, they find it hard to disobey orders or to expose the wrongdoings of others because they may feel that doing so would be an act of disloyalty or betrayal. When fellow-soldiers are killed by the enemy, they feel enraged and have the urge to take revenge. Prisoners and civilians have been killed as a result of such feelings. (Chan, 2012: 78)

Professionals may later regret the decisions they made and these feelings of anger may change over time, as does ethical awareness both in children and adults. In this sense, it would be of interest to apply some of Kohlberg's findings about the development of ethical judgment in adults to professionals such as interpreters, doctors or soldiers in conflict areas, by setting up a longitudinal study. Like Piaget (1932) before him, Kohlberg (1973) presented moral dilemmas to children and adults of various ages in order to study their problem-solving strategies, using longitudinal data, every three years. His aim was to prove whether the change in moral judgment in the same subjects occurred in the ways postulated by theory, an experiment later replicated by Rest (1994) for the Defining Issues Test[9]:

> There were the usual findings of gains in moral judgement with age, but it was also found that education is a far more powerful predictor of moral judgement development than merely chronological age, per se. The general trend is that as long as subjects continue in formal education, their DIT scores tend to gain; when subjects stop their formal education, then their DIT scores plateau. Consequently, if you wanted to predict the DIT scores of adults, you would do best by knowing their education level, not age or gender. (Rest, 1994: 15)

This finding, which may now seem natural to us, was somewhat unexpected at the time, and changed the way that psychologists and philosophers alike viewed moral development in every aspect of the discipline of ethics, including applied ethics to the professions. The acceptance that education may bring human beings to a higher degree of moral development gave rise to a whole branch of studies in ethics, which will be explored in the next section.

Others might argue that professionals in conflict areas will always encounter inescapable ethical dilemmas in the practice of their profession, regardless of experience and despite having received thorough ethical training. The mere existence of true moral dilemmas demonstrates that the theories we base any moral education upon are always imperfect and must be left open to improvement:

> The explanation for this may lie in these philosophers' beliefs about what implications would follow from the admission that genuine moral dilemmas are possible. They worry that the admission that there are, or could be, genuine moral dilemmas could have problematical implications both for the intelligibility of our moral concepts and the coherence of our moral theories. The admission that there could be moral dilemmas might lead us to conclude that the moral concepts we use are untenable, or that the logical structures we take to underlie them are incoherent or otherwise fatally flawed. (Davis, 2003: 487)

There is also the question of whether people's reports about their personal experiences provide us with sufficient grounds for believing there are genuine moral dilemmas (Davis, 2003). By definition, true moral dilemmas are unsolvable, however rhetorical this definition may be. Thus, trainee interpreters learning from their lecturer through precedent (or what experts in applied ethics call the strategy of retrospective assessment) should be given the tools to distinguish true dilemmas from a variety of reappearing ethical quandaries. This challenge is especially visible in the literature on ethics in the interpreting profession (see, for example, Baker, 2010 or Pym, 2001).

Perhaps, as Davis (2003: 493) asserts, 'when we appeal to retrospective assessments, we are reminded both that humans are prey to ineliminable vulnerabilities and inevitable distortions of judgment and perception [...]. [The limitations can] explain why the moral quandaries seemed insoluble to him or her and to provide us with a basis for denying that they truly were insoluble'. Retrospective assessment would only provide us, then, with a personal or, at most, internalist perspective of a given situation.

Beauchamp (2003) distinguishes three modern approaches to applied ethics in any given profession: internalism (ethical approaches to deontology construed by the professionals themselves), externalism (for example, public opinion, laws or philosophical ethics) and, thirdly, mixed internalism and externalism described as follows:

> Members of the professions and other trusted institutions are bound by moral standards that are fixed not merely by their membership (an internal morality), but also by the moral standards of the broader culture or community (an external morality) [...] Internal moralities in the professions will vary accordingly because they are in significant measure dependent upon the external moralities. (Beauchamp, 2003: 6)

This third, modern approach, which combines internalism and externalism, remains largely unnoticed in some professions, including interpreting. Most literature on ethics in translation and interpreting studies still tends to ignore previous externalist works in moral development (psychology), education, theories of ethics and applied ethics to professions which acquired the third level of ethical thought long before ours did. Arguably, research in translation and interpreting studies and educators in these disciplines would benefit from further consideration of meta-ethics (the ethics of ethics, or the structure of the way we think and talk about ethics). The following section outlines the ways in which this might be achieved.

Meta-Ethical Consequences of the Absent Curriculum

In 1994, McNeel wrote a paper in which he published the results of a study he had undertaken over many years on his students' moral development. He had noticed earlier that, in most universities across the US, ethics was being treated as a subject that was spoken of, when included in the curriculum, but not effectively implemented (McNeel, 1994), notably due to the rise of disciplinary specialisation and an emphasis on 'value-free inquiry' in the 20th century (Sandin, 1989). He measured moral judgment through the use of the Defining Issues Test, or DIT (Rest, 1994), first on his own freshman students, following which the results were compared with those of sophomore students. He then compared his college to other colleges throughout the US, and his results to those obtained in other fields of study. He also contrasted the results obtained in the DITs by students who had done volunteer work to those who had not, and those who had spent a year abroad to those who had stayed in the US before completing their degree, as well as other variables. He found, among a number of interesting conclusions, that students of certain professions scored higher in the moral development test than others.

McNeel's findings about the positive influence on ethical development of both living in other countries and helping others selflessly are of special interest to the translation and interpreting community because most students in that field are required to have knowledge of other cultures, including spending time abroad, and many of the translation and interpreting tasks or internships that students undergo in universities are for non-governmental organisations (NGOs). Empathy and the understanding of the Other are paramount in the education of translators and interpreters in general, and particularly interpreters in conflict areas.

Rest (1986) also administered the DIT to people of different ages and education in 40 different countries. In every country, the DIT scores increased with age and, most importantly, education, proving Kohlberg's theory that certain ideas are so basic to human interaction in society that they are relevant regardless of culture (Rest, 1994). This research provides a basis for future studies concerning ethics in cross-cultural contexts, from different *Weltanschauung* (world views), including unanswered questions about the translation of those tests into different languages in the 1980s.

I attempted to measure the acquisition of ethical awareness in the interpreting classroom, using a simple experiment consisting of addressing the lack of ethical awareness in a group of students who, despite having received theoretical ethical training, did not seem capable of applying this knowledge to specific case studies in a critical manner. The main objective of the exercise was to improve the teaching and learning of ethics in the interpreting classroom by trying to take the students to a third level of ethical thought, that of meta-ethics.[10] In order to do this, the students were asked to perform tasks that developed their ethical awareness and strengthened their capacity for empathy in a professional situation (Brander de la Iglesia, 2012).[11]

Similar attempts at measuring or quantifying ethics-related constructs in professional settings include testing accuracy, measuring ethical awareness in patients and health workers, quantifying the importance given to ethics by businessmen, etc. When exploring the literature on ethics in other professions, the general impression is that a significant difference emerges in ethical approaches, values and the importance given to ethical dilemmas between two sets of professions: the first includes medicine, healthcare-bioethics, humanitarian action, social work and so on; the second comprises business, journalism and engineering (Brander de la Iglesia, 2010a, 2010b). Whether the field of translation and interpreting belongs to the first or the second set of professions remains to be proved empirically. Translators and interpreters can also become entrepreneurs, or business owners. They could be considered communicators, mediators or social workers and thus, depending on the task at hand, they may have to abide by different values and codes. Much has been written on the ethics of all these professions, and even on the ethics of volunteer work.

McNeel (1994: 29) *was* able to prove that the fields of business and education were more likely to show significant decreases in principled reasoning, due to an ethical crisis of sorts in certain disciplines where 'an emphasis on teaching technical competence in a narrow area was associated with less concern about broader questions of human values and morality'. Interestingly, McNeel's next (meta-ethical) move was to administer the DIT to university lecturers. Based on the results, he created a specific course in the college where he worked, so that they, in turn, could teach their students about ethical issues. On the impact of university education on moral judgment, he wrote: 'Growth in moral judgment appears to occur through mechanisms that fit nicely in a college or university community' (McNeel, 1994: 28), provided that the college or university purposely includes ethics in its curriculum. This poses the problem of whether ethics is included in the curriculum and how.

Eisner (2002), for example, distinguishes between the explicit curriculum, the implicit curriculum and the null, or absent, curriculum, which is his way of saying that an institution or indeed, any teacher, may, at any point, be sinning by omission. It is not only what we choose to teach, but also what we choose to omit that shapes the moral character of our students and their actions in the world. When applied to the acquisition of ethical awareness in translation and interpreting, this idea is concisely captured in the following extract:

> University-level translator and interpreter trainers have long instructed their students to follow professional codes of ethics unquestioningly, and have been slow to provide them with the profound understanding of ethical issues. (Baker & Maier, 2011: 2)

Deontological codes are to ethics what the law is to justice. Rules are necessary, as are traffic lights on a road, in any society or community. Codes of conduct provide the norms by which soldiers, doctors or interpreters should abide when doing their job. Yet, regardless of the legal or deontological framework that they work in, humans are moral beings and must therefore be responsible for the ethical decisions they make, whether these decisions correspond to what is expected of them by their peers or not. The same applies to legal systems: any law-abiding citizen who, under normal circumstances, would never hurt a fly, may encounter a situation in which the fairest, or less unjust, decision turns out to be illegal, either because that law is unfair, or because the legal system, though generally accepted as good, does not allow for that specific situation to be solved legally *and* in fairness. Much like laws and traffic signs, the rules and codes that are essential to keep the peace in any community need to be revised, improved and, at times, changed when the day-to-day use by professionals in the field requires it.

Ad hoc interpreters, for instance, are especially vulnerable in conflict situations (Tipton, 2011). Institutions and associations have, at times, tried to provide codes of practice to attenuate such difficulties. Red T,[12] FIT[13] and AIIC[14] (2013) have created a practical guide for interpreters in war zones aimed both at them and their clients, in a pedagogical attempt to improve the working and living conditions of these civilians-turned-interpreters for an army, journalists or NGOs. The document includes the rights and responsibilities of the actors involved, though it is still unclear whether these minimal guidelines will be acknowledged and respected in the field, and included in training.

It is not easy to find information on the subject of training interpreters for conflict situations. Riega Arrieta (2015), for instance, experienced difficulties in obtaining information about the ethical education available to interpreters in war zones. But whether they come from countries where they have been able to study translation and interpreting or recruited in the conflict area itself by foreign troops, there is evidence of a militarisation of ethics in the profession of interpreting, at least when it comes to interpreting for US troops. In Spain, Riega Arrieta was not allowed to access any army data; in other countries, however, this information was freely available on the internet, or had even resulted in the creation of formal training schemes in universities (namely well-known schools of interpreting in Geneva and Monterrey).

Professional interpreters around the world are put into precarious situations and are fighting to create a legal basis to protect their profession. These are two different, non-exclusive debates: it is a moral obligation for professionals to support the protection of workers by means of laws and codes, but every so often, laws may fail to protect citizens, and flaws in the system may prevent those laws from being revisited or changed. Arguably, lecturers have a moral obligation to make students aware of both deontological and ethical issues in their profession.

The amount of available literature on applied ethics in other subjects and professions underscores the lack of meta-ethical thought in interpreting studies and interpreter education and, most importantly, the need for research into the meta-ethics of 'academia as a professional setting' in translation and interpreting. Works by philosophers such as Cortina Orts (2005) on the ethics of education and citizenship; the monograph entitled *Professional Ethics for Translators and Interpreters* by Hortal Alonso (2007); or Martinez Navarro (2010) whose research explores the ethics of the teacher/lecturer as a professional, may provide the basis for a discussion of these issues in an academic context.

Conclusion

Despite efforts to broaden awareness of ethical issues and their theorisation in the interpreting classroom, students often find it conceptually convenient to consider a code of conduct as a single set of rules, as though carved in stone. Perhaps, as with the Ten Commandments, a single code would support the notion of the good and virtuous interpreter who will remain forever morally righteous if these rules, that are set in stone and given to mankind by some heavenly being, were simply obeyed. In truth, however, there is not one single code of conduct, in the same way that there is not one single law for the good people that inhabit this vast world. Interpreters belong everywhere, in every culture, in different places, for every profession, straddling different worlds at the same time.

The codes available in each institution or association can only provide much-needed guidance for students and *ad hoc* interpreters on general issues; but, educators have a duty and responsibility to make sure that students understand that, like laws, codes can and *should* be revised and improved. When a given rule or law clashes with morality or ethics, with common sense or simply fails to protect the community, it is perhaps the moment to abandon previous conceptions of ethics as a one-off, all-encompassing process. It might very well be possible to conceive of a situation-based workplace ethics that evolves through time. Like laws, codes are not carved in stone; their purpose is to help professionals, to protect them and to simplify their job, not the opposite. Like laws and traffic regulations, not one of the rules of a code of conduct in any given profession is without exceptions.

The question of how the contrast between (Stage 4) prescriptive deontology and (Stage 6) meta-ethical considerations can be dealt with in the interpreting classroom has not been sufficiently addressed in interpreting studies. Whether education plays a central role remains open to question. As we have seen in the previous section, Rest (1986) proved that ethical judgment increases with education across groups of different cultures and countries, showing that certain shared values are relevant regardless of culture. In light of these findings, some could perhaps argue that a universal code for translators and interpreters could be attempted. The only reply that I can think of lies in Rest's (1994: 20) own self-critical results of his experiment: 'The instruments used in many of the cross-cultural studies involve translations of the DIT. Translating is a very vexing enterprise, and we do not know the equivalence of test scores from various translated tests'.[15]

Moral dilemmas may, or may not, be the same in every culture and language and thus they may, or may not, need to be adapted to the target audience for educational purposes. It seems that even James Rest remains in awe at the meta-meta-ethical experience (for a full definition, see McCloskey, 1969/2013: 3) of ascertaining that, what he perhaps thought was the simple task of translating a moral dilemma (with the purpose of measuring ethical judgment in peoples of different cultures, so as, in turn, to prove it increased universally with education), ended up becoming an ethical double-bind in itself.

This does not change the fact that moral judgment increases with education (moral judgment can be taught to healthy individuals); it *does*, however, force us to ask ourselves how to educate translators and interpreters on ethical issues and develop their moral judgment. It also raises the question of who is positioned to develop others' moral education and how this can be achieved. In the case of the absence of ethics in the translation studies curriculum at undergraduate or postgraduate level, including the education of lecturers, we may very well be in need of importing concepts from a variety of other disciplines rather than reinventing the wheel in the form of normative efforts. There are many ways to include (absent) ethical education in the curriculum in an interpreting lecture (Brander de la Iglesia, 2012). Constructing ethical awareness as part of the collective knowledge or shared decision-making processes taught in a class, department or school, is an exercise in reflective self-critical thought, and requires the effort of the actors involved if they wish to remain ahead of the times, technically and with regard to meta-ethics.

With or without the help of codes, interpreters do take arms against a sea of troubles, whether they are working on a luxury cruise ship, on a dingy boat or have been forced to learn to swim in order to survive. It is our obligation and responsibility as lecturers *not* to throw them a life-saver... carved in stone.

Notes

(1)   'Life is short, and Art long; the crisis fleeting; experience perilous, and decision difficult.' (Hippocrates, 5 BC).

(2)   For further discussion of the Hippocratic Oath, see Bragg *et al.* (2011).

(3)   Ethics could be roughly defined as the branch of philosophy which deals with morality (Etxeberría, 2002); deontology as the branch of ethics that studies moral codes or rules of a given profession (Hortal Alonso, 2002); and applied ethics as the branch of ethics that deals with moral problems in society and in professional ethics (Beauchamp, 2003).

(4)   Certain authors distinguish between normative ethics, divided further into normative theory and applied ethics (see, for instance Darwall, 2003) and meta-ethics. Meta-ethics could be described as the structure of the way we think and talk about ethics (Etxeberría, 2002), and dealing with it would arguably take ethics to a third level of ethical thought in the field of translation and interpreting, as in any other field or profession.

(5)   Darwall (2003) distinguishes the following approaches to the study of ethics: 'contractarianism' (which formulates that 'whether an action is right or wrong depends on whether it accords with or violates principles that would be the object of an agreement, contract, or choice made under certain conditions by members of the moral community'. According to this view making the right choice depends on what rules are in everyone's interest.); 'contractualism' (the difference between 'contractarianism' and 'contractualism' is that in the former the choice of values is self-interested and in the latter the choice of principles is grounded in reciprocity or fairness); 'consequentialism' ('the moral rightness and wrongness of acts are determined by the non-moral goodness of relevant consequences'); 'deontology', which we have defined previously and 'virtue theory' (Darwall, 2003).

(6)   'Virtue ethics' is presently, together with deontological and consequential approaches, one of the three most important methodologies in normative ethics. It highlights the virtues, or moral character, of the actors involved, while deontology emphasises duties or rules and consequentialism deals with the consequences of actions (Hursthouse, 2013).

(7) 'The law or right to war', the criteria that should be debated before deciding to initiate a war (Hallet, 1999: 283).

(8) 'The law or right in war'. The criteria that should be debated before deciding to use this or that strategy, tactic or weapon during a war (Hallet, 1999: 283).

(9) Rest, working on and adding upon Kohlberg's model, discovered that there are at least four components determining moral development: moral sensitivity, moral judgment, moral motivation and moral character. This division helped him instrumentalise his theory in order to create a test that measures moral judgment, a test called the Defining Issues Test: 'The DIT uses a Likert-type scale to give quantitative ratings and rankings to issues surrounding five different moral dilemmas, or stories. Specifically, respondents rate 12 issues in terms of their importance to the corresponding dilemma and then rank the four most important issues. It is important to note that the issue statements that respondents respond to are not fully developed stances which fall on one side or another of the presented dilemma' (Rest, 1994: 11).

(10) See Note 3 for the definitions of the three levels; Deontology, Ethics and Meta-ethics (not to be confused with Kohlberg's six stages of moral development).

(11) The group's initial training in ethics involved the traditional method used in many Spanish universities such as Salamanca, where the students attend a maximum of six hours of theoretical sessions (not specifically on ethics, but including some workplace issues), as well as a newly introduced seminar called Deontology for Translators and Interpreters, which focuses on deontological codes and tips to enter the translation market. Year after year, it seemed that interpreting students had no intellectual problem with memorising the theoretical difference between ethics and deontology, but that this was not improving their use and development of ethical awareness and empathy skills in practice.

Thus, I designed an action-research spiral in order to quantify ethical awareness in a group of fourth-year students. In the interpreting class, I explained the difference between deontology and ethics, including many examples, then gave students a different written case study based on a real-life situation. I asked the students to identify, in writing, as many ethical issues as they could.

I had previously identified at least 10 ethical issues in the case study. Significantly, only one student found at least 7 ethical problems; three students identified 5, three more students spotted 4 and the remaining four students noticed just 3 out of 10, in spite of the fact that the case study was similar to the examples we had seen in class. The results showed that careful explanation of theoretical concepts, together with practical examples, did not improve ethical awareness in that specific group of students, and that they had a tendency to identify only breaches of 'the deontological code' (for full results, see Brander de la Iglesia, 2012).

As the main objective of the exercise was to measure the acquisition of ethical awareness, in order to improve the teaching and learning of ethics in the interpreting class, I then undertook two action research sessions in which the case study was discussed, and students were asked to role-play, adopting the position they had least identified with. By the end of the session, the students were capable of putting themselves in the shoes of people whose intentions and interests they had completely ignored at first, and to identify all the ethical issues in the case study (for further conclusions, see Brander de la Iglesia, 2012).

(12) See http://red-t.org/.

(13) See http://www.fit-ift.org/.

(14) See http://aiic.net/.

(15) See Rest (1986: chapter 4) for further discussion of cross-cultural studies.

References

AIIC (2013) Conflict Zone Field Guide for Civilian Translators/Interpreters and Users of Their Services. See http://aiic.net/page/3853/aiic-red-t-and-fit-introduce-the-first-conflict-zone-field-guide/lang/1 (accessed 1 July 2015).

Baker, M. (2010) Interpreters and translators in the war zone: Narrated and narrators. *The Translator*, special issue on *Translation and Violent Conflict* 16 (2), 197–222.

Baker, M. and Maier, C. (2011) Ethics in interpreter and translator training: Critical perspectives. *The Interpreter and Translator Trainer* 5 (1), 1–14.

Beauchamp, T.L. (2003) The nature of applied ethics. In R. Frey, G. Wellman and C. Heath (eds) *A Companion to Applied Ethics* (vol. 26; pp. 1–17). Malden, MA: Blackwell.

Bragg, M., Nutton, V., King, H., Pormann, P. and Morris, T. (2011) *Hippocratic Oath*. In Our Time. See http://www.bbc.co.uk/programmes/b014gdqq (accessed 1 July 2015).

Brander de la Iglesia, M. (2010a) Ethics in translator and interpreter training: From intention to freedom in the digital era. In B. López-Campos, C. Balbuena and M. Álvarez. (eds) *Traducción y Modernidad* (pp. 391–402). Córdoba: Universidad de Córdoba.

Brander de la Iglesia, M. (2010b) From 'should' to 'could' in the ethos of the interpreting community: Landscaping the critical garden. Unpublished paper Critical Link 6: Interpreting in a Changing Landscape, Birmingham, 26–30 July.

Brander de la Iglesia, M. (2012) Fit to be shared? Measuring the acquisition of ethical awareness in interpreting students. In I. García-Izquierdo and E. Monzó (eds) *Iberian Studies on Translation and Interpreting* (pp. 91–102). Oxford: Peter Lang.

Camayd-Freixas (2008) Statement to the profession: Interpreting after the largest ICE raid in US history. *The Gotham Translator Newsletter*, New York Circle of Translators National Association of Judiciary Interpreters and Translators.

Chan, D.K. (2012) *Beyond Just War. A Virtue Ethics Approach*. New York: Palgrave Macmillan.

Cortina Orts, A. (2005) *Ciudadanos del Mundo. Hacia una Teoría de la Ciudadanía*. Madrid: Alianza.

Darwall, S.L. (2003) Theories of ethics. In R. Frey, G. Wellman and C. Heath (eds) *A Companion to Applied Ethics* (vol. 26; pp. 17–37). Malden, MA: Blackwell.

Davis, N.A. (2003) Moral dilemmas. In R. Frey, G. Wellman and C. Heath (eds) *A Companion to Applied Ethics* (vol. 26; pp. 487–497). Malden, MA: Blackwell.

Eisner, E.W. (2002) *The Arts and the Creation of Mind*. New Haven, CT: Yale University Press.

Etxeberría, X. (2002) *Temas Básicos sobre Ética de las Profesiones*. Bilbao: Desclée de Brouwer.

Hallett, B. (1999) Just war criteria. In L. Kurtz (ed.) *Encyclopaedia of Violence, Peace and Conflict* (2nd edn). Toronto: Academic Press.

Hortal Alonso, A. (2002) *Ética General de las Profesiones*. Bilbao: Descleé de Brouwer.

Hursthouse, R. (2013) 'Virtue Ethics'. In E.N. Zalta (ed.) *The Stanford Encyclopaedia of Philosophy* (Fall 2013 Edition). See http://plato.stanford.edu/archives/fall2013/entries/ethics-virtue/ (accessed 15 February 2016).

Inghilleri, M. (2010) You don't make war without knowing why. *The Translator*, special issue on *Translation and Violent Conflict* 16 (2), 175–196.

Kohlberg, L. (1973) Continuities in childhood and adult moral development revisited. In P.B. Baltes and K. Schaine (eds) *Life-Span Developmental Psychology: Personality and Socialisation* (pp. 93–120). New York: Academic Press.

Kohlberg, L. (1976) The Quest for Justice in 200 Years of American History and in Contemporary American Education, in Contemporary Education, 48.1 (Fall 1976), 5.

Kohlberg, L., Colby, A., Speicher, B., Hewer, A., Candee, D., Gibbs, J. and Power, C. (1987/2011) *The Measurement of Moral Judgment*. Cambridge: Cambridge University Press.

Martínez Navarro, E. (2010) *Ética Profesional de los Profesores*. Vol. 12 Ética de las profesiones. Bilbao: Desclée de Brouwer.

McCloskey, H.J. (1969/2013) *Meta-Ethics and Normative Ethics*. London: Springer.

McNeel, S.P. (1994) College teaching and student moral development. In J. Rest and D. Narváez (eds) *Moral Development in the Professions: Psychology and Applied Ethics* (Chapter 2). Hillsdale, NJ: Lawrence Erlbaum.

Piaget, J. (1932) *Le Jugement Moral Chez l'Enfant*. Paris: Librairie Felix Alcan.

Pöchhacker, F. (2006) Going social? On pathways and paradigms in interpreting studies. In A. Pym, M. Shlesinger and Z. Jettmarová (eds) *Sociocultural Aspects of Translating and Interpreting* (pp. 215–232). Amsterdam/Philadelphia, PA: John Benjamins.

Preston, J. (2008) An interpreter speaking up for migrants. *The New York Times*, 11 July. See http://www.nytimes.com/2008/07/11/us/11immig.html?_r=0 (accessed 16 February 2016).

Pym, A. (2001). The return to ethics. Manchester: St Jerome. Special issue of The Translator 7 (2).

Rest, J. (1986) *Manual for the Defining Issues Test*. Minneapolis, MN: Centre for the Study of Ethical Development, University of Minnesota.

Rest, J. (1994) Background: Theory and research. In J. Rest and D. Narváez (eds) *Moral Development in the Professions: Psychology and Applied Ethics* (pp. 1–26). Hillsdale, NJ: Lawrence Erlbaum.

Riega Arrieta, C. (2015) La ética en la formación para el intérprete en zonas de conflicto. Videoanálisis del reportaje *Afghanistan, Lost in Translation*. Un estudio de caso. Unpublished undergraduate dissertation, Universidad de Salamanca.

Sandin, R.T. (1989) *Values and Collegiate Study*. Atlanta, GA: Mercer University.

Tipton, R. (2011) Relationships of learning between military personnel and interpreters in situations of violent conflict: Dual pedagogies and communities of practice. *The Interpreter and Translator Trainer* (ITT), special issue on *Ethics and the Curriculum: Critical Perspectives* 5 (1), 15–40.

Part 2

Experiences From the Field

6 Ethical Codes and Their Impact on Prison Communication

Carmen Valero-Garcés

Introduction

If the number of seminars and calls for papers or articles related to aspects concerning not only the interpreter's or translator's role, but also the perception that providers and clients have of ethics and the language service provider's means of carrying out his/her role are any indication, research on ethical and ideological issues is a relevant topic in the field of interpreting and translation, particularly in the area at the centre of our focus in this study: public service interpreting and translation (PSIT).

Taking into account the idea that all professions are regulated by certain rules and ethical principles, my aim is threefold: first, to investigate what happens when more than one code of ethics come into play simultaneously; then, to examine the ethical conflicts that may arise in such a scenario; and, finally, to explore how such conflicts are resolved. My focus will be on a field that has received little attention from researchers to date: the prison system and communication with members of the foreign population therein who do not share the majority language and culture, thus requiring the presence of a third party – the interpreter.

The following steps aim to achieve this goal: first, a brief introduction on the meaning of *ethics* and other related terms, followed by a brief description of the general context in which the study was carried out (i.e. the field of law). This will allow us to then focus on the more specific context of the penitentiary system. The next step will be to present the project carried out in various penitentiary centres and to discuss the qualitative analysis of the results according to the main objective. The analysis will focus on the reported behaviour of prison staff and interpreters in relation to their respective professional conduct, as well as potential ethical dilemmas and their consequences.

Ethics and Moral Principles in Play

Ethics is a complex term with numerous definitions, often used to describe concepts such as deontology, morals or values, and it may even be used interchangeably with these terms. In the first quarter of the 20th century, Kohlberg (1975: 58) spoke of 'moral principles', which he defined as 'a universal code of choosing, a rule of choosing which we want all people to adopt in all situations'. Years later, Abbott (1983: 856) spoke of 'codes of ethics', which he described as 'the most concrete cultural form in which professionals acknowledge their societal obligations'. More recently, Rachels and Rachels (2006: 24) have written of 'morals', which they consider to be the foundation for ethical codes that guide professionals in day-to-day ethical decisions, concluding that 'ethics and moral principles affect and play a fundamental role in every sphere of public and private life'.

Even more recently, Cortina (2010: 30) has suggested that 'it is important to remember, first of all, that a profession is a type of social activity', and that 'the professional, in entering his profession, makes a commitment to pursuing the goals of that social activity, whatever private motives he may have for entering into it'. Cortina also observes that, in the case of civil servants who provide direct services to the public, professional ethical conduct carries an even greater importance because of the consequences that these employees' decisions may have. This observation by Cortina also applies to the work of interpreters and translators in contexts such as the justice system.

Most ethical codes are based on a series of meta-ethical principles, which are sometimes referred to as *prima facie duties*. The following list includes classic examples of such meta-ethical principles (Ross, 1930/2002: 33):

(1) Do no harm (nonmaleficence).
(2) Do good (beneficence).
(3) Fidelity (keeping one's promises and contracts and not engaging in deception).
(4) Reparation (repairing the injuries that one has caused to others).
(5) Gratitude.
(6) Justice and equality.
(7) Self-improvement.

Other researchers (Humphrey, 1999; Humphrey *et al.*, 2004) add to Ross's list of *prima facie duties* the principles of protection of the weak and vulnerable, responding with care, self-improvement and informed consent.

These meta-ethical principles are at the core of studies on ethics in different contexts within the field of PSIT: Camayd-Freixas (2013), Baixauli-Olmos (2013), Inghilleri (2012) and Laster and Taylor (1994) focus on the field of law, while Dougherty and Atkinson (2006), Dysart-Gale (2005) and Kaufert and Putsch (1997) focus on healthcare. Rudvin and Tomassini (2011) are concerned more generally with the workplace in the context of PSIT, and Baker and Maier (2011) and Brander (in this volume) focus on training.

The aforementioned principles also serve as the foundation for the two codes of ethics implicated in this study: the code of ethics for civil servants working in prisons and the code of ethics for institutional translator-interpreters in Spain. *TITLE III. Rights and Duties. Civil Service Code of Conduct. Chapter VI. Duties of Civil Servants. Codes of Conduct* (Spanish Official Bulletin of the State [BOE], edition updated 1 April 2015), reads in Article 52:

> Article 52. Duties of Civil Servants. Code of Conduct.
> Civil servants must carry out the tasks assigned to them with diligence and protect general interests by remaining faithful to and observing the Constitution and all other requirements of the law. Furthermore, they must act according to the following principles, which inform the Code of Conduct for civil servants: objectivity, integrity, neutrality, responsibility, impartiality, confidentiality, dedication to public service, transparency, exemplariness, austerity, accessibility, efficacy, honor, promotion of cultural and environmental contexts, and respect for gender equality. These principles are shaped by the ethical principles and conduct set forth in the articles that follow. The principles and rules established in this Chapter will inform the interpretation and application of disciplinary measures for civil servants. (My translation)

Ethics and principles of conduct are differentiated in the subsequent Articles 53 and 54 (see BOE, 1 April 2015). The *Libro Blanco de la traducción y la interpretación institucional* (*White Paper on Institutional Translation and Interpreting*, 2010: 89–93), in Chapter VIII, titled 'Code of Ethics and Best Practice', highlights the following principles:

(1) Fidelity and integrity of the message.
(2) Adequate competency and preparation.
(3) Communication of circumstantial limitations.
(4) Impartiality.
(5) Confidentiality.
(6) Responsibility.
(7) Ethical or moral integrity.
(8) Continuing education.
(9) Professional solidarity.

In comparing these two codes, it is easy to observe certain similarities and differences in terms of the foremost ethical principles. As Mendoza argues:

If a professional is faced with a situation that has competing meta-ethical principles, such as respect for autonomy and do no harm, professionals are expected to draw on their own values and personal ethics and apply those to the situation at hand. (Mendoza, 2002: 60)

Likewise, Hortal (2007), professor of ethics and author of the book *Ética profesional de traductores e intérpretes* (*Professional Ethics for Translators and Interpreters*), writes of professional ethics:

Professional ethics are standards and duties that are generally set forth in a code that has been approved by a corresponding professional association. These ethics, whether outlined in a code or not, reflect what professionals do, ought to do, or what is advisable for them to do in order to practice their profession ethically. (Hortal, 2007: 41)

In this more specific definition, Hortal's emphasis on whether or not guidelines are outlined in a code is key. Indeed, situations vary, as do the individuals involved, making each communicative event unique. This leads us to believe that while the interpreter should obey professional ethics within the communicative triangle, he or she must also adapt his or her behaviour and the message to be delivered based on the situation at hand. It is not the same to interpret for a victim of gender violence or an asylum seeker (where emotions of fear, anger, pain or low self-esteem tend to present themselves), as it is to interpret in a courtroom, with the police, or in a prison, where the aforementioned emotions do not tend to arise. Ultimately, all participants in the communicative act (prison staff, interpreters and inmates) must be aware of the context and what is required of them.

Among the many factors that have an impact in the context of PSIT, culture is one that deserves special mention, as suggested by Language and Culture Worldwide (LCW):

Ethics and culture are linked so tightly that it is nearly impossible to discuss one without the other. In fact, it could even be said that ethics are a direct reflection of a culture's core values—a strong belief of what is right or wrong is, almost by definition, a belief in what is ethical. (http://lcwmail.com/culture-ethics)

These statements lead to the conclusion that codes of conduct are a clear reflection not only of the organisational culture that influences their creation, but also of the national culture and other cultures that influence the drafting organisation. Carrying these codes over to another culture is not always easy, particularly when fundamental values differ. Undoubtedly, conflict or ethical dilemmas may arise when diverse cultures come into contact, as Rudvin (2007) clearly exemplifies in her article 'Professionalism and Ethics in Public Service Interpreting'.

Gert (2012) goes even further, preferring to use the term *morality* instead of *ethics* to refer to the codes of conduct of different societies. He defines morality as a code of conduct that is established by a society and that most members of that society use as their guide. But he also indicates that members of the society who are also members of other specific groups (religious, racial or ethnic) may treat both guides as defining elements of morality, and they may differ with respect to which of the conflicting elements of the moral guide they consider most important. There are likely to be significant moral disputes among those who consider different elements to hold more value.

In the end, every profession has its own standards for professional conduct that guide actions. These principles may be influenced by a number of factors, such as the society in question, the culture(s) that the society is in contact with and even personal or private ethics. When two different professions with respective codes coexist in the same context, there may be overlap, disagreement or misalignment when it comes to achieving or carrying out the ethical principles that guide each respective profession. This can lead to ethical conflicts or give rise to more than one solution for a single problem.

Hypothesis

Based on the discussion above, the present study hypothesises that the existence of two unique codes of professional conduct for these two professional figures (i.e. civil servants and interpreters) has a great impact on the differing perceptions of both parties in relation to inmates' rights to communicate in their own language, not only with relatives and friends but also with 'official representatives of organizations and institutions' (Organic Law 1/1979 [*Ley Orgánica 1/1979*] of September 26, Chapter VIII, Article 51). These differences may give rise to dilemmas or possible clashes when it comes to expectations for professional conduct in situations where civil servants and interpreters cross paths and where different languages and cultures come into play.

The Study

The prison setting within the field of law and regulations

PSIT is carried out in institutions and in a number of different fields (law, healthcare, education and social services), all of which possess distinct characteristics that determine the nature of the interpretation.

Within the field of law there are numerous interrelated settings: namely, law enforcement, courts and prisons.

Law (and the court system in particular) is the setting that enjoys the greatest visibility and recognition – a fact that suggests that this is the area of PSIT that has achieved the greatest advancement towards professionalisation (Ortega Herraez, 2010). Nevertheless, there are certain contexts in the field that have been overlooked and that remain in the shadows in terms of translation and interpreting, as is the case with the prison system. This claim is supported by a brief review of the current legislation and the scarcity of existing jobs in Spain (Almeida Herrero *et al.*, 2006; Baixauli, 2012; Martínez-Gómez, 2008; Valero-Garcés & Mojica, 2014).

The current Penitentiary Regulations (*Reglamento Penitenciario*), approved by Royal Decree 190/1996 (*Real Decreto 190/1996*) of February 9, which implements and enforces Organic Law 1/1979 (*Ley Orgánica 1/1979*) of September 26, sets forth several provisions that make explicit reference to the treatment of foreign inmates (Articles 4(1), 15(5), 26, 27, 41(1,7), 43(2), 46, 49 (3), 52(2, 3, 4, 5), 62(4), 118(2), 123(1), 127(3), 135(2) 197 and 242(2)(j)). Of these articles, only a handful make reference to services of translation and interpreting:

Art. 46. Written communications: documents will be submitted to management for translation and subsequent processing when the language cannot be translated in the penitentiary institution.
Art. 52. Information:

3. For these purposes, management seeks to edit documentation in languages spoken by inmates belonging to representative foreign groups found in Spanish penitentiary institutions. Foreign inmates who do not understand the language in the documentation will be provided with an oral translation by prison staff or by other inmates who speak their language. If deemed necessary, foreign inmates' consulates may be asked to cooperate.
4. In any case, when Spanish or foreign inmates cannot understand written information, the same information will be provided by other appropriate means.
5. The libraries and Admissions Department of Spanish penitentiary institutions will provide foreign inmates with several copies of the General Organic Law for Penitentiaries, the Penitentiary Regulations and the internal regulations that govern the prison. The Management Board seeks to provide the General Organic Law for Penitentiaries and the Penitentiary Regulations in the inmates' native language. Collaboration from the corresponding diplomatic authorities will be sought to this end.

Art. 242. Appointment of instructor and statement of objections (2): 'A civil servant or inmate may be asked to act as interpreter when foreign inmates do not speak Spanish'. (My translation)

The references to translation and interpreting in the extract above mainly focus on the translation of informational documents. With regard to interpreting, this task is usually delegated either to civil servants whose duties are unrelated to the task of interpreting, or to inmates themselves, as indicated by the aforementioned studies (Baixauli, 2012; Martínez-Gómez, 2008; Valero-Garcés & Mojica, 2014).

This fact raises questions regarding the quality of the interpretation, which, as Martínez-Gómez (2008) observes, 'depends on the helpfulness and availability of prison staff and foreign inmates who speak different languages'. Efforts to improve the situation are often driven by circumstances. To give one example, after the attacks on 11 March 2004, the Spanish Ministry of the Interior became aware of the precarious situation of interlinguistic communication in prisons, which depended on the goodwill of multilingual staff and inmates (Gutiérrez et al., 2008). Alarmed by Islamist terrorist activity, the ministry hired 30 Arabic interpreters. One of these professional interpreters serves as a source of data for the present study.

Similarly, the transposition of Directive 2010/64/EU of the European Parliament and of the Council, regarding the right to interpreting and translation in criminal proceedings, establishes common minimum rules in the area of interpreting and translation with the aim of improving mutual trust among Member States of the European Union and guaranteeing the right to a fair trial. The Directive also establishes that Member States must ensure that the quality of translation and interpreting be sufficient in order for the persons involved to understand the charges against them and to exercise their rights of defence. In Spain, the transposition of this Directive resulted in Organic Law 5/2015 (*Ley Orgánica 5/2015*) (Spanish Official Bulletin of the State [BOE], 27 April 2015), which reads:

Organic Law 5/2015 of 27 April 2015, which modifies the Code of Criminal Procedure (*Ley de Enjuiciamiento Criminal*) and Organic Law 6/1985 of 1 July, of the Judiciary, to transpose the Directive 2010/64/EU of 20 October 2010 regarding the right to interpreting and translation in criminal proceedings and the Directive 2012/13/EU of 22 May 2012 regarding the right to information in criminal proceedings.

Nevertheless, according to documents published by professional translation and interpreting associations and other entities representing legal translation and interpreting, these modifications are insufficient. One such example is the press release titled 'Missed Opportunity: Legal Interpreting without Guarantees' (*Oportunidad perdida: interpretación judicial sin garantías, Nota de Prensa 17/4/2015*), published by APTIJ, Vértice and CCDUTI. Although the aforementioned law does not directly affect the prison system, it does provide evidence of the evolving value of translation and interpreting and the recognition of professionals in this field.

The prison system

The prison system is a context with peculiarities – most notably its confined spaces that are guarded with tight security – that distinguish it from other settings in the field of law (i.e. law enforcement and the courts). It is also a unique context in that it encompasses all of the branches of PSIT, from interviews with lawyers, doctor's visits and training sessions, to encounters with social workers – a variety of fields each with their respective professional codes of conduct, the overlapping of which presents significant potential for conflict.

According to the Spanish National Institute of Statistics (*Instituto Nacional de Estadística*; INE), the Spanish prison population housed a total of 68,597 inmates in 2012, of which 22,893 (approximately 33%) were foreigners. This means that one of every three inmates in Spain was a foreigner in 2012. This is a high figure, particularly taking into account that foreigners account for about 10% of the general population in Spain in 2013 (during this year, 4,676,021 of the total population of 46,507,760 were foreign-born).

International studies dedicated to exploring the problems unique to foreign inmates in prisons have been scarce. Within Europe, there are those by Bhui (2003, 2004, 2006), Cheney (1993), Ellis (1998), Green (1991, 1998), Pourgourides *et al.* (1996), Tarzi and Hedges (1990, 1993) and Van Kalmthout *et al.* (2007); and in Spain the doctoral theses and research cited earlier by Baixauli (2012), Martínez-Gómez (2008) and Valero-Garcés and Mojica (2014).

Bhui (2006), in her comparative study of six prisons in the United Kingdom, identifies the foremost problems faced by foreign inmates and provides information regarding the general situation in prisons:

(1) Lack of information (e.g. regarding the legal system or the prison).
(2) Problems related to immigration (e.g. deportation orders and indefinite detention by Immigration Services).
(3) Language barriers (a factor that intensifies other problems).
(4) Isolation (particularly that of families).
(5) Lack of preparation for reintegration to society and the workforce once a term is served.
(6) Poor treatment, racism and disrespectful attitudes on the part of staff.

These results are corroborated by remarks from Škvain (2007):

Knowledge of language plays the key role; otherwise a prisoner does not have the opportunity to communicate with others and it will be easier to end up in social isolation. Such a prisoner is not able to understand what his/her obligations are in prison and he/she is treated differently not only by prison staff, but by his/her fellow prisoners too. (Škvain, 2007: 193)

Van Kalmthout *et al.* (2007) also observe that

[t]he most common and significant problem faced by foreign prisoners is the lack of knowledge of the national language. As a result, verbal and written communication is severely hampered and that causes feelings of social isolation, uncertainty and helplessness [...] Daily interactions between foreign prisoners and staff are crucial and it often depends on the goodwill of prison staff and fellow prisoners and the availability of an interpreter. Language barriers are often the main source of other problems that foreign prisoners face in penitentiary institutions. (Van Kalmthout *et al.*, 2007: 17)

These same problems have been described in research on Spanish prisons (see studies cited earlier).

Pilot project: Objective and methods

In 2011, the University of Alcalá (UAH) in Madrid began to establish ties with the Spanish Directorate General for Penitentiaries through the Masters in Intercultural Communication and Public Service Interpreting and Translation (MA in IC and PSIT) with the aim of establishing the Directorate General for Penitentiaries as one of the institutions belonging to the university's internship programme. As such, students would be able to visit Spanish prisons and offer services there as interpreters. When months had gone by without a response from the Directorate General, a direct agreement was signed with one of the prisons located in Madrid (Madrid V – Soto del Real) in June 2012. This agreement made it possible to send one student to complete his or her internship at the institution. Research was also carried out by means of interviews with staff members, which revealed the need for translation and interpreting services. After this development, interest grew in widening the scope of the project, and in late 2012 the agreement was extended to include another prison: Alcalá Meco Mujeres I (a women's prison). In 2013, the agreement was extended again to four additional prisons (Centro Penitenciario de Botafuegos in Algeciras,

Centro Penitenciario de Zuera, Centro Penitenciario de Daroca and Centro Penitenciario de Teruel).

The objective of these projects was to explore communication within the prison population among inmates who were unfamiliar with the contact language and culture in order to determine shortcomings in language access and how these shortcomings were being approached in order to propose joint solutions. The preliminary results, based on surveys and interviews carried out with staff, interpreters and inmates, were published in Valero-Garcés and Mojica (2014).

The current study, in addition to complementing the existing research, serves as a qualitative study based exclusively on interviews carried out with prison staff and interpreters in the aforementioned projects. Interviews were carried out with prison staff, interpreters and inmates in the original studies; in the present study only data from the first two groups are taken into account.

Data come from the pilot project conducted in two CPs: CP Madrid I (Women), also known as the Alcalá Meco Prison, and CP Botafuegos in Algeciras. Data used for the present study were collected between February 2013 and June 2014. This undertaking has highlighted key synergies between research and training for PSIT, and it also falls within the research themes of the FITISPos Group and the postgraduate training programme in PSIT at the University of Alcalá in Madrid.

Results

Once permission was granted by the Secretary General of Penitentiary Centers, the two aforementioned centres (Alcalá Meco and Botafuegos) collaborated closely for the purposes of this research. Apart from interviews and surveys carried out with the three groups involved in the study (staff, interpreters and inmates), the prisons also provided statistics that granted a more precise understanding of the multilingual and multicultural reality of this confined environment.

Staff who completed surveys were males aged between 40 and 50 years who serve as members of prison staff, either as part of the facility's disciplinary commission or as social workers who help inmates maintain contact with family members. The professional interpreters who participated in the study were aged between 30 and 40 years and held high school diplomas or a bachelor's degree in language studies or translation and interpreting. Individuals serving as *ad hoc* interpreters in the prisons are often inmates themselves or staff who know additional languages and who either volunteer or are paid to interpret when required. In all instances, staff reported communicating with inmates through interpreters more than 20 times a year. Inmate interpreters also reported having interpreted between zero and 20 times a year. Both inmates and interpreters reported that the most common interpreted encounters were those with lawyers, doctors and prison staff, whereas the most common encounters with staff were with social workers and educators.

The perspective of prison staff on the interpreter's role

According to members of prison staff who responded to the survey, the most common communicative situations requiring an interpreter involved administrative matters, although communication with other professionals appeared to be covered by different means, as suggested by the response of a staff member at CP Botafuegos, who describes communication with lawyers:

Example 1:

I (interviewer):	When there is a serious topic like a meeting with a lawyer, for example, what is the communication like?
R (prison staff member):	We don't know. We are never present for meetings with lawyers.
I:	Does that mean the lawyer brings his own interpreter, then?
R:	Yes, the lawyer usually brings his own interpreter. We are unable to comment on the matter.

The following exchange regarding interpreting during medical appointments in the prison adds further information regarding encounters with other professionals:

Example 2:

I:	So what is communication with doctors like?
R:	Of course in the nursing unit it is the inmates themselves who interpret.
I:	And this type of communication tends to be effective?
R:	Always, above all because the visits are only in outpatient care. In an emergency, inmates are taken to the hospital, where they have the same rights to interpretation as any other citizen. The prison only offers primary care visits and the inmates who interpret do not need to have medical knowledge.

The above exchange indicates that the staff member complies with his profession's code of ethics by guaranteeing inmates 'the same rights as any other citizen'. Another matter, however, is the quality of the guaranteed communication when compared to the professional interpreter's code. As we will see in the following section, achieving such quality requires full comprehension of the original message and a complete transfer thereof, which means possessing a command of both languages at the very least. Nevertheless, it appears that amidst the chaos, when prison staff evaluate the success of the communication, they place more value on whether they trust a particular inmate to serve as an interpreter rather than in the inmate's true capacity to interpret, and they therefore fail to question the accuracy of the content. This conclusion supports Pym's (2004) notion of 'translational trust' discussed in his article 'Propositions on Cross-Cultural Communication and Translation', in which he argues that the related concepts of complexity, success conditions and risk can describe not only the act of translating as a mode of cross-cultural communication, but also certain features of the professional intercultures to which translators belong.

Furthermore, the prison staff member's response above confirms that foreign inmates themselves who possess knowledge of the majority language often provide interpreting services on a voluntary basis, outside of normal procedures for assigning interpreted visits or contracting interpreting services, although it appears that in some instances there is a possibility of remuneration:

Example 3:

I: So do the inmates themselves who perform this work receive payment?

R: Sometimes yes, sometimes no. They receive pay for tasks referred to as 'productive'. It's not a lot of pay, but enough to cover their expenses. But sometimes inmates interpret in a given moment just to be of help, the same as any other person would do on the street; out of neighbourliness, you could say.

For prison staff, the question of quality or faithfulness to the original message in the transfer of information does not pose an ethical debate or dilemma, given that the staff member's fundamental duty lies in guaranteeing the proper operation of the facility and protecting basic rights, as we have seen in the civil servant's code of ethics cited earlier. Hence, staff consider the level of understanding to be high between themselves and inmates who do not speak Spanish. They affirm that 'despite the fact that [the inmates] are not professionals, they carry out their functions correctly when necessary'. Nevertheless, this belief is not shared by the inmates themselves, who consider their understanding to be very low (not only in prison but in general) and claim that they 'hardly understand anything', according to data collected from interviews with inmates (Granados, 2014: 65).

These comments lead us to believe that regardless of whether the service is provided by inmates who act as volunteers or by prison staff who know the second language, confidence in the service fluctuates between moderate and high either 'because although prison staff are unfamiliar with the language, experience tells them that the inmates are satisfied with the interpreters, or because there simply do not seem to be many incidents' (Granados, 2014: 72). The following response to the question about the faith that staff members put in inmate interpreters leaves no room for doubt:

Example 4:

R: Complete [confidence], of course, given that the circumstances are not extraordinary. We are not mounting a case for defenselessness because an inmate says he needs a toothbrush. These are everyday things. When there are rights involved, we have a disciplinary commission for offenses or other events that arise in prison where we have the aid of an unofficial interpreter. However, there are certain educated inmates who hold university degrees and are not your stereotypical inmate. These individuals receive a higher level of trust than others and they are able to help on the spot. We make things work with what we have. The most delicate matters that arise occur within the disciplinary commission, because in these cases the inmate must defend himself. However, because the supervising judge must approve sanctions in advance, we do not see cases where inmates fail to receive proper representation.

The existence of different ethical codes or disparities among the ethical principles that guide each profession is clearly illustrated in the following response:

Example 5:

I: Alright. I understand that having truly qualified interpreters does not seem to be important to you.
R: Yes, it would seem important to me if the inmate's life were easier, but there are other more important deficiencies, so if there were a budget, yes (...). Right now, for example, we are experiencing some serious security issues due to lack of personnel. Among other things, the security of the facilities has been seriously undermined, endangering the lives of the inmates. So certainly we can make a sacrifice when *it comes to an inmate using correct language to request bread* while another might have a serious safety issue. (Author's emphasis)

This response is consistent with the civil servant's code of ethics in that security and ensuring the rationing of resources are primary principles (as indicated in point 4 of Article 53. Ethical Principles, below), unlike in the case of the interpreter's code of ethics, where quality of communication takes priority.

4. Conduct will be based on respect for fundamental rights and public liberties, avoiding any behaviour that may produce discrimination based on birth, racial or ethnic origin, gender, sex, sexual orientation, religion or belief, opinion, disability, age or any other personal or social condition or circumstance.

Furthermore, point 5, Article 54. Principles of Conduct, indicates the following:

5. Public resources and goods will be managed with austerity and not for personal gain or for the gain of acquaintances. Furthermore, the duty of ensuring the conservation of these resources must be upheld.

The foremost principle that civil servants must observe as representatives of the law is that of demonstrating and enforcing respect for the law (Article 53. Ethical Principles: '1. Civil servants will respect the Constitution and all other requirements of the law'). There already exist certain mechanisms for this purpose which one staff member describes in his response to the question of how communication with inmates is carried out in the prison when no inmate interpreter or other *ad hoc* interpreter is available:

Example 6:

R: All inmates receive legal assistance prior to entering prison. Communication with lawyers is carried out with an interpreter and once they arrive at prison, if there is no one who speaks Bulgarian or Croatian—well, they adapt little by little. Normally, a Bulgarian or Croatian who goes to prison here has spent time living in Spain and because they have committed a crime here, they enter prison here already knowing some Spanish.

Thus, the responsibility of offering interpreting services, whether inside or outside the prison, is diverted away from prison staff. The first strategy is to leave the responsibility of communication to the inmate himself/herself, despite the fact that he/she only 'knows some Spanish'. Resorting to translating necessary materials is another strategy that allows staff to satisfy the code of conduct that guides their professional ethics, as is observed in the following response:

Example 7:

I: In the case that no one else speaks the inmate's language, how do they communicate and become integrated in the prison?

R: We have brochures in almost every language so that they are able to understand their rights and duties. But they never need the brochures; they all communicate just fine and participate in all the different activities.

This staff member's response reflects point 4 of Article 54. Principles of Conduct:

Civil servants will inform citizens of matters that they have the right to know and will help them to exercise their rights and satisfy their obligations.

However, from the point of view of the interpreter or translator, the statement 'they communicate just fine' raises questions about what 'just fine' truly means, given that foreign inmates for whom these materials exist do not have an advanced command of Spanish. As for the staff, having satisfied the legal requirements for communication, their next duty is to administer resources as indicated in point 5 in Article 54. Principles of Conduct mentioned earlier. The following excerpt from the interview reflects this point:

Example 8:

I: How do you believe that the service of interpreting could be improved once basic needs are met?

R: I believe that it would be most productive for staff to be trained. In fact, this has been done through small classes in order for staff to be able to communicate with the most common population. Arabic classes are organized annually to train staff so they can read and communicate in basic Arabic, but I think there should be more advanced training. That would be the most productive solution in the prison setting.

I: Just one language then?

R: Yes, the majority language in each center. A translator for each language is a utopic idea. Perhaps in a bigger city, but it is just not economically feasible because even travel time must be paid.

In the following excerpt, the interviewer asks whether the transposition of the Directive 2010/64 and the need to create a registry of professional translators and interpreters may serve as a solution for issues of communication. Again, the interviewee's response refers back to the established rules of conduct for his profession, in Chapter 4. Duties of Civil Servants. Code of Conduct:

Example 9:

I: Sure, it may not be the most productive for less common languages, but what would happen, for example, if there were an internal or external bank of interpreters for more common languages? I think it could be very useful to have some sort of registry or database to refer to in these cases.

R: It would be useful. In fact, I am not sure how they do it, but I know that other departments within the Ministry of the Interior have their own translators. When it comes to assisting inmates or individuals who have been arrested or convicted, it is a different story. Ideally, in my opinion, each country's consulate would assist its own nationals. Consulates are located all over the world, but they also tend to be located in accordance with the number of nationals residing in each country.

The respondent avoids commenting on the creation of a registry of translators and interpreters – a topic that has also been left unanswered in the recent passing of Organic Law 5/2015 (Spanish Official Bulletin of the State [BOE], 27 April 2015), wherein Preamble IV indicates the following:

The Law includes a final provision that refers to the creation of a Registry of court translators and interpreters as a necessary means for guaranteeing the adequate execution of this task, which is fundamental for the trial process. This is also a follow-up to the Directive 2010/64/ EU regarding the right to interpreting and translation in criminal proceedings. The rules of operation for this Register will be created by law and enforced in accordance with regulations.

The staff member's final answer again reflects the professional code of conduct and ethical principles to which he is expected to adhere.

Example 10:

R: (...) It would be ideal to have a body of translators who were able to assist when necessary, but who would pay them? Plus there are other priorities. We only have four or five translators out of the ten that there ought to be. Now *that* affects the health and life of inmates. Inmates receive legal assistance outside of prison. Prison translators would be better placed with the disciplinary commission because they deal with rights such as the deprivation of liberty. I think that someone who enters a Spanish prison without speaking even a word of Spanish is someone who was not integrated into Spanish society, someone who has committed a crime here based on circumstance. Our penal code states that inmates are allowed to serve sentences of less than six years in their country of origin. There is also that possibility. Inmates have the right to communicate to their consulate that they are in prison but they almost never want to. They do not want their country or family to know that they are in prison. We assist everyone up until their trial simply because of the presumption of innocence. Nobody is without defence and everyone receives basic care. There is no social exclusion. I think that isolated cases should be resolved with the help of consulates.

Ultimately, prison staff appear to consider the presence of professional translators and interpreters in the prisons to be worthwhile; however, the current situation complies with current legislation and falls within what is permitted by the law. As a result, communication with the non-Spanish-speaking population is adequate and does not pose serious problems given the existence of procedures that guarantee the minimum required rights:

(1) Basic communication with the inmate who knows some Spanish or staff who know some of the inmate's language.
(2) Communication with the help of an *ad hoc* inmate interpreter.
(3) Communication through written material regarding necessary basic matters on coexistence and the guarantee of inmate rights.

The perspective of interpreters on the interpreter's role

The introduction to the previously cited Code of Conduct in the *Libro Blanco de la Traducción e Interpretación Institucional* (2010) (henceforth LB) reads:

In order to regulate any branch of translation or interpreting—in this case institutional—a code of ethics is fundamental. Thus, all parties affected by the translator's or interpreter's work are able to trust them, knowing, for example, that they will observe the requirements of confidentiality and impartiality and that there are procedures to identify and address cases where these requirements are violated. (LB, 2010: 99)

The answers provided by the professional interpreter in one of the CPs studied will serve to illustrate the situation in relation to the Code of Conduct in the LB. The respondent is a 40-year-old man who has substantial experience interpreting and translating for the Spanish Civil Guard (Guardia Civil),[1] which, like the Secretary General of Penitentiary Institutions (Secretaría General de Instituciones Penitenciarias), operates within the Ministry of the Interior. The interviewee was hired at the prison in response to the attacks of 11 March 2004 in Madrid. His working languages are Arabic and several of its dialects, and as he reports: 'I translate classic Arabic and interpret phone taps or testimonies or interviews in *Darija*'.[2] The interview with the interpreter touches on the first principle outlined in the aforementioned LB (2010) – that of fidelity and integrity of the original message:

> The message should be interpreted and translated truly and faithfully to the best of one's ability without altering the content or the intention of the original message. This section includes matters such as maintaining the tone of the message (formal or colloquial) and the preservation of cultural terms that have no immediate equivalent in the target language. (LB, 2010: 99)

The following excerpt from the interview demonstrates the interpreter's (T&I) overall fulfilment of this principle:

Example 11:

I: I understand that you have also worked in the courts. Has the judge ever requested that you summarize?

T&I: I have always interpreted everything that is said.

I: Do you believe that to be common? It is my understanding that many interpreters summarize in order to save time.

T&I: I have always tried to be literal, although I do remember a time that someone got angry with me and said that I was not translating everything. There were a lot of laws and they thought I was simplifying them because I thought they would not understand them. In reality I transmitted all of the important information.

This final comment, nevertheless, indicates a deviation from the principle of fidelity, albeit justified in this case, and demonstrates the difficulty of applying principles literally. However, this example is also in keeping with Hortal's (2007: 41) aforementioned argument that '(...) [professional] ethics, whether outlined in a code or not, reflect what professionals do, ought to do, or what is advisable for them to do in order to practice their profession ethically'. Observations by other interpreters (gleaned by the author through conversations or personal experience) on judges' instructions to condense defendants' statements in order to save time are also worth mentioning. There are other factors that may also interfere with the concept of 'fidelity' as literal translation, as illustrated by the following excerpt:

Example 12:

I: Do you believe that one's level of education may have an impact and that it may be necessary to adapt the message?
T&I: Yes, of course. I believe that the delivery should be complete.

Other extralinguistic elements also come into play which further confirm Hortal's remark regarding the potential influence of the situation:

Example 13:

I: How do you usually do your job?
T&I: Like that, of course. Although, sometimes, I have also had to take on the role of mediator. In court, the judge wants answers to be concise and asks me to interrupt because there isn't enough time. In this case I let the person know that they will have the floor at the end in order to explain themselves. Sometimes they arrive very nervous and you have to calm them down. This is not the interpreter's role, but it is the reality of the situation.

The interpreter's involvement in this scenario goes well beyond merely transmitting the message, as is prescribed by the interpreter's code of ethics, but the influence of situation discussed by Hortal can lead to this sort of departure. In fact, firm adherence to the principles of fidelity and accuracy is a topic currently under debate, as is reflected in research in various settings within the field of translation and interpreting (Angelelli, 2004; Baraldi & Gavioli, 2010; Dougherty & Atkinson, 2006; Tribe & Raval, 2014). In comparing the interpreter's answers with those of the prison worker, we observe that both strive to follow their professional codes of conduct. The difference lies in their moral principles or in establishing the limits of what is understood by 'communication': in one case, it is understood to be a general transfer of content whereas in the other it means pursuing a complete transmission of the original message. The second basic principle recommended by the LB (2010) is that of sufficient competency and preparation:

Interpreters and translators should have an understanding of what the assignment involves before accepting it. They should be sure that they possess sufficient competency in order to perform the task and that they have the time and materials necessary to carry out any prior preparation or research. They should also have access to sources of necessary information and reference materials. (LB, 2010: 100)

The following excerpt demonstrates the interpreter's professionalism, even though this is not a matter that the prison worker takes into account when considering the interpreter's role in facilitating communication:

Example 14:

I.   There is also burnout syndrome, where the interpreter (who speaks in first person) becomes involved in the suffering of the person they interpret for.

T&I: I work mostly with Islamic terrorism and I see a lot of videos of terrorists in which the degree of persuasion is such that, without training or experience, you might end up becoming involved. The most difficult experience I had was around 2003 when I worked for the Spanish National Police over the summer and a small boat of children arrived. Listening to them was heart wrenching. I admit that I took my work home with me that week, but at the end of the day you realize that you cannot let your profession become something personal. I have gone through so many emotions: from insulting myself to kissing my own feet, but without a doubt, that particular experience was the most difficult thing I have had to do.

The final sentences of the above quote illustrate the diverse reactions that the interpreter's work can elicit. Thus the need arises for robust training in order to give the interpreter the skills to face difficult situations with professionalism. However, the necessary preparation to become a professional is not always guaranteed or understood in the same way by members of other professions, even when the two are expected to work as a team or collaborate.

Example 15:

I: What technical difficulties have you encountered over the years?

T&I: A lack of material, first and foremost. Although that is not the case right now: I have my dictionary that I ordered upon arriving, since with the Arab Spring so many new concepts have surfaced. I have my computer with an Arabic-Spanish keyboard that no one uses but me, my own office, a voice recorder...

I: Would you receive information before interpreting for a trial, for example?

T&I: No, I would have to improvise, but I have always asked all the questions I could.

I: I think that ignorance is to blame—they are not familiar with the interpreter's job. If at any point you needed a dictionary, would they allow you to use one?

T&I: No, not at all. I had no choice but to resort to my own ingenuity.

A close reading of this statement exposes certain truths: first of all, the disparity of opinions between the two groups of professionals with regard to training and the availability of resources. In the case of civil servants, it is circumstance that drives change (e.g. the Arab Spring and the need for professional interpreters), whereas in the case of professional interpreters, the inability to access materials or resources leads them to resort to tactics like 'ingenuity' or improvisation, with all of the potential risks that come with doing so. The following example, nevertheless, seems to compromise the principle of fidelity, in addition to those of confidentiality and impartiality, and may even pit personal and professional ethics against one another:

Example 16:

I: Have you ever been in a position where a prisoner has confessed to you having committed a crime that he has been denying?

T&I: Personally, I try to be impartial and professional. I would never protect a criminal.

The interpreter's clarification that she would 'never protect a criminal' suggests that she would reveal the disclosed information, whether by an obligation to her own moral principles or to the authorities. In this case, the interpreter's action is consistent with both her own code of ethics and that of the civil servant. She explains her motives, which can be summed up as safeguarding her personal safety:

Example 17:

I: Right, but because there is no regulation or code of ethics, the protocol is a bit ambiguous.

T&I: Yes, it would be different if there were regulations. I limit myself to the questions they ask the prisoner. I have heard of cases where interpreters have covered themselves at work so they cannot be recognized...

Discrepancies in terms of the knowledge and consideration that one profession has for the other or the type of training that they ought to have are illustrated in the final statement made by the interpreter below. These discrepancies also shed light on the comment made earlier by the member of prison staff who placed more importance on experience and trust in the interpreter than on the interpreter's training.

Example 18:

I: What status do you think interpreting has in this area of public services?

T&I: Well, it is looked down upon, poorly paid and there is a lot of joking around about interpreters being tattletales for the police. It is not even considered a profession because anyone can do this work, although there are a lot of well-prepared people who have bothered to learn what to do and how to do it. For temporary contracts, say just three to four months, they will hire anyone; that is where I have seen real deficiencies. There should be regulations and they should understand that you cannot just hire someone because they know a language. I earn 1,100 euros a month here and I have spent many years studying and training.

The assertion that 'interpreters [are] tattletales for the police' suggests the lack of awareness surrounding this professional figure and the distrust she is met with. On the other hand, the interpreter must take into account that the civil servant is subject to a code of public service, and that as long as the laws do not change, he/she is exercising his/her role in the manner that he/she deems most correct.

Conclusion

Ethics are present in almost all aspects of our lives. Every profession is governed by ethics outlined in codes of conduct or best practice guides. The present study has analysed communicative situations involving professionals from different fields in order to determine what happens when multiple codes of ethics overlap, the ethical conflicts that arise and how these conflicts are resolved. I have focused on the little-studied context of CPs within the field of law, and communication with the foreign population therein. This is a unique context that combines every branch of PSIT, from interviews with lawyers, doctor's visits and training sessions, to encounters with social workers as just a few examples of the diversity of communicative situations that occur.

As for framing the present study in a greater context based on prior research on the prison setting, past studies have indicated that communication in this setting suffers from a lack of information and complications related to immigration or language, and that furthermore there is a risk of isolation, racism and a lack of preparation for reintroduction to society after sentences are served. The current qualitative study is based solely on interviews carried out with prison staff and interpreters in these projects and their results.

Data come from the pilot study carried out in Spanish prisons and from the analysis of the behaviour reported by prison staff and interpreters in interviews. The results indicate that while both codes of ethics explored agree on fundamental principles, there are nevertheless certain disparities in principles that may lead to conflict and disagreement when evaluating whether certain ethical principles have been met in each of the professions. The greatest difference lies in establishing the limits of what is understood by 'communication'. In one case (that of prison staff) it is defined as a general transfer of content, whereas in the other (interpreters), a complete transfer of the message is expected.

From the point of view of prison staff, the presence of translation and interpreting professionals in prisons is advisable, although the current situation, where inmates may serve as *ad hoc* interpreters, meets regulations, and the staff's behaviour is consistent with what is permissible by law. As a consequence, communication with the non-Spanish-speaking population is adequate and does not pose serious problems, as there are procedures that guarantee the minimum required rights, such as basic communication with prisoners who know some Spanish or staff who know some of their language; communication through an *ad hoc* inmate-interpreter; and communication through written material on basic necessary information for coexistence and observance of inmate rights. Trust in the interpreter based on his/her experience or mere knowledge of contact languages is valued above training, without taking into account fidelity or impartiality, as long as the basic rights of the inmate are satisfied and conflicts are avoided.

From the point of view of the interpreters, fidelity to content and impartiality are fundamental principles that must be adhered to, as is possessing adequate training that allows him/her to behave professionally. The interpreter believes that the quality of service offered is generally poor, although it continues to improve. He/she advocates for the use of professional language service providers who are adequately qualified.

Certainly, communicative, socio-professional and ethical issues do not pose problems for prison staff, given that their foremost goal is to guarantee basic rights and avoid conflict. They do not question the professionalism of an inmate who acts as an *ad hoc* interpreter, nor is the *ad hoc* interpreter held to any standards, given that there is no code of ethics that regulates his/her efforts. Thus, if the *ad hoc* interpreter alters a message or includes his/her own opinion, these issues are never brought to light. Professional interpreters, on the other hand, are committed to the fidelity and impartiality that are so vital to their task and they suspect that the distrust towards members of their profession may be due to general ignorance about their work.

In conclusion, it is suggested that greater familiarity with both professional codes of ethics, continuing education and collaboration between prison staff and interpreters will help to guarantee greater success in fulfilling the objectives of both professions.

Notes

(1) The Civil Guard, a military force charged with police duties, holds both a national role and also undertakes specific foreign peacekeeping missions. In general, the Civil Guard patrols rural areas (including highways and ports) and investigates crimes, while the *Policía Nacional* (National Police) deals with significant urban situations (see http://en.wikipedia.org/wiki/National_Police_Corps_of_Spain). Most cities also have a *Policía Local* (Local Police), which concentrates on crime prevention, traffic control, settling minor incidents and, crucially, intelligence gathering. Locally, all three forces work closely, and are nationally coordinated under the Ministry of the Interior.
(2) *Darija*, also written as *ad-darija, derija* or *darja*, refers to the colloquial variety of Arabic subsumed under Maghrebi Arabic.

References

Abbott, A. (1983) Professional ethics. *American Journal of Sociology* 88 (5), 855–885.
Almeida Herrero, C., Lucena García, M. and Rodríguez Enríquez, F.J. (2006) *Situación de los presos extranjeros en el Centro Penitenciario de Topas (Salamanca)*. Salamanca: Cáritas diocesana de Salamanca. See http://docplayer.es/11472058-Situacion-de-los-presos-extranjeros-en-el-centro-penitenciario-de-topas-salamanca.html (accessed 3 November 2016).
Angelelli, C. (2004) *Revisiting the Interpreter's Role: A Study of Conference, Court, and Medical Interpreters in Canada, Mexico and the United States*. Amsterdam: John Benjamins.
Baixauli, L. (2012) La interpretació als serveis públics desde una perspectiva ética. La deontologia professional i l'apliccació al context penitenciari. PhD thesis, Universitat Jaume I. See http://repositori.uji.es/xmlui/handle/10234/74752 (accessed 20 June 2015).
Baixauli-Olmos, L. (2013) A description of interpreting in prisons – Mapping the setting through an ethical lens. In C. Schäffner, K. Kredens and Y. Fowler (eds) *Interpreting in a Changing Landscape. Selected Papers from Critical Link 6* (pp. 45–60). Amsterdam: John Benjamins.
Baker, M. and Maier, C. (2011) Ethics in interpreter and translator training. *The Interpreter and Translator Trainer* 5 (1), 1–14.
Baraldi, C. and Gavioli, L. (eds) (2010) *Coordinating Participation in Dialogue Interpreting*. Amsterdam: John Benjamins.
Bhui, H.S. (2003) 'Foreign Nationals in Prisons', *Guardian Society*. See http://www.europris.org/expert-groups/foreign-nationals-in-prison/ (accessed 20 June 2015).
Bhui, H.S. (2004) The resettlement needs of foreign national offenders. *Criminal Justice Matters* 56, 36–37, 44.
Bhui, H.S. (2006) *Going the Distance: Developing Effective Policy and Practice with Foreign National Prisoners*. See http://www.prisonreformtrust.org.uk/uploads/documents/GOING_THE_DISTANCE_book3.pdf (accessed 3 November 2016).
Camayd-Freixas, E. (2013) *US Immigration Reform and its Global Impact. Lessons from the Postville Raid*. New York: Palgrave Macmillan.

Código de la Función Pública, Estatuto básico del empleado público. BOE, Edición actualizada a 1 de abril de 2015. See www.boe.es/legislacion/codigos/ (accessed 2 November 2016).

Collin, J. and Morris, R. (1996) *Interpreters and the Legal Process*. Winchester: Waterside Press.

Cortina, A. (2010) *¿Para qué sirve realmente la ética?* Madrid: Paidos.

Cheney, D. (1994) Policy and practice in work with foreign nationals. *Probation Journal* 41 (4), 1–6.

Dougherty, D. and Atkinson, J. (2006) Competing ethical communities and a research's dilemma. The case of a sexual harasser. *Qualitative Inquiry* 12 (2), 292–315.

Dysart-Gale, D. (2005) Communication models, professionalization, and the work of medical interpreters. *Health Communication* 17 (1), 91–103.

Ellis, R. (1998) *Asylum-Seekers and Immigration Act Prisoners. The Practice of Detention.* London: Prison Reform Trust.

España. Real Decreto 190/1996, de 9 de febrero, por el que se aprueba el Reglamento Penitenciario. *Boletín Oficial del Estado,* de 15 de febrero de 1996, núm. 40, pp. 5380–5435. See http://www.boe.es/boe/dias/1996/02/15/pdfs/A05380-05435.pdf (accessed 20 June 2015).

Gert, B. (2012) The definition of morality. In E.N. Zalta (ed.) *The Stanford Encyclopedia of Philosophy* (Fall 2012 edition). See http://plato.stanford.edu/archives/fall2012/entries/morality-definition (accessed 20 June 2015).

Granados, F. (2014) Interpretación en los servicios públicos ámbito jurídico: jurisdicción penal policía, juzgado, prisión. Algeciras. MA thesis, Máster Universitario en Comunicación Intercultural, Interpretación y Traducción en los Servicios Públicos ,University of Alcalá.

Green, P. (1991) *Drug Couriers*. London: Howard League for Penal Reform.

Green, P. (1998) *Drugs, Trafficking and Criminal Policy: The Scapegoat Policy*. Winchester: Waterside Press.

Gutiérrez, J.A., Jordán, J. and Trujillo, H. (2008) Prevención de la radicalización yihadista en las prisiones españolas. Situación actual, retos y disfunciones del sistema penitenciario. *Athena Intelligence Journal* 3, 1–9.

Hortal, A. (2007) *Ética Profesional de Traductores e Intérpretes*. Bilbao: Editorial Desclee De Brouwer.

Humphrey, J.H. (1999) *Decision? Decisions!* Amarillo, TX: H&H Publishers.

Humphrey, E., Janosik, S.M. and Creamer, D.G. (2004) The role of principles, character, and professional values in ethical decision-making. *NASPA Journal* 41, 675–692.

Inghilleri, M. (2012) *Interpreting Justice – Ethics, Politics, and Language*. New York: Routledge.

Kaufert, J.M. and Putsch, R.W. (1997) Communication through interpreters in healthcare: Ethical dilemmas arising from differences in class, culture, and power. *The Journal of Clinical Ethics* 8 (1), 71–87.

Kohlberg, L. (1975) Moral education for a society in moral transition. *Educational Leadership* 32 (6), 13–16.

Laster, K. and Taylor, V.L. (1994) *Interpreters and The Legal System*. Annandale, VA: The Federation Press.

Libro Blanco de la Traducción e Interpretación Institucional. 2010. Ministerio de Asuntos Exteriores y Cooperación. http://ec.europa.eu/spain/pdf/libro_blanco_traduccion_es.pdf (accessed 3 November 2016).

Martínez-Gómez, A. (2008) La integración lingüística en las instituciones penitenciarias españolas y europeas. Proceedings of the International Conference *El español, lengua de traducción* (pp. 485–500). *ESLETRA*. Universidad de Castilla-La Mancha. See http://cvc.cervantes.es/lengua/esletra/pdf/04/051_martinez.pdf (accessed 20 June 2015).

Mendoza, R. (2012) Thinking through ethics: The processes of ethical decision making by novice and expert interpreters. *International Journal of Interpreter Education* 4 (1), 59–70.

Ministerio de Asuntos Exteriores y Cooperación (2010) *Libro Blanco de la Traducción e Interpretación Institucional*. See http://ec.europa.eu/spain/pdf/libro_blanco_traduccion_es.pdf.

Oportunidad perdida: interpretación judicial sin garantías – Nota de Prensa 17/4/2015). See www.aptij.com (accessed 20 June 2015).

Ortega Herraez, J.M. (2010) *Interpretar para la Justicia*. Granada: Comares.

Pourgourides, C.K., Sashidharan, S.P. and Bracken, P.J. (1996) *A Second Exile: The Mental Health Implications of Detention of Asylum Seekers in the UK*. Birmingham: University of Birmingham/Cadbury Trust.

Pym, A. (2004) Propositions on cross-cultural communication and translation. *Target* 16 (1), 1–28.

Rachels, J. and Rachels, S. (2006) *The Elements of Moral Philosophy*. New York: McGraw-Hill.

Richards, M., McWilliams, B., Batten, N., Cameron, C. and Cutler, J. (1995) Foreign nationals in English prisons: I. Family ties and their maintenance. *Howard Journal* 34 (2), 158–175.

Ross, W.D. (1930/2002) *The Right and the Good*. P. Straton-Lake (ed.). New York: Oxford University Press.

Rudvin, M. (2007) Professionalism and ethics in public service interpreting. *Interpreting* 9 (1), 47–69.

Rudvin, M. and Tomassini, E. (2011) *Interpreting in the Community and Workplace. A Practical Teaching Guide*. Basingstoke: Palgrave MacMillan.

Ruthven, D. and Seward, E. (2002) *Restricted Access: Legal Information for Remand*. London: Prison Reform Trust.

Samba, M. (2007) Behind closed doors. *The Linguist* 46 (1), 6–7.

Škvain, P. (2007) Czech Republic. In A.M. van Kalmthout, F.B.A.M. Hofstee-van der Meulen and F. Dünkel (eds) *Foreigners in European Prisons* (pp. 169–206). Nijmegen: Wolf Legal Publishers.

Solomon, E. and Edgar, K. (2003) *Having Their Say: The Work of Prisoner Councils*. London: Prison Reform Trust.

Tarzi, A. and Hedges, J. (1990) *A Prison Within a Prison*. London: Inner London Probation Service.

Tarzi, A. and Hedges, J. (1993) *A Prison Within a Prison – Two Years On: An Overview*. London: Inner London Probation Service.

Tribe, R. and Raval, H. (2014) *Working with Interpreters in Mental Health*. Amsterdam: John Benjamins.

Valero-Garcés, C. (ed.) (2014) *(Re)considerando ética e ideología en situaciones de conflicto/ (Re)visiting ethics and ideology in situations of conflicto*. Alcalá de Henares: Servicio de Publicaciones de la Universidad de Alcalá.

Van Kalmthout, A.M., Hofstee-Van Der Meulen, F.B.A.M. and Dünkel, F. (eds) (2007) *Foreigners in European Prisons*. Nijmegen: Wolf Legal Publishers.

7 Virtual Presence, Ethics and Videoconference Interpreting: Insights from Court Settings

Jérôme Devaux

> *By simply doing my job and following my code of ethics to the letter, I, like the rest of the participants, had facilitated the wrongful demise of hundreds of impoverished workers and vulnerable families.*
> Camayd-Freixas, 2013: 17

Introduction

In the 1970s, telephone interpreting was first used in Australia to facilitate intercultural communication in emergency cases in public service settings (Kelly, 2008). Since then, and with the advent of further technological developments and the increasing demand for access to interpreters in Europe, the use of new technologies has developed into an integral part of the public service interpreter's work, whether it be via videoconference interpreting (VCI) (in which the interpreter is present with one of the parties, and the two [or more] locations are linked by a video and audio feed) or remote interpreting (RI; in which the equipment is similar to that of VCI, but all parties are in the same room, except the interpreter who is in another location). Despite the fact that new technologies have been in use for over 45 years, research on ethics in interpreting studies, and more particularly public service interpreting (PSI), has been carried out chiefly in relation to face-to-face interpreting. However, as discussed below, some of the findings (such as emotional attachment) raise questions about ethics in VCI and how they are investigated.

This chapter examines ethical conflicts as perceived by spoken-language court interpreters in England and Wales in VCI. In reporting on the perceptions of the three interpreters interviewed, it does not aim to generalise about the interpreters' experiences and instead it seeks to identify and theorise the range of ethical issues reported. To this end, the first section of the chapter briefly reviews the use of videoconference (VC) equipment in mono- and multilingual settings. The second section critically evaluates Camayd-Freixas' (2013) study, which constitutes the theoretical framework used to analyse the data that were gathered during three semi-structured interviews with qualified court interpreters in England and Wales in 2013. It is posited that the ethical issues that occur in VCI can be categorised in terms of deontology, consequentialism, moral sentiments and virtue ethics, some of which are similar to those encountered in face-to-face interpreting, whereas others arise as a result of the use of VC equipment. It is also posited that these issues are often mode based (i.e. VCI A or VCI B), and they can be partially explained by the absence of guiding principles in the National Register of Public Service Interpreters' (NRPSI) *Code of Professional Conduct*, and the interpreters' tendency to perceive and resolve ethical issues mainly through this code.

The Use of Videoconference Systems in Legal Settings

Videoconferencing technologies and their use are provided for in legal instruments at a European level (e.g. the Convention on Mutual Assistance in Criminal Matters between European Countries, 2000; Directive 2010/64/EU, 2010) and through policies in England and Wales (such as the Crime and Disorder Act, 1998; the Youth Justice and Criminal Evidence Act, 1999). Some studies have investigated the impact that such systems have on court proceedings. For instance, Plotnikoff and Woolfson (1999, 2000) conducted two pilot studies in courts in England in which they sought the opinions of various court stakeholders on the use of VC equipment. Although these studies focus on VC use in monolingual court settings, they also yield important insights for studies on multilingual settings. The sections that follow provide a brief overview of the research in mono- and multilingual legal settings.

VC research in a monolingual legal setting

At the beginning of the 1990s, studies by Raburn-Remfry (1994) and Thaxton (1993), for example, investigated the use of VC systems in monolingual settings, and the discussions focused on two main issues: court participants' perceptions of VC systems and their potential impact, and the type of equipment used and its technological shortcomings. The physical absence of the defendant, for instance, raised questions regarding fairness and the court participants' perceptions of the legal proceedings. When examining the literature on the use of VC systems in courts in the USA, Raburn-Remfry (1994: 836) argues that physical absence could lead to 'an emotional detachment by those sworn to uphold the rights of the accused', suggesting that legal practitioners may act differently when VC systems are used. In a similar vein, McKay (2015) examines the impact that the use of VC equipment has on the defendant, concluding that sensorial restrictions inherent in the use of VC systems lead the defendant to feeling more disengaged and isolated. Reporting on its increasing use within the European Union, Hodges (2008: para. 15) holds the view that 'there are questions about whether witnesses who provide evidence via [videoconference systems] treat the court process with the same gravitas as if they were in attendance'. Although the extent to which earlier research informed her study is unclear, she claims that VC equipment may impact on the kind of working relationship that is established between the solicitor/ barrister and the suspect/defendant.

Further to the question of perception of court participants, studies have also revealed technological shortcomings. Drawing on findings from a mixed methods study involving observations, interviews and questionnaires in Manchester Crown Court (United Kingdom), Plotnikoff and Woolfson (2000) highlight concerns about equipment performance and reliability, courtroom layout and confidentiality issues arising from client/lawyer consultations. Based on an experiment with 60 volunteers in a UK-based university, it also emerges from Fullwood et al.'s (2008) study that the use of screens and microphones renders it more difficult for parties involved to visualise non-verbal cues and body language. In order to minimise the effect of VC equipment and make it as much a 'true-to-life' experience as possible, the European Commission (2009) published some guidelines in the Guide on Videoconferencing in Cross-Border Proceedings. However, the extent to which these recommendations have been implemented in courts in England and Wales remains unclear. Finally, Licoppe et al. (2013) highlight the technical difficulties of adjusting the video frame when various participants speak at the same time.

Studies such as the above appear to suggest that the use of VC systems is flawed. However, Fullwood et al. (2008) argue that their findings are in line with other studies such as the one conducted by Joudo and Taylor (2005) in Australia using an experimental approach, in the sense that at macro-levels, there is no evidence to suggest that a hearing outcome differs whether the hearing is conducted in the physical presence of a witness/ defendant, or if he/she is at another location. Indeed, in their experiment, Fullwood et al. (2008) conclude that VC equipment did not impact on the participants' evaluation of the eyewitness testimony delivered by an actor. However, these studies, and others such as Licoppe (2014) and Rowden et al. (2013), indicate that the use of VC systems does impact on court proceedings at micro-levels (such as intimacy cues, managing turn-taking and technical shortcomings), as a result of which many scholars (such as Federman, 2006; Haas, 2006; Harvard Law School, 2009; Poulin, 2004) highlight the need for more empirical research. It is important to note that scholarly work in this field tends to be primarily anchored around literature reviews or experiment-based methodologies, suggesting the need for more empirical research based on real-life observations, as used in Plotnikoff and Woolfson's (2000) study.

VC research in a multilingual legal PSI setting

Research on VCI use in multilingual legal settings has been mainly carried out through the AVIDICUS projects that have been funded by the European Commission. Their aim is not limited to VCI, as they also explore RI. The studies carried out within the scope of Avidicus 1 (2008–2011) covered several research areas ranging from the legal frameworks underpinning the use of VC systems to training needs (Braun & Taylor, 2012a). Avidicus 2 (2011–2013) further developed the work undertaken during the project's first phase and offers some guidance as to when VCI is to be used. Based on a mixed methods approach (lab experiments, court observations and interviews), the projects have illuminated issues specific to VCI and RI, which range from the type and frequency of linguistic errors and interpreters' delivery (e.g. Braun & Taylor, 2012b; Miler-Cassino & Rybińska, 2012) to the impact that VC equipment has on spatial organisation, as discussed in the Avidicus 2 (2013) research report. Finally, Avidicus 3 (2013–2015) takes stock of pan-European solutions used in various legal institutions. Its aim is to assess their suitability when interpreters are part of VC court interactions, and to further develop training in this area.

Other studies have focused more specifically on VCI in court settings. For instance, using linguistic ethnography, Fowler's studies (2007, 2012, 2013) examine VCI in courts in England and Wales. She asserts that interpreters make their presence felt considerably more in VCI-mediated interaction than in face-to-face interpreting, based on the observation that interpreters sought more repetitions in VCI than during face-to-face hearings, and they interpreted consecutively in front of the court (instead of using whispered simultaneous interpreting performed at the back of the courtroom). Similarly, Licoppe and Verdier (2013) use video ethnography and conversation analysis to examine four VCI-mediated hearings. More specifically, they focus on the interactions involved when prosecution lawyers present their case during pretrial remand hearings. They conclude that the prosecution's discourse in court is more fragmented when the defendant is situated in a remote location. As a result, there are more opportunities for other participants to intervene, which leads to a greater need to manage turn-taking.

Using the sociological framework of Translation (Callon, 1986), and more specifically the concepts of problematisation, interessement and enrolment, Devaux (2016) investigates the effect of VC equipment on the court interpreters' perceptions of their role. This sociological framework makes it possible to consider VC equipment as a fully fledged actor in the interpreter-mediated court hearing, to the extent that it modifies the networks that court interpreters usually create in face-to-face court interactions. As a result, the interpreters' role perception is altered, depending on whether they are interpreting in VCI A or VCI B.

The findings of the literature on monolingual settings suggest that VC equipment can influence various aspects of a court hearing, whether it be emotional attachment, body language or gravitas. By contrast, the literature that addresses multilingual settings highlights specific issues in which the interpreter is the focal point. Although these studies do not specifically concentrate on ethics, their findings raise ethical questions as to the use of VC equipment. Indeed, the issue of emotional attachment or the different perceptions that arise in relation to the mode of VCI used raise specific questions as to the impact that VCI has on the interpreter's rationalisation of the ethical decision-making process.

Camayd-Freixas and Ethics in Interpreting Studies

Ethics have been studied in various PSI settings, such as in medical and legal settings (Baixauli-Olmos, 2013; Dysart-Gale, 2005; Laster & Taylor, 1994). Within these different settings, research is moving away from examining ethics solely through the lens of deontology towards other theoretical perspectives (e.g. Baker & Maier, 2011; Chesterman, 2001). Camayd-Freixas' (2013) study is an example of this shift in emphasis, as he explores an interpreter-mediated situation not only from the perspective of pre-existing rules (or deontology), but also from the perspective of consequentialism, moral sentiments and virtue ethics. His study draws on an interpreting assignment that took place in 2008 during an immigration raid in Postville, Iowa, USA, in which he acted as a court interpreter. During this assignment, Camayd-Freixas and 35 other court interpreters were called to interpret for several weeks between various legal bodies (prosecution, defence lawyers, etc.) and South American illegal immigrants who were working in a slaughterhouse. The immigration raid resulted in hundreds of arrests. Although such a situation may not be unusual, this American case was unique since the illegal immigrants were charged with 'the antiterrorism crime of "aggravated identity theft"' (Camayd-Freixas, 2013: 17), a more serious offence than that of working illegally, in order to force the illegal workers to plead guilty to a lesser charge.

Camayd-Freixas reflects on his personal experience in Postville as a case study which serves as a basis for recommended revisions to interpreter codes and the role that professional organisations play. He argues that ethics cannot be considered solely through the prism of deontology and that interpreters would benefit from the application of complementary theories of ethics to their practice, such as consequentialism, moral sentiments and virtue ethics. Although his study does not analyse ethical issues arising from one specific code of ethics (possibly since many codes include similar tenets such as confidentiality and impartiality), he draws on examples from a selection of court interpreters' codes of ethics issued by bodies such as the federal government or the National Association of Judiciary Interpreters and Translators.

When analysing the event retrospectively from a deontological perspective, Camayd-Freixas highlights various shortcomings arising from interpreters' codes of conduct, which can be explained by the fact that codes cannot pre-empt all potential ethical conflict. This observation concurs with work by other scholars on interpreters' codes of ethics and neutrality or impartiality (e.g. Inghilleri, 2012; Kaufert & Putsch, 1997; Rudvin, 2002, 2007).

Drawing on theories of consequentialism (e.g. Bentham, 1878), Camayd-Freixas reflects on his own experience and explores ways in which the shortcomings in the codes can be circumvented. In his study, consequentialism is described as follows: 'an act is moral only if its foreseeable consequence brings "the greatest happiness to the greatest number"' (Camayd-Freixas, 2013: 23). According to this definition, interpreters would be encouraged to rationalise ethical issues based on the consequences that an action or non-action on their part would have. Therefore, an action or non-action contrary to a particular tenet in a code of conduct may still be deemed ethical if done for the greater good. However, Camayd-Freixas (2013: 23) warns that 'consequences (...) are not always clear-cut or easy to foresee, let alone quantify'. The extent to which an individual's subjectivity plays a part could also be questioned. Indeed, interpreters may not reach the same conclusions. Camayd-Freixas therefore concludes that similar to deontology, consequentialism should not be the only type of ethical theory that informs interpreters' rationalisation processes.

Another ethical facet concerns moral sentiments. Grounded in the work of the philosopher Smith (1790), Camayd-Freixas (2013: 24) states that 'the moral sentiments of sympathy (empathy), compassion, and benevolence are primary to any rationalization of ethics', which 'require presence or affective immediacy'. For Camayd-Freixas (2013: 24), this means that interpreters must identify themselves 'morally and culturally' with each speaker in order to interpret not only the speaker's informational content, but also the manner in which it was delivered. However, in the context of VCI, the interpreter is not physically present with one of the parties, and the extent to which VCI equipment enables affective immediacy is open to question. Furthermore, Camayd-Freixas argues that as the court interpreter, he believed that he could not show any emotions. However, one could question the feasibility for interpreters of rationalising their decision process using moral sentiments, if they have to suppress such feelings. For Camayd-Freixas (2013: 25), it was more of an 'after-thought' rather than an *in-situ* rationalisation mechanism. Although showing emotions in courts seems to be unacceptable for interpreters, showing empathy may be beneficial, in therapeutic sessions for instance, even though it can be perceived by interpreters as conflicting with most codes of conduct's tenets of impartiality and neutrality (McDowell *et al.*, 2011; Splevins *et al.*, 2010).

Finally, Camayd-Freixas reflects on his experience through the paradigm of virtue ethics. Anchored more specifically within Confucian collectivism, Camayd-Freixas (2013: 26) defines virtue ethics as 'the enlightened pursuit of positive values' whereby the understanding of 'positive values' may differ from one interpreter to another. Therefore, to further define his approach, he asserts 'the values to be pursued in virtue ethics must not be individual values, but those sanctioned by a collective of body' (Camayd-Freixas, 2013: 27). However, the extent to which a collective body such as a professional organisation can suppress individual values could be called into question (Rudvin, 2007). As a means of mitigating the impact of individual values, Camayd-Freixas (2013: 27) argues that professional organisations need to define virtue ethics through guiding principles, as it is the case in the code of ethics for the Massachusetts Trial Courts. These guiding principles, for Camayd-Freixas, must precede any ethical tenets. By defining them first in a code of conduct, they will underpin the interpretation of all of the articles that follow. Although this approach may help the interpreter contextualise the tenets in his/her particular code, the extent to which the interpreter's subjectivity and prior cultural experience may affect his/her rationalisation process through virtue ethics remains unclear.

Camayd-Freixas, then, uses deontology, consequentialism, moral sentiments and virtue ethics to analyse the ethical issues that he encountered during the Postville immigration raid. In his reflection, he does not accord more importance to one ethical theory over another, but he sees them as complementary in rationalising the ethical decision-making process. However, he does not seem to differentiate overtly between morality and ethics, and the extent to which these theories are mutually compatible is unclear; as a result the extent and ways in which public service interpreters apply them when rationalising their own ethical decision-making warrant further investigation.

Data Analysis and Discussion

The following section discusses a selection of findings from the author's doctoral study. Specifically, the discussion focuses on semi-structured interviews that were conducted in 2013 with three public service interpreters in England and Wales, following ethical approval at the University of Salford. Although the study's primary focus was on the court interpreter's perception of their role in VCI, the interpreters reported spontaneously on ethical issues they encountered during VCI court assignments.

In terms of the participants' profiles, each interpreter had over 10 years of experience, and they were registered on the National Register of Public Service Interpreters. In order to preserve anonymity, the interpreters will be referred to as P1, P2 and P3. The participants had experience in both VCI A and VCI B, and P1, P2 and P3 interpreted through these modes on three, two and four occasions, respectively.

In terms of methodology, the data were collected in line with the Actor-Network Theory's tenets of agnosticism, symmetry and free association (Callon, 1986; Devaux, 2016). As argued by Devaux (2016), this approach enables the researcher to consider VC equipment as a potential non-human actor that may influence an interaction. The data were then analysed thematically, and each theme was categorised according to deontology, consequentialism, moral sentiments or virtue ethics, in keeping with Camayd-Freixas' study (2013).

Pre-existing rules and deontology

In Camayd-Freixas' study, deontological issues arose when he had to face a situation in which reality conflicted with codes of ethics. This section reports on instances in which ethical issues arose in court, which led to a divergence between the prescribed behaviour in the interpreter's code and the actions of the interpreter. During the interviews, four main deontological concerns were identified by the interpreters: providing summaries, shortfalls within their code of conduct, interactions with the defendant and impaired communication.

It is worth noting firstly that, according to P1, public service interpreters have 'masses of codes' of conduct when the various professional bodies and interpreting and translating agencies operating in England and Wales are taken into account. However, the three participants clearly referred to the NRPSI (2011)'s *Code of Professional Conduct* as their main code for court interpreting, which will therefore be the code used to examine pre-existing rules and deontology.

While interpreting during a court hearing, P1 said that she was once asked to provide a summary of the proceedings to the defendant. She refused to do so as she stated that she was present to interpret everything that was said. Indeed, in the *Code of Professional Conduct*, Clause 5.4 states that '[p]ractitioners shall interpret truly and faithfully what is uttered, without adding, omitting or changing anything'. However, this clause further states that 'in exceptional circumstances a summary may be given if requested'. It is worth noting that although the code allows for summaries, it fails to define how 'exceptional circumstances' should be interpreted. Moreover, as the interpreter perceived an ethical conflict not only between what the code states and the situation, but also ethical conflicts within the code (i.e. full rendition vs. summary), the interpreter decided that a full rendition was the only ethically acceptable means to proceed. This example illustrates that within a code of conduct, there are 'situations where different tenets conflict or lead to divergent conclusions' (Camayd-Freixas, 2013: 21). In this case, the divergence arises from the fact that there is no clear understanding of what constitutes 'exceptional situations', and whether VCI qualifies as an 'exceptional situation' or not.

Furthermore, P1 believed that there were some shortcomings in the NRPSI's code. She first mentioned that, in general, codes of ethics for interpreters and translators were not very lengthy. As a consequence, P1 felt that the codes were superficial, and they did not encompass the various situations in which interpreters are called to work. P1 further suggested that 'there are all sorts of things that need to be done to strengthen the codes and make them more thorough (...). There are still, kind of, grey areas'. To illustrate this particular point, she highlighted that the NRPSI's *Code of Professional Conduct* did not make any specific reference to VCI and telephone interpreting. However, she believed that most of the code's tenets still applied to VCI or telephone interpreting. She therefore suggested that guidelines could be developed and incorporated to make specific references to the use of VCI.

In order to shed light on the underlying reasons why codes cannot provide for all situations, Camayd-Freixas (2013) claims that:

> [S]ooner or later, experienced interpreters will confront the inherent limitations of such purportedly 'universal' codes. This is bound to happen whenever codified, pre-existing rules are tested against new social, political, and legal realities. (Camayd-Freixas, 2013: 21)

It can be argued that the NRPSI's *Code of Professional Conduct* falls within 'universal codes' since it is stated in its Preamble that the code is 'intended to regulate the professional conduct of members of the registrants on the National Register of Public Service Interpreters'. As such, the code's clauses do not differentiate between any settings (medical, legal or even business) or interpreting modes (such as liaison or whispered interpreting) that its members may encounter, which can leave them feeling unsettled, as discussed below.

With regard to interaction with the defendant, P2 reported on a case where she was called to interpret from the prison where the defendant was located, and had to wait for a VC link to be established. As there were technical issues, the hearing was delayed and the defendant started talking to her. She felt uncomfortable, since, had she not engaged with the defendant, she was conscious that she would have been perceived as being rude. However, the NRPSI's code expressively stipulates in Clause 5.9 that '[p]ractitioners (...) shall not enter into discussion, give advice or express opinions or reactions to any of the parties that exceed their duties as interpreters'. In this context, she perceived that VCI B put her in a situation that conflicted with the code, as she felt that she had to talk to the defendant. This contrasts to a different experience reported by P3 in which during a similar situation involving a VCI B set-up, the defendant was only brought in when the equipment was working, and therefore, the ethical issues expressed by P2 did not arise. No similar issues were reported by either interviewee in relation to VCI A. This suggests that a timely coordination and organisation between the parties could alleviate what P2 perceived as a conflicting ethical situation.

Lastly, all of the interpreters perceived that VC equipment impaired various aspects of communication. In terms of non-verbal communication, the interpreters reported that they encountered difficulties reading the participants' body language on the screen where VCI A was used. As P1 said, body language is of particular importance to interpreters as it is a means of verifying whether the participants understand what the interpreter is saying for instance. This concurs with Fullwood *et al.*'s (2008) study discussed previously, and regardless of the setting (mono- or multilingual), VC equipment hampers the ability to read body language.

In terms of verbal communication, the three interpreters also expressed some concerns. P2 compared the VC set-up to a tunnel or one-way communication channel in the sense that some parties would not participate in the interaction. To illustrate this point, the interpreters perceived that in VCI A, the defendants were 'like a statue'. Indeed, since the defendants were so distanced from the courtroom, P1, P2 and P3 felt that the defendants did not participate in their own hearing. In such instances, the interpreters found establishing communication with the defendant very difficult. In VCI B, however, the interpreters believed that it was very difficult if, in addition to interpreting, they wanted to communicate with the parties in the courtroom, especially when they were talking between themselves as they tended to forget that the interpreter and the defendant were on the other side of the screen. Consequently, such situations resulted in ethical issues, where interpreters were aware of the importance of communication, as it related to their code (Clause 4.1 for instance), but felt powerless to act in such circumstances.

Baker and Maier (2011: 3) argue that '[t]he disjuncture between [the] challenging reality and the traditional professional ethos of neutrality and non-engagement, as expressed in numerous codes of practice (...), can leave many practitioners with a sense of unease or disorientation'. The three interpreters in this study also reported a sense of unease when they worked in VCI. This could be due to the fact that, as discussed above, the NRPSI code can be classed as 'universal', and some tenets could be interpreted as conflicting. However, interpreters felt that the main ethical issues in VCI arose from their interaction with the defendant (in VCI B) and impaired communication. Although such issues could be encountered in a face-to-face situation, the interpreters felt that they are more dominant in VCI. This could be due to the fact that interpreters have developed coping mechanisms in face-to-face interpreting, which are in line with their deontology. For instance, P2 and P3 would pretend to be on the phone to avoid interacting with the defendant, or, when they needed to intervene, they would wave their hand to attract the attention of the judge or clerk, who would be sitting opposite the interpreter. However, it seems that they have not yet developed coping strategies in VCI and they tend to turn a blind eye to most deontological issues arising from the use of VCI.

Consequentialism

As defined by Camayd-Freixas, consequentialism is based on evaluating the ethical impact that an action or a non-action from the interpreter may have on a situation. When analysing the interpreters' interviews, it became apparent that they perceived that VCI greatly constrained the range of actions open to them, and that they lacked sufficiently broad ethical decision-making frameworks to account for this problem. To some extent, this impacted on the 'greater good' since it was perceived that due process in court, for instance, could be called into question. In this study, consequentialism was used to illuminate the ethical issues arising from introductions, positioning, intervention and technological difficulties and role boundaries, which are discussed in this section.

The interpreters unanimously agreed that it was of paramount importance for them to introduce themselves, or be introduced/ sworn in as the court interpreter. As P2 mentioned, the introduction allows her to say that 'I have a role here and I set out my stall, if you like'. This introductory process gives them the opportunity to remind all the parties of the interpreter's *Code of Professional Conduct* in terms of their role, confidentiality and impartiality. It also allows them to verify whether they can understand/be understood by the other participants. In other words, this formal introduction sets up certain expectations for all the other parties. The three participants agreed that to some extent, they could introduce themselves/be introduced to the other court actors that are physically present in the same room, but this was not the case with those on the other side of the screen. They also mentioned that in VCI A, the defendant did not always see the interpreter being sworn in, and in VCI B, it was not always possible to swear in the interpreter. This impacted on the interpreter's self-perception as an actor in the interaction. As P2 said, 'I could have been the court cleaner as far as anyone was concerned (...). The woman with the microphone'.

Furthermore, the use of VCI also restricts the interpreter in terms of her/his physical space and position in courts. P2 reported that due to the lack of space, she had to sit next to the prosecution barrister in VCI A. For her, this raised an ethical issue, as she perceived that by sitting next to him she was 'sending the wrong signal'. She believed that the defendant would not see her as a neutral actor in court. To remedy this situation, she decided to slightly turn her shoulder away from the barrister in an attempt to create a physical barrier between the two of them and, by so doing, she tried to restore a visual clue as to her neutrality in the proceedings.

The next theme that arose from the interviews was the interpreter's concern about how to intervene. When giving an account of an event in VCI B, P2 stated that 'if I intervene, I am breaking down the process of communication'. In line with the communication-related deontological issue discussed above, she was referring more specifically to the fact of trying to interact with the parties on the other side of the screen. However, P2 would not hesitate to intervene in a face-to-face interaction, which further suggests that VC equipment limits the interpreter's perceived range of actions. Furthermore, and echoing Hodges' study (2008) in a monolingual setting, VC equipment impacts on the other participants' actions in a multilingual context. P2 argued that interactions between the defendant and his solicitor team, for instance, were also affected, due to the perceived difficulty of intervening: '[personal interactions] are not happening anymore because what are you going to do? Are you going to talk to the screen? Are you going to take the microphone off the person?' The perceived impossibility of acting was particularly apparent in relation to VCI A. P2 stated that the process 'is inherently flawed because [the defendant] can ask me to explain if I have said [something] in a strange way, but they can't with a video-link because as soon as they say something, the whole courtroom hears them, and they are interfering with the court proceedings'.

Furthermore, technological issues were also encountered. As P2 said in VCI B, 'while I am in the courtroom, I have much more control over things so if the video-link is dodgy, how am I going to tell them in court?' Again, this was not only felt by the interpreters, but also by other parties. In VCI A, P1 explained that the screen froze when the defendant closed his eyes, and 'we thought he was asleep and if the client had been sitting next to us, we would have been able to elbow him in the stomach or had he not been closed to us, we could have given him a note to say wake up, you are in the middle of a hearing!' This seems to suggest that technological problems appear to further limit the interpreter's range of actions, regardless of the VCI A or VCI B mode. Finally, P1 mentioned that VCI can also force the interpreter to take actions that she considered undesirable and unethical. In VCI B, she said that:

Sometimes, I'm actually having to go in, go out of my role I feel as an interpreter and perform a different role by trying to alert the court that the client wants to say something (...). So I am having to take on an additional role here of being some kind of advocate if you like and in the general meaning of the word, by trying to convey to the court that the defendant is not happy or that he can't hear or he wants that repeated. (...) So I am having to take on extra roles that I don't really feel I should be taking on.

The ethical issue of taking on extra roles may be as a result of the 'tunnel communication' described by P2 earlier and the participants' inability to intervene. P1 felt in this case that her role usually aligned with the role prescribed in the *Code of Professional Conduct*; however, she felt that VCI B forced her to breach the code on occasions. This particular example demonstrates further how VC equipment can force interpreters to take certain actions, knowing that their consequences conflict from a deontological perspective.

To summarise, the interviews suggest that various consequentialist issues arise because the use of VC equipment seems to limit the interpreters' actions. Firstly, the interpreters felt that they could not introduce themselves or be introduced, and this impacted on the perception of themselves as court interpreters. In VCI A, they raised concerns that the defendant did not know who they were for instance, or that they could not verify whether the interpreter and the defendant could understand each other. In VCI B, they were not always sworn in, which raised questions regarding how other court participants would perceive them. The fact that interpreters have limited physical space in VCI also impacts on the perception of impartiality, especially from the viewpoint of the defendant when the interpreter is positioned next to the prosecution in VCI A. However, from the perspective of the parties in court, such an issue was not mentioned by the interpreters in VCI B. This could be due to the fact that interpreters usually sit next to defendants in courts, and VCI B mirrors their close proximity. Technological faults also meant that the interpreter was unable to communicate with the other parties, which could lead to deontological conflicts, especially in VCI B if the defendant and the interpreter are together, as discussed above. However, VC equipment could also force the interpreter to take action (especially in VCI B), which could lead to other consequentialist conflicts, as was the case with P1. Interestingly, the participants seemed aware of the consequences and ethical issues that arise from the use of VC equipment. However, unlike in Camayd-Freixas' study, it seems that the participants felt that they could not act upon them. Therefore, they could not resolve ethical problems through consequentialism alone.

Moral sentiments

When analysing the interpreters' interviews through the lens of moral sentiments, two themes arose: the perceived conflict between the

Code of Professional Conduct and moral sentiments, and the absence of affective immediacy in VCI. P3, for example, recalled an assignment in which she was asked to comfort a distressed defendant and reported to the court staff: 'I am not allowed by my code of ethics to take part in anything like this, as I would no longer be unbiased'. P2 shared a similar experience. During a case where two court interpreters where needed, she recalled that the other interpreter was commissioned by the defence to interpret during private conferences with the legal team. This interpreter started building a certain rapport with the defence team and, on being acquitted, the defendant hugged the interpreter. P2 pointed out that 'that's why you need to keep your distance; otherwise you can't be professional if you start being emotionally involved'. Finally, some defendants and witnesses can also be 'hostile' to the interpreter, as P3 added. In this case, it may be more difficult for the interpreter to feel any empathy towards the defendant/witness. Although these assignments were conducted in the face-to-face mode, the interpreters stated that such situations could occur in VCI. It is interesting to note that the participants in this study perceived that any sentiments such as empathy and compassion were in total contradiction to the NRPSI's *Code of Professional Conduct*.

Furthermore, the fact that participants may not be able to show any compassion or empathy in VCI could be exacerbated by the perceived absence of participants' physical presence and/or affective immediacy. Indeed, VCI intrinsically implies the physical absence of at least one of the participants and affective immediacy could be impacted. P1 stated that when interpreting in VCI A, 'I feel like there is a barrier between myself and [the defendant]. (...) It is a bit clinical because you are so divorced from the other person's presence'. In such circumstances, parties may feel an 'emotional detachment' due to the use of VC equipment (Raburn-Remfry, 1994: 832). The participants also seem to suggest that by affecting physical presence and affective immediacy VCI could prevent rapport-building. When comparing it to a face-to-face situation, P1 said that:

> You can see fear, you can see alarm, you can see distress. And when you put a video screen quite a distance up on the wall, unless they are actually crying or you can hear in their voice that they are very sad or whatever, you just can't tell.

As a potential remedy, interpreters were asked whether VCI B would be a more suitable alternative, as they would be next to the defendant. However, they disagreed on such an option, as they claimed that the deontological (e.g. communicating with the court) and consequentialist (e.g. role boundaries) issues discussed in the previous sections of this chapter could arise. Finally, when discussing VCI with other colleagues, P1 observed that it was a common perception among interpreters that establishing a working relationship with other participants was difficult. P2 also asserted that 'even well-versed, outspoken business people tend to be very quiet at the end of the video-link if they are not present in the meeting room'. These suggest that VCI may not only impact on affective immediacy in a court setting, but other interpreting fields (such as business interpreting) as well.

Overall, the data suggest that the three interpreters in this study do not tend to rationalise ethical issues through moral sentiments as this ethical paradigm could conflict with their code of ethics, to which they would default. The data also suggest that potentially hostile defendants could hinder such a rationalisation process. Finally, the absence of physical presence and affective immediacy could also serve as a barrier, especially in VCI A. However, rationalising through moral sentiments is further impeded by the extent to which this ethical paradigm is taught as part of court interpreters' preparatory courses, if at all, or whether this would be deemed an acceptable ethical rationalisation process in court. To some extent, this explains why the three interpreters in this study appear ill-equipped to rationalise through moral sentiments.

Virtue ethics

Anchored within Confucian collectivism, Camayd-Freixas (2013: 27) argues that 'the values to be pursued in virtue ethics must not be individual values, but those sanctioned by a collective body'. When examining the values which the British legal system espouses through the Ministry of Justice website, fairness and due legal process are promoted as being of the utmost importance as indicated in the objectives and content of the first statement in the Criminal Procedure Rules (Ministry for Justice, 2005). However, the achievement of fairness and due process in VCI is less clear. Indeed, P2 said that '[the defendants] tend to be like static because they are not involved. Probably half of them are not even listening. Because they are just so removed. And I think it's a human rights' issue' (sic). This suggests that VC equipment impacts on the extent to which a defendant experiences due process and is involved in his/her own hearing, and on the interpreters' perceptions of virtue ethics.

Furthermore, Camayd-Freixas argues that the values to pursue in virtue ethics should be laid down in the interpreter's code of ethics. They are to be framed as representing those of society and those of the interpreter's profession, and they form part of a set of 'guiding values' (Camayd-Freixas, 2013: 27). Such guiding values could enable the interpreter to resolve some of the deontological and consequentialist conflicts that were discussed earlier. To illustrate this point, Camayd-Freixas refers to the Massachusetts' *Code of Professional Conduct for Court Interpreters of the Trial Court* (2009). Unlike other codes, this one first and foremost establishes 'guiding principles' to frame the way in which the tenets of the code are to be interpreted (Camayd-Freixas, 2013: 27). Indeed, Article 1.01.1 states that the code 'seeks to accomplish the following: assure meaningful access to court proceedings (...), protect the constitutional rights (...) [by providing] the assistance of a court interpreter during court proceedings, ensure due process in all phases of litigations (...), ensure equal protection of the law (...)'. Camayd-Freixas argues that the code's tenets that follow these guiding principles are very similar to other codes of ethics. Indeed, they deal with recurring themes that can be found in many codes, such as impartiality, confidentiality and the interpreter's demeanour. However, in the Massachusetts' code, impartiality and confidentiality, for instance, are to be interpreted according to its guiding principles, which are designed to preserve 'meaningful access to court proceedings'. This may permit a certain degree of fluidity in interpretation and action that may not be possible through a strict interpretation of the code's tenets alone.

Similarly, the NRPSI's *Code of Professional Conduct* also offers a general framework and overarching principles in Clauses 2 and 3. However, the code differs from the Massachusetts' code in terms of the informational content, as these two clauses do not establish guiding principles according to which the deontological tenets that follow are to be interpreted. Instead, it prescriptively establishes what is expected from an NRPSI interpreter, which could lead to the deontological, consequentialist and moral sentiments issues discussed above.

To conclude this section, the literature review in the first section highlighted that VC equipment affected court hearings in relation to various micro-level aspects, but it had no impact at macro-levels. However, from the interpreters' viewpoint, it was argued that VC equipment *could* impact at the macro-level since due process could be called into question. Furthermore, based on Camayd-Freixas' (2013) study, it could be suggested that as the *Code of Professional Conduct* does not include guiding principles, it would be difficult for the interpreter to rationalise ethical issues on the basis of virtue ethics (such as the use of VC equipment being unconducive to due judicial process, as discussed above). This is based on the hypothesis that guiding principles are beneficial to the rationalisation process but there is a lack of empirical research on how guiding principles improve the interpreters' perception of 'positive values' in virtue ethics. In order to validate Camayd-Freixas' claims about the benefits of virtue ethics, more empirical studies assessing the merits of guiding principles in the Massachusetts' code and interpreters' ability to interpret and implement them are needed.

Conclusion

This study examined court interpreters' perceptions of ethics in VCI and the extent to which the interpreters interviewed encountered similar or different ethical conflicts in relation to VCI A and VCI B. To achieve this, four paradigms of ethics theory were drawn on: deontology, consequentialism, moral sentiments and virtue ethics. This study demonstrates that some of the ethical issues found to occur in monolingual settings are encountered when interpreters are present (e.g. technical issues). Furthermore, based on the sociological concept of Translation, VC systems were considered to be fully fledged actors that interacted with the interpreters' rationalisation processes, and specific ethical shortcomings and conflicts, arising from the use of VC equipment, were identified in VCI A and/or VCI B. The three participants seemed to privilege a deontological approach when they rationalised ethical issues in face-to-face interactions, although they did not manage to resolve some deontological issues arising from the use of VCI. Therefore, further empirical studies on how well-equipped interpreters are to rationalise decision-making through consequentialism, moral sentiments and virtue ethics, and the role of education, qualifications, social and cultural understanding of the interpreter's role are needed.

Finally, despite certain limitations (only three participants were used who presented similar profiles in terms of qualifications, years of experience and the number of VCI assignments), this study paves the way for further research in which a larger sample of interpreters with different qualifications, years of experience and a wider range of VCI assignments would permit a more comprehensive picture to emerge.

References

Avidicus 2 (2013) Assessment of Video-Mediated Interpreting in the Criminal Justice System – Research Report. See http://wp.videoconference-interpreting.net/wp-content/uploads/2014/01/AVIDICUS2-Research-report.pdf (accessed 14 September 2015).

Baixauli-Olmos, L. (2013) A description of interpreting in prisons – Mapping the setting through an ethical lens. In C. Schäffner, K. Kredens and Y. Fowler (eds) *Interpreting in a Changing Landscape. Selected Papers from Critical Link 6* (pp. 45–60). Amsterdam: John Benjamins.

Baker, M. and Maier, C. (2011) Ethics in interpreter and translator training. *The Interpreter and Translator Trainer* 5 (1), 1–14.

Bentham, J. (1878) *An Introduction to the Principles or Morals and Legislation* [1823]. Oxford: Claredon.

Braun, S. and Taylor, J.L. (eds) (2012a) *Videoconference and Remote Interpreting in Criminal Proceedings*. Guilford: University of Surrey.

Braun, S. and Taylor, J. (2012b) AVIDICUS comparative studies – Part I: Traditional interpreting and remote interpreting in police interviews. In S. Braun and J. Taylor (eds) *Videoconference and Remote Interpreting in Criminal Proceedings* (pp. 99–118). Guildford: University of Surrey.

Callon, M. (1986) Some Eelements of a Sociology of Translation: Domestication of the Scallops and the Fishermen of St Brieuc Bay. See http://www.vub.ac.be/SOCO/tesa/RENCOM/Callon%20%281986%29%20Some%20elements%20of%20a%20sociology%20of%20translation.pdf (accessed 28 September 2015).

Camayd-Freixas, E. (2013) Court interpreter ethics and the role of professional organizations. In C. Schäffner, K. Kredens and Y. Fowler (eds) *Interpreting in a Changing Landscape* (pp. 15–30). Amsterdam/Philadelphia, PA: John Benjamins.

Chesterman, A. (2001) Proposal for a Hieronomyc oath. *The Translator* 7 (2), 139–154.

Devaux, J. (2016) When the role of the court interpreter intersects and interacts with new technologies. In P. Henry-Tierney and D. Karunanayake (eds) *Intersect, Innovate, Interact*. CTIS Occasional Papers. Manchester: Centre for Translation and Intercultural Studies, University of Manchester.

Dysart-Gale, D. (2005) Communication models, professionalization, and the work of medical interpreters. *Health Communication* 17 (1), 91–103.

European Commission (2009) *Guide on Videoconferencing in Cross-Border Proceedings*. See http://bookshop.europa.eu/en/guide-on-videoconferencing-in-cross-border-proceedings-pbQC3012963/ (accessed 20 June 2015).

Federman, M. (2006) On the media effects of immigration and refugee board hearings via videoconference. *Journal of Refugee Studies* 19 (4), 433–452.

Fowler, A.Y. (2007) Interpreting into the ether: Interpreting for prison/court video link hearings. Proceedings of the Critical Link 5 Conference, Sydney, 11-15/04/2007. See http://www.criticallink.org/files/CL5Fowler.pdf (accessed 15 April 2015).

Fowler, A.Y. (2012) Non-English-Speaking Defendants in the Magistrates Court: A Comparative Study of Face-To-Face and Prison Video Link Interpreter-Mediated Hearings in England. PhD thesis, Aston University. See http://eprints.aston.ac.uk/19442/1/Studentthesis-2013.pdf (accessed 20 January 2015).

Fowler, A.Y. (2013) Business as usual? Prison video link in the multilingual courtroom. In C. Schäffner, K. Kredens and Y. Fowler (eds) *Interpreting in a Changing Landscape. Selected Papers from Critical Link 6* (pp. 226–248). Amsterdam: John Benjamins.

Fullwood, C., Judd, A.M. and Finn, M. (2008) The effect of initial meeting context and video-mediation on jury perceptions of an eyewitness. *Internet Journal of Criminology*. See http://www.internetjournalofcriminology.com/Fullwood,%20Judd%20&%20Finn%20-%20Video%20Mediation.pdf (accessed 1 August 2012).

Haas, A. (2006) Videoconferencing in immigration proceedings. *Pierce Law Review* 5 (1), 59–90.

Harvard Law School (2009) Access to courts and videoconferencing in immigration court proceedings. *Harvard Law Review* 122 (1151), 1181–1193.

Hodges, L. (2008) Towards a European e-Justice Strategy – A Review of the Communication from the Commission in May 2008. See http://www.ecba.org/cms/index.php?Itemid=71&id=201&option=com_content&task=view (accessed 1 August 2013).

Inghilleri, M. (2012) *Interpreting Justice – Ethics, Politics, and Language*. New York: Routledge.

Joudo, J. and Taylor, N. (2005) The impact of pre-recorded video and closed circuit television testimony by adult sexual assault complainants on jury decision-making: An experimental study. *Research and Public Series Australian Institute of Criminology*. See http://aic.gov.au/documents/5/3/4/%7B53472FA7-7F7B-48E8-B0E6-32D816852F89%7DRPP68.pdf (accessed 15 August 2014).

Kaufert, J.M. and Putsch, R.W. (1997) Communication through interpreters in healthcare: Ethical dilemmas arising from differences in class, culture, and power. *The Journal of Clinical Ethics* 8 (1), 71–87.

Kelly, N. (2008) *Telephone Interpreting – A Comprehensive Guide to the Profession*. Victoria (BC): Trafford Publishing.

Laster, K. and Taylor, V.L. (1994) *Interpreters and the Legal System*. Annandale, VA: The Federation Press.

Licoppe, C. (2014) Two modes of referring to the case file in the courtroom: The use of indirect reported text and text-as-addressed speech in case summaries. *Language and Communication* 36, 83–96.

Licoppe, C. and Verdier, M. (2013) Interpreting, video communication and the sequential reshaping of institutional talk in the bilingual and distributed courtroom. *The International Journal of Speech, Language and the Law* 20 (2), 247–275.

Licoppe, C., Verdier, M. and Dumoulin, L. (2013) Courtroom interaction as a multimedia event: The work of producing relevant videoconference frames in French pre-trial hearings. *The Electronic Journal of Communication* 23 (1–2). See http://www.cios.org/EJCPUBLIC/023/1/023125.HTML (accessed 28 July 2016).

Massachusetts' Code of Professional Conduct for Court Interpreters of the Trial Court (2009). See https://ia802501.us.archive.org/35/items/professionalcond00mass/professionalcond00mass.pdf (accessed 12 May 2015).

McDowell, L., DeAnne, K. and Dawson Estrada, R. (2011) The work of language interpretation in health care: Complex, challenging, exhausting, and often invisible. *Journal of Transcultural Nursing* 22 (2), 137–147.

McKay, C. (2015) Video links from prison: Court 'appearance' within carceral space. *Law, Culture and the Humanities* 1–21.

Miler-Cassino, J. and Rybińska, Z. (2012) AVIDICUS comparative studies – Part III: Traditional interpreting and videoconference interpreting in prosecution interviews. In S. Braun and J.L. Taylor (eds) *Videoconference and Remote Interpreting in Criminal Proceedings* (pp. 117–136). Guildford: University of Surrey.

Ministry of Justice (2005) The objectives and content of the first Criminal Procedure Rules. See http://www.justice.gov.uk/courts/procedure-rules/criminal/notes (accessed 10 June 2015).

National Register of Public Service Interpreters (2011) *Code of Professional Conduct*. See https://www.scribd.com/document/81992567/Code-of-Conduct-07 (accessed 20 November 2014).

Plotnikoff, J. and Woolfson, R. (1999) Preliminary Hearings: Video Links Evaluation of Pilot Projects – Final Report. See http://lexiconlimited.co.uk/wp-content/uploads/2013/01/Videolink-magistrates.pdf (accessed 15 August 2014).

Plotnikoff, J. and Woolfson, R. (2000) Evaluation of Video Link Pilot Project at Manchester Crown Court – Final Report. See http://lexiconlimited.co.uk/wp-content/uploads/2013/01/Videolink-Crown.pdf (accessed 15 August 2014).

Poulin, A.B. (2004) Criminal justice and videoconferencing technology: The remote defendant. *Tulane Law Review* 78 (1089), 1089–1167.

Raburn-Remfry, P. (1994) Due process concerns in video production of defendants. *Stetson Law Review* 23, 805–838. See http://www.stetson.edu/law/lawreview/media/due-process-concerns-in-video-production-of-defendants.pdf (accessed 12 June 2015).

Rowden, E., Wallace, A., Tait, D., Hanson, M. and Jones, D. (2013) Gateways to Justice: Design and Operational Guidelines for Remote Participation in Court Proceedings. University of Western Sydney: Sydney. See http://researchdirect.westernsydney.edu.au/islandora/object/uws%3A15505/datastream/PDF/view (accessed 28 July 2016).

Rudvin, M. (2002) How neutral is 'neutral'? Issues in interaction and participation in community interpreting. In G. Garzone, M. Viezzi and P. Mead (eds) *Perspectives on Interpreting* (pp. 217–223). Bologna: CLUEB.

Rudvin, M. (2007) Professionalism and ethics in community interpreting. The impact of individualist versus collective group identity. *Interpreting* 9 (1), 47–69.

Smith, A. (1790) *The Theory of Moral Sentiments* [1759] (6th edn). London: A. Millar.

Splevins, K.A., Cohen, K., Joseph, S., Murray, C. and Bowley, J. (2010) Vicarious posttraumatic growth among interpreters. *Qualitative Health Research* 20 (12), 1705–1716.

Thaxton, R. (1993) Injustice telecast: The illegal use of closed-circuit television arraignments and bail bond hearings in federal court. *Iowa Law Review* 79, 175–202.

Statutes

Crime and Disorder Act, 1998.

Directive 2010/64/EU on the right to interpretation and translation in criminal proceedings in Europe by the European Parliament and the Council, 2010.

European Convention on Mutual Assistance in Criminal Matters between European Countries, 2000.

Youth Justice and Criminal Evidence Act, 1999.

8 Participants' and Interpreters' Perception of the Interpreter's Role in Interpreter-mediated Investigative Interviews of Minors: Belgium and Italy as a Case

Heidi Salaets and Katalin Balogh

Introduction: The Co-Minor-IN/QUEST Project: Its Scope and Background

As the project name (Cooperation in Interpreter-Mediated Questioning of Minors) indicates, the research topic in question concerns investigative interviews with minors, i.e. children under the age of 18. For the purpose of this chapter, however, the term 'children' will also be used, because it is less closely connected to the idea of a particular legal majority age (in comparison to the word 'minors'). The term 'children' also appears in Directive 2012/29/EU (establishing minimum standards on the rights, support and protection of victims of crime), the UN Convention on the Rights of the Child (UNCRC) and the Guidelines of the Committee of Ministers of the Council of Europe on child-friendly justice: they commonly define children as people under the age of 18. The same age limit serves as a reference for the CO-Minor-IN/QUEST study, although we are well aware of the fact that the range in age between 0 and 18 is relatively large in terms of definition. We are also aware that the chronological and mental age of an interviewee do not necessarily correspond, and that several other factors can also influence child development and the communication process: advanced or reduced mental capacities, behavioural problems, disabilities and all kinds of diseases.

The CO-Minor-IN/QUEST project (JUST/2011/JPEN/AG/2961) focuses on pretrial interviews with children in the context of criminal cases. The pretrial phase is an essential part of criminal procedure: any type of inaccuracy that occurs during this stage of the investigation inevitably has an impact on the rest of the procedure and on any future trial phase. The very first interview by the police provides the most valuable opportunity to collect evidence. It must be noted that the actual number of interview instances involving children are limited as much as possible. Therefore, interviews (especially those with child victims and witnesses) are also often recorded for future use in court: if necessary, these recordings can then be used as official evidence so that the child will no longer have to appear in person in the courtroom. This factor also adds to the key role played by pretrial child interviews.

Our study of the interview setting has revealed that in addition to age (children under the age of 18 are generally considered to be in need of extra protection) two factors affect the vulnerability of child interviewees: the child's procedural status (either as a victim, witness or suspect) and the child's language, i.e. whether it differs from the language of procedure.

Regarding the procedural status of child interviewees, the research team broadened its scope and, in addition to victims (i.e. the only category of interviewees mentioned in the 2012/29/EU Directive), also included child witnesses and suspects. It is true that the procedural status of an interviewee inevitably has an impact on the way the questioning is conducted, but the main point of similarity shared by all three types of interviewee (victims, witnesses and suspects) is their vulnerability. The scope to safeguard children is also clearly expressed in the new Directive 2016/800/EU of the European Parliament and of the Council of 11 May 2016 on procedural safeguards for children who are suspects or accused persons in criminal proceedings.[1] Moreover, the procedural status of an interviewee may not always be that clear from the start or might even change during the course of the interview (e.g. a child suspect who himself/herself turns out to be a victim of neglect), as the new directive states.[2] Thirdly, an interviewee's native language can be regarded as another vulnerability factor: if the child's first language differs from the language of procedure, he/she will also need extra assistance (i.e. linguistic support – interpretation and/or translation) to participate fully in the interview process.

The right to interpretation and translation is explicitly enshrined in European law, including Directive 2010/64/EU on the right to interpretation and translation in criminal proceedings and the above-mentioned Directive 2012/29/EU. Moreover, another important legal source is the UNCRC, which explicitly mentions the right to free assistance by an interpreter, yet only for child offenders (cf. art. 40[2] VI). Closely related key requirements included in the UNCRC are the right of every child to express their views freely and their right to be heard (cf. art.

12), in addition to the priority principle of the best interest of the child (art. 3). We can conclude that a child-sensitive approach is indispensable for any of these interviews, precisely because of the inherent vulnerability of young interviewees.

To implement this child-friendly interview approach and to ensure that each child's needs are met, close cooperation between all professionals involved in the interview process is needed. For that reason, promoting knowledge exchange between all professional groups concerned is the most important aim of this research, which brings together specialists from a number of different areas of work (interpreters, police officers, lawyers, judges, psychologists, psychiatrists, behavioural scientists, child support workers [CSW], etc.), the purpose being the sharing of expertise. This idea of knowledge exchange is also in line with article 25 of Directive 2012/29/EU, which states that practitioners working with children in legal contexts should be properly informed and trained.

Through international collaboration between several member states of the European Union (Belgium, France, Hungary, Italy, the Netherlands and UK), researchers and experts from all of the aforementioned disciplines were not only able to share their knowledge and thus improve interpreter-mediated child interview practices, but also to express their specific opinions, doubts and needs in a questionnaire. For more detailed information on the partners, content, questionnaire and results of the project, we refer the reader to the project website at https://www.arts. kuleuven.be/english/rg_interpreting_studies/research-projects/co_minor_ in_quest and the publication that is mentioned in the references (Balogh & Salaets, 2015): https://www.arts.kuleuven.be/tolkwetenschap/projecten/ co_minor_in_quest/children-and-justice

Background and Literature: A Summary

As mentioned earlier, this chapter focuses on the role of the interpreter as viewed by the interpreters themselves and by the other professionals in an ImQM (Interpreter Mediated Questioning of Minors). The Co-Minor-IN/QUEST questionnaire concerns the role of the interpreter and other issues such as briefing and debriefing, seating arrangements, particular challenges related to highly specific ImQM settings and needs identified by the respondents. For a comprehensive analysis of the questionnaire and findings, we refer readers to the relevant chapter in the aforementioned volume that was published at the end of the project (Salaets & Balogh, 2015a: 175–227) and to the contribution by Amato and Mack (2015: 247–280) on briefing, debriefing and support. In this chapter, particular attention will be paid to the role of the interpreter, because it is a much discussed and often polemic topic both in basic and applied interpreting research. Moreover, the role of the interpreter is one of the key issues in the gradual professionalisation of community interpreting, which also includes legal interpreting, for the precise reason that 'the type of intra-social interpreting with the strongest historical roots is interpreting in courts of law' (Pöchhacker, 2004: 29). We have to keep in mind that this professionalisation process is very different from professionalisation in conference interpreting (Baigorri, 2014), as Pöchhacker illustrates with this striking metaphor:

> Compared to the 'wave' of professionalization that swept conference interpreting to thigh international prestige after the 1950s, the professionalization of interpreting in community-based settings appears more like a pattern of ripples. (Pöchhacker, 2004: 29)

This situation is the result of some very specific features, which are typical of community interpreting work, as Hertog (2010) clearly describes:

> In other words, it is not the modes or strategies that set the community interpreter apart from the conference interpreter but it is the institutional settings – usually sensitive, delicate and private, sometimes downright painful or antagonistic – and the working arrangements: the interpreting is bi-directional between the service provider and the client; moreover the proxemics, the participant parties, the level of formality and range of registers are completely different; and it is as yet on the whole a solitary profession with a very different social aura, professionalization and remuneration. (Hertog, 2010: 49)

In early research, the interpreter's role was understood as entailing much more than translating alone: in his/her work, he/she serves as 'a guide, adviser, trader, messenger, spy or negotiator' (Pöchhacker, 2004: 28). It is known to the research community that this 'role' – also redefined as 'positioning' (Mason, 2009) because of its continuously changing nature during the interpreted interaction – has changed several times over the last 50 years. Firstly, there was a radical change from the multifunctional model or even 'helper model' (in the case of sign language interpreters see Cokely, 2005; Wilcox & Shaffer, 2005) to the 'machine/conduit/ invisible interpreter' model. The lack of correspondence between the 'invisible' model and the realities of the workplace led to alternative conceptualisations of the interpreter as a 'communication facilitator' and active participant (Roy, 2000; Wadensjö, 1998) in the interaction or 'triad', followed by a bilingual–bicultural model (Kent, 2009) and the very recent 3D model of the interpreter's role-space (Llewellyn-Jones & Lee, 2014).[3]

Yet, in many training programmes and codes of conduct the strongly normative expectation of the interpreter's neutrality largely still appears to prevail or as Hertog (2010: 51) observes: 'in many training programmes and professional codes the equilibrium between prescriptive rules and real-life practice is still shaky'. Consequently, interpreters not only continue to struggle with their role(s) and responsibilities (see Valero-Garcés & Martin, 2008), but also 'direct users' of interpreters either do not really know what to expect from an interpreter or have unrealistic expectations. It is also the case that research rarely sheds light on the expectations and experiences of direct users or clients and their dealings with an interpreter. In our case, the direct users would have been the minors themselves whom, for obvious reasons, we could not interview.

If we look specifically at police interpreting, a considerable amount of research has emerged, although it is characterised by a limited body of data-driven empirical research. The reasons behind this lack of fieldwork are clear: the intrinsically delicate and private, often traumatising or confidential character (in the case of investigation) of these interviews seldom allow researchers to be present or to use recorded materials for research purposes, let alone when a minor is present. Exceptions include, for example, Berk-Seligson (2009) and Nakane (2014), but also Russel (2002) who uses tape-recorded data from Police and Customs interviews within the UK legal system and discusses the interpreted interview as a linguistic event, before examining some of the effects which the presence and participation of the interpreter has/may have upon the turn-taking system. Berk-Seligson (2009) draws on an earlier work (Berk-Seligson, 1990) and shifts from the bilingual (Spanish–English) US courtrooms to bilingual police interrogations, which is explained as follows:

> The role of interpreters in legal settings has become relatively formalized for proceedings that take place at the tail end of the judicial process, that is, in speech events that are bound to the courtroom. At the front end of judicial process, however, were the crime scene and police station hold centre stage, no such guarantee exists for the person in need of interpreting services. (Berk-Seligson, 2009: 15)

In Nakane (2014), a discourse pragmatic approach is applied to three interviews with Japanese nationals in 1992 and one in 2002, which shows how difficult authentic material is to obtain, despite guarantees of confidentiality and anonymisation. Other approaches are experimental; for example, Böser (2013) who investigates the impact of interpreting within the discursive frame of the free recall element in forensic interview formats, or concern training of the users of interpreters, e.g. more specifically the necessity of teamwork between the interpreter and the police officer (Perez & Wilson, 2007). Other more psychology-oriented police studies put forward a simplistic view of the role of police interpreters as a passive word-for-word translating device. This explains in part their continuing resistance of the use of interpreters (Shepherd, 2007).

Finally, our review of the literature shows emphasis on the strict protocols used by police officers when interviewing child victims and witnesses, for example the PEACE method of investigative interviewing[4]; or the widely studied National Institute of Child Health and Human Development (NICHD) Protocol developed by Lamb *et al.* (2008) which 'has been designed to "dovetail" into existing interviewing procedures developed in many countries and legal jurisdictions, and has informed the development of similar methods' (La Rooy *et al.*, 2015: 125). Examples of such methods include good practice memoranda by Davies and Westcott (1999) or the 2011 *Achieving Best Evidence in Criminal Proceedings*. As far as we know, only Nilsen (2013) has studied – again on an experimental basis – interpreter-mediated encounters with minors, in order to identify from what age children are able to communicate efficiently through an interpreter and how they perceive/understand the nature of the interpreter's specific task during the encounter. A similar experiment but one that focused on the preferred mode of interpreting (simultaneous in the booth or simultaneous whispering) has been carried out by Solem (2015). Yet, there are no empirical results available on interpreter-mediated interviews with police officers, which can be very intimidating and even traumatising.

It is clear that the role of the interpreter in police interviews is still subject to debate despite the research that has been conducted. As stated before, the role of the interpreter in authentic police interviews with minors has never been studied before. This is why the Co-Minor questionnaire was designed to be a first modest step to map gaps, challenges and needs, not only through the voice of the interpreters themselves but also through the eyes of the other interpreter users, i.e. the service providers involved in the interpreter-mediated child interviewing. We will come back to the weaknesses and drawbacks of this methodology later.

Since we deal with a specific North–South focus in this chapter (Belgium and Italy), theorisations of the interpreter's role are even more complex and require terminological differences to be addressed, as well as the various concepts and tasks described by this terminology. For instance, a question arises as to the so-called *mediatore linguistico* in Italy and what it is that they do. In Italian, many different terms are used to (try to) capture the actual tasks of these 'mediators': *mediatore linguistico-culturale, mediatore interculturale, mediatore linguistico e interculturale*. Apparently, they all refer to a task that is no longer exclusively linguistic (interpreting) but also (inter) cultural. The most complex and confusing job title we found is probably *interprete e traduttore mediatore linguistico culturale e interculturale,*[5] which broadly translates as 'linguistic, cultural and intercultural interpreter, translator and mediator' all brought together in one person.

The figure of the linguistic or/and cultural mediator has its roots in a long, embedded history during which Italy changed from being an emigrant country to an immigrant country (Bettin & Cela, 2014). Italy experienced mass migration from the 19th century on – mainly from the period of the *Risorgimento* (Italian Unification) in 1861 – with a decline during and immediately after the First World War:

> The combined effect of two world conflicts, the Great Depression in-between, and the simultaneous launch of restrictive immigration policies by the US government, which introduced literacy tests and immigration quotas from Southern Europe, caused a sharp drop in European emigration. (Bettin & Cela, 2014: 40)

Although there was a 'revival' in emigration after the Second World War, destinations had changed in the meantime from the Americas and Australia to Northern Europe and regions within Italy itself (from the South to the North). It was only in the 1970s that Italy started to receive immigrants. Since 2000, massive flows of immigrants have continued to arrive mostly in Lampedusa, which is considered as the border of Europe by many African refugees.

According to Amato and Garwood (2011), Italy was confronted at the turn of the century with an increasing migration flow that was not anticipated by the authorities because 'no immigration policy had been planned'. According to the same authors, this situation also had an impact on 'mediators':

> While most countries have developed accredited, certified interpreting services to facilitate communication between migrant populations and public service providers, in Italy service providers turned to the associations created to assist the migrant populations. Rather than just interpreting, the people sent by the associations also wished to act on the migrants' behalf as cultural mediators. (Amato & Garwood, 2011)

This also explains to a great extent the initial role of these cultural mediators when they were sent out by civil society organisations, mostly as volunteers:

> The people these organizations sent to assist the public service providers were not trained interpreters, but members or friends of the associations (often fellow migrants) who did not just interpret for the

newly-arrived migrants, but also pursued the goals of these voluntary organizations by supporting the migrants, advising them and helping them to claim their rights, basing their role on empathy and advocacy. (Amato & Garwood, 2011)

The aim of these mediators was mostly to help their fellow migrants, sometimes because of a natural inclination to help others but also because of empathy: the mediators often had gone through the same experiences of hardship and difficulties in the integration process (Rudvin & Tomassini, 2008: 252). The following extract perfectly illustrates the difficulty that a country like Italy has in defining the role of the mediator/interpreter:

> Paradoxically, then, the global political positioning on migrants, culture, cultural differences and the need to mediate in order to achieve integration – which in our view is very positive – has, as mentioned, led to a rather stressful role confusion regarding cultural and professional aspects of interpreting and mediating. Indeed, it is precisely in countries like Italy and Spain that a vigorous debate is emerging about the figure of mediator vs. interpreter and the conduit vs. communicator. (Rudvin & Tomassini, 2008: 249)

In relation to LIT (Legal Interpreting and Translation), the situation in Italy is even more complex and there is a complete lack of institutionalisation. The term 'legal interpreter' as such does not even exist in Italy. Instead, the more general term of *linguistic expert* is employed, which is further subdivided into *ausiliario* ('assistant' of the judicial police), *consulente tecnico d'ufficio* (appointed by and acting as technical expert for the prosecutor) and *perito* (appointed by and working for the judge in court) and finally freelance interpreters (ImPLI report, 67–68, 91–95). The former three categories (that fall under the term *linguistic expert*) are selected by public competition and cover 11 languages; for the latter, there is no specific training, recruitment or quality requirements. However, there are sporadic (nationally recognised) training classes, e.g. organised by Annalisa Sandrelli in Rome (UNINT) and Mette Rudvin in Bologna (University of Bologna). There is no national register of sworn interpreters and translators, and remuneration is extremely low (a gross hourly rate of €14.68 for the first hour, and €8.15 for the hours that follow). This explains why there appears such a low level of interest in professionalisation on the part of freelance interpreters, not to mention limited willingness to participate in a specialised training programme on interpreting for minors.

If we then look at Belgian history and narrow it down to its relationship with Italy and migration – which is of particular interest here – it is well known that the migration along the South–North axis has played an important role: many Italian immigrants came to Belgium to work in the mining industry after the Second World War and especially from the Golden sixties to the mid-seventies:

> The economic boom and the consequent labour shortages in the early 1960s led some countries to open their labour markets to foreign workers (the so-called 'guest workers') through programmes of active recruitment. France, Germany, United Kingdom, Switzerland, Belgium and the Netherlands all recruited workers from Southern European countries (Italy, Spain, Portugal, Greece, Turkey, Yugoslavia) and North Africa (Morocco, Tunisia, Algeria). The main direction of the flows, within Europe, became therefore the South-North axis. (Bettin & Cela, 2014: 40)

Historiography does not seem to pay particular attention to how the integration of these migrants was accomplished. This lack of interest was further compounded by the simple fact that most of the immigrants had the intention of returning to their home country after a certain time and they were even actively encouraged to do so after the oil crisis and global recession of 1973 (Bettin & Cela, 2014: 40). In Belgium, professionalisation of the public service interpreting (PSI) sector is a very recent phenomenon (from the late 1990s and the year 2000), but in this country the different roles are more clearly defined than in Italy. There is an explicit distinction between the tasks and skills of intercultural mediators and 'social interpreters' (the Dutch term for public service interpreters). The former have a fixed set of tasks (Verrept, 2008) comparable to those of the *mediatore linguistico-culturale*, which also includes interpreting (which remains problematic because they are not specifically trained to do so, in contrast to their other tasks). The latter, on the other hand, have had to comply with an officially standardised set of competencies since 2008 (SERV, *Sociaal-Economische Raad van Vlaanderen* or Social and Economic Council of Flanders) if they want to become a PSI interpreter. Moreover, chapter VII of the Decree of the Flemish Community of 30 April 2009 on Flemish integration policy is entirely dedicated to 'social interpreters and translators' (equivalent to Public Service Interpreting and Translation [PSIT] interpreters) and their support organisations.

When we examined the job description of the PSI interpreter in Belgium, we discovered that legal interpreting is not part of it. Contrary to other parts of the world – such as the UK and Australia for example – PSIT and LIT are separated. To be clear, the separation of PSI and LIT is meant as a mere observation, not as a quality judgment for one of these countries. For the latter, in Belgium some courses (three or five days on legal matters) are organised by the Belgian Chamber of Translators and Interpreters

(CBTI/BKVT). There is also a more extensive course of 150 hours, which is (unfortunately) the only one in Flanders. This course is organised by KU Leuven, Antwerp campus and contains the following modules: Law, Legal Dutch and Legal Terminology, Legal Translation, Legal Interpreting, Police Questioning. It is preceded by admission tests and concluded with final exams (written exams for law, terminology and translation and a role-play exam for legal interpreting). However, there is still no uniform national or legal basis for becoming a sworn interpreter – only in the judicial district of Antwerp, is the KU Leuven (formerly Lessius) LIT certificate an 'official' requirement if one wishes to be included in the local register. There are as yet no national quality standards, quality control mechanisms or national register (ImPLI report, 59–60, 73–77). On 19 December 2014, the *Belgian Official Gazette* (*Belgisch Staatsblad/Moniteur belge*) published the Law of 10-4-2014 on 'The establishment of a National Register for legal experts and the establishment of a National Register for sworn translators, interpreters and translators/interpreters' that will enter into force in December 2016. In the meantime, many amendments are being proposed by several expert groups.

Methodology

For a detailed report on the methodology used in the study, we refer readers to the aforementioned chapter on the survey results (Salaets & Balogh, 2015a: 176–183) where the survey design, distribution, respondents and the mixed methods (quantitative and qualitative) used for data processing (Hale & Napier, 2013: 12 & 51–81) are described in detail. Here, we limit ourselves to a summary of the most important key methodological features.

The questionnaire was distributed using the snowballing and networking method initially only in the six Member States in the project consortium (Belgium, France, Hungary, Italy, the Netherlands and the United Kingdom) and was sent more specifically to professionals and professional organisations of the five categories we wanted to elicit views from about ImQM encounters: interpreters, justice and policing professionals, psychologists, CSW and other professional groups (e.g. paediatricians). The introductory part of the questionnaire consisted of a participant information section (language of the questionnaire, country, area of work) with a separate questionnaire for signed language and spoken language interpreters, followed by questions on job title, training, personal experience and frequency of working with children, as well as questions about the age of the children and the type of cases involved.

The survey questions in the middle section were ranked in chronological order (before, during and after the encounter) and asked about briefing (*before*), the role of the interpreter and seating arrangements (*during*) and debriefing (*after*). Before answering the final set of questions, respondents were asked to list any problems or needs they had encountered in an ImQM. Finally, all respondents were asked for additional demographic information, such as gender, age and highest level of qualification, and possible membership of professional organisations and their strongest language or mother tongue and the language combinations they work in (for the interpreters). This final part was not compulsory, but respondents were encouraged to complete it so that the researchers could more easily contextualise their responses. All the information gathered was treated anonymously.

Six hundred and ten forms were completed, but not all professions were equally represented in the different countries. In France, the largest professional group consisted of interpreters, CSW in Italy and justice and policing professionals in Belgium. This is also the reason why we wanted to examine the answers of these categories of respondents in detail. The large number of responses from justice and policing representatives in Belgium can probably be explained by the fact that one of the experts in the project is a Belgian youth lawyer and also by the close contacts with the Behavioural Science Department of the Federal Police via Hans De Wiest, who sent the questionnaire to all his Dutch- and French-speaking colleagues. When we looked at the responses from all participants, we noted that justice and policing professionals and interpreters were equally represented (35% and 37%, respectively). Sixteen and thirty-nine interpreters in Belgium and Italy, respectively, completed the questionnaire: this relatively low response rate could be explained by the lack of a national register for sworn interpreters or a national educational programme for court interpreters in both countries, as was explained above. Even if basic skills are to be covered in training, it is unreasonable to expect there to be specialised training for legal interpreters on how to work with minors. When we look at the overall experience of all respondents in working with minors, the picture is reassuring: 56% of the respondents have 10 years or more of experience and another 21% have between 4 and 9 years of experience. Seventy percent of the respondents have had more than 5 professional encounters with minors in the last 3 years, and 39% of them even had more than 40 recent professional encounters.

The choice of questionnaire method has clear limits, including the way questions are formulated and structured. Other limitations include the lack of access to the respondents' thought processes when he/she is answering the questions (how does he/she understand the question, which concrete case does he/she have in mind) and the context in which he/she is answering the questionnaire (in a quiet moment, quickly without time to think about the answer etc.). These are some of the reasons that needed to be taken into account when seeking justification for (sometimes) divergent answers. It is clear that further, in-depth research is needed for which a number of recommendations are made in the conclusion.

In this chapter, we will only discuss the question: 'In your view, what is the interpreter's function when working with minors?' Ten statements had to be evaluated on a Likert scale (I completely disagree – I rather disagree – I neither agree nor disagree – I rather agree – I completely agree), which were merged into three categories for analytical purposes: disagree – neither agree nor disagree – agree. We will discuss the following seven statements in our analysis.

(1) The interpreter supports the minor (through his/her interpretation and initiative).
(2) The interpreter supports the interviewer's purposes (through his/her interpretation and initiative).
(5) The interpreter takes the initiative to explain sociocultural differences.
(6) The interpreter takes the initiative to explain technical terminology.
(7) The interpreter takes the initiative to adjust the language to the level of the minor.
(8) The interpreter takes the initiative to put the minor at ease.
(9) The interpreter takes the initiative to keep the communication flowing.

These statements were the result of preparatory work, namely a literature review, but also discussions and debates during a workshop with all professionals involved in the ImQM (Interpreter Mediated Questioning of Minors). They were drafted in English by the consortium partners (of which the Scottish members checked the wording for clarity). Subsequently, the whole questionnaire was translated into Dutch, French, Hungarian and Italian by the consortium partners, all professional translators.

For reasons of space, we mainly discuss the data from a quantitative point of view: the results of the quantitative analysis will be presented by means of cross tables. Some of the key ideas repeatedly mentioned in the narratives (qualitative part) will be used in the discussion section to illustrate (confirm or deny) the quantitative findings, which will allow us to put these into perspective. Moreover, these narratives are the only resource used to collect information on the specific needs of the different professional groups (there were no closed questions regarding existing needs) and for that reason, they will be briefly mentioned in the discussion as well. We are aware of the fact that the qualitative discussion is rather arbitrary, but reasons of space force us to limit this part to an illustrative one. The data are too extensive to be discussed as a whole.

The aim of this chapter is to compare the results of our study of the North–South axis, taking into account the aforementioned history of emigration and immigration, the complex terminology and conceptualisation of legal interpreting *stricto sensu* and PSI interpreting as a whole. The results of the North–South analysis can be summarised as follows: most respondents disagree with statements 1 and 2 above, thereby confirming the generally accepted idea of an interpreter's impartiality; but interestingly, the same respondents are much more divided on statements 5–9. At this point, we explicitly want to stress the wording of the statements: the interpreter *takes the initiative to* (explain sociocultural differences and technical terminology; adjust the language to the level of the child; put the minor at ease; keep communication flowing). Some of the answers therefore seem to threaten the so-called impartiality of the interpreter, or at least illustrate the confusion that still exists about the role of the interpreter both among the service providers and the interpreters themselves.

For a more detailed discussion of the findings, we refer to the aforementioned contribution by Salaets and Balogh (2015a) in the final publication of the Co-Minor-IN/QUEST *Children and Justice: Overcoming Language Barriers. Cooperation in Interpreter-mediated Questioning of Minors.* In the next section, we will only compare the findings of the North–South axis (Belgium and Italy) and more specifically the responses of the interpreters, legal and child support professionals to the statements on the function of the interpreter.

The Role of the Interpreter in ImQM in Belgium and Italy: A Quantitative Analysis

In the section that follows, we provide an overview of how interpreters perceive themselves in an ImQM and of how legal practitioners and CSW perceive them. What tasks and responsibilities do they assign to the legal interpreters? What are the interpreter's role boundaries (if any) and what requirements do interpreters need to satisfy?

Here, we will only present the Belgian and Italian results, and more specifically the answers provided by the Belgian ($n=16$) and Italian ($n=41$) legal interpreters (in total $n=57$), legal professionals ($n=86$ in Belgium and $n=45$ in Italy) and Italian CSW (in total $n=121$). In the present analysis, we limit ourselves to the answers of the Italian CSW, because only one Belgian child support worker completed the questionnaire. His/her answers are therefore not representative. However, as we will see later, Italian CSW play a very important role during interviews with minors. Their presence influences the way in which legal interpreters and legal professionals work.

As mentioned earlier, not all legal interpreters are officially certified or trained in either of the two countries. Furthermore, neither Belgium nor

Italy has a national register for legal interpreters. But we do know whether the respondents of our questionnaire had training in legal matters and/ or interpreting techniques. In Belgium, only 2 of the 16 legal interpreters (12.5%) did not take part in training for legal interpreters.[6] In Italy, the response rate was the following: only 2 of the 41 interpreters (4%) had not participated in any training for legal interpreters. Of course, we cannot make further judgments on the kind, length or content of the concept 'training for legal interpreters' in Italy since we do not know what kind of training is meant by the respondents. It seems rather contradictory that in Italy where there is (at least, as far as reported in the ImPLI report) no systematic training, most respondents claim to have had training. Nevertheless, 'training' can represent all kinds of education programmes: a one-day workshop, a two-day course or a fully fledged course on legal interpreting which is uncommon in Italy, as we stated before. Although we specifically inserted a box to answer the open question: 'Please indicate what kind of training', few respondents did.

From the answers to the introductory set of questions, it becomes clear however that the majority of the respondents in the interpreting group have extensive experience in working with minors. Twenty-two percent of the interpreters have more than 4 years of experience in encounters with minors and 50% of the interpreters have even more than 10 years of experience in working with minors.

On the other hand, we can assume that most of the legal professionals did take part in regular training, since they can only start to work in the profession (i.e. as a police officer, judge, youth lawyer, etc.) if they have the necessary qualifications – this is in contrast to the interpreting profession, where one can start to work without any qualification at all. The legal professionals in this sample showed that they had considerable experience in ImQM encounters (63% in Belgium and 46% in Italy). The results of our questionnaire show whether they received any specific education or training on working with minors. Seventy-five of the 86 Belgian legal professionals (87%) received special training in questioning minors. The Italian response rate was the following: 100 of the 121 legal professionals (82%) received special training and only 21 did not (18%).

To allow for a clear and valid comparison with the respondents in the interpreting category (who almost all had experience with ImQM), we decided to only select the answers of the legal professionals who also had experience with ImQM. The answers of the other professionals (legal actors and CSW) without ImQM experience were thus excluded from the data sample used in this chapter. As a result, we analysed the answers given by the Italian and Belgian legal interpreters, and compared these to the expectations of the Italian and Belgian legal professionals and more specifically also to those of the Italian CSW, both with ImQM experience.

Statements 1 and 2

Most interpreters did not agree with the first statement and also clearly disagreed with the second statement. The overall majority of the interpreters think that supporting the interviewer during an ImQM is not part of an interpreter's task (Figure 8.1).

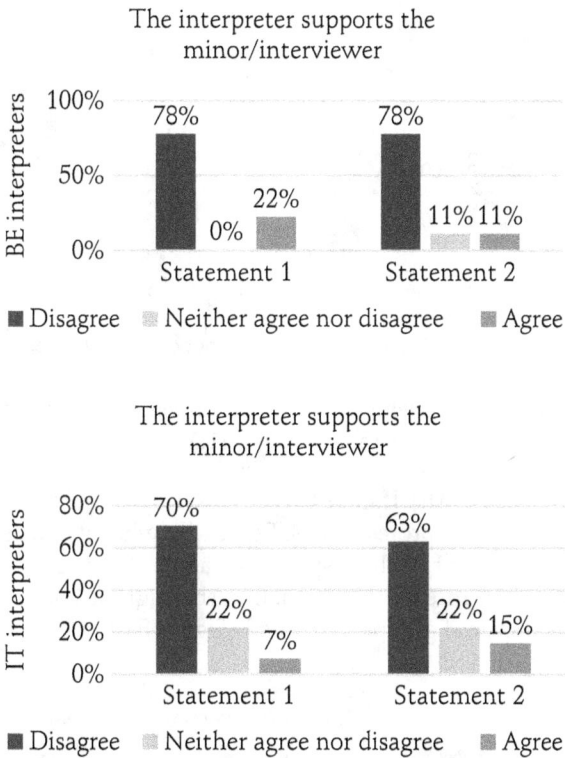

Figure 8.1 Chart 1: Statements 1 and 2 interpreters (BE). Chart 2: Statements 1 and 2 interpreters (IT)

When we examined the answers of the Belgian and Italian legal professionals (Charts 3 and 4), we observed the same tendency. It is particularly interesting to note that the answer of the Italian legal professionals to statement 1 is very straightforward: they all disagree (Figure 8.2).

The interpreter supports the
minor/interviewer

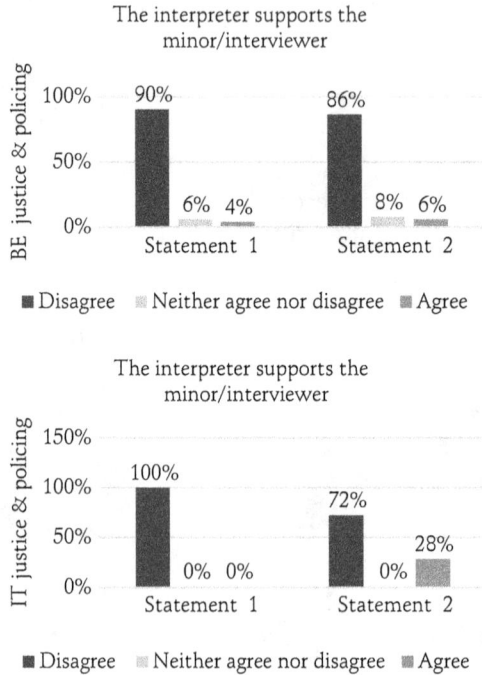

Figure 8.2 Chart 3: Statements 1 and 2 justice/police respondents (BE). Chart 4: Statements 1 and 2 justice/police respondents (IT)

The responses of the Italian CSW (Chart 5) are nevertheless different from those of the legal professionals. Especially when it comes to the second statement, almost half of the respondents agree that the interpreter should rather support the interviewer, which is the highest confirmation rate of the three professional groups examined (Figure 8.3).

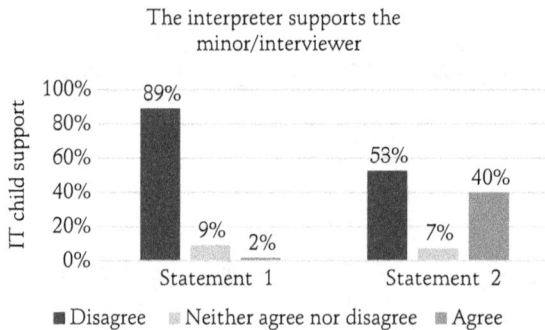

Figure 8.3 Chart 5: Statements 1 and 2 CSW (IT)

Statements 5 and 6

The respondents' opinions show a clear difference of perspective in relation to the Belgian and the Italian legal interpreters for both statements (Charts 6 and 7). The Belgian interpreters seem to adopt a neutral position towards the interpreter, taking the initiative to explain social-cultural differences or technical terminology with some unsure about which position to take, while almost all of their Italian colleagues think that a legal interpreter should explain sociocultural differences and technical terminology (Figure 8.4).

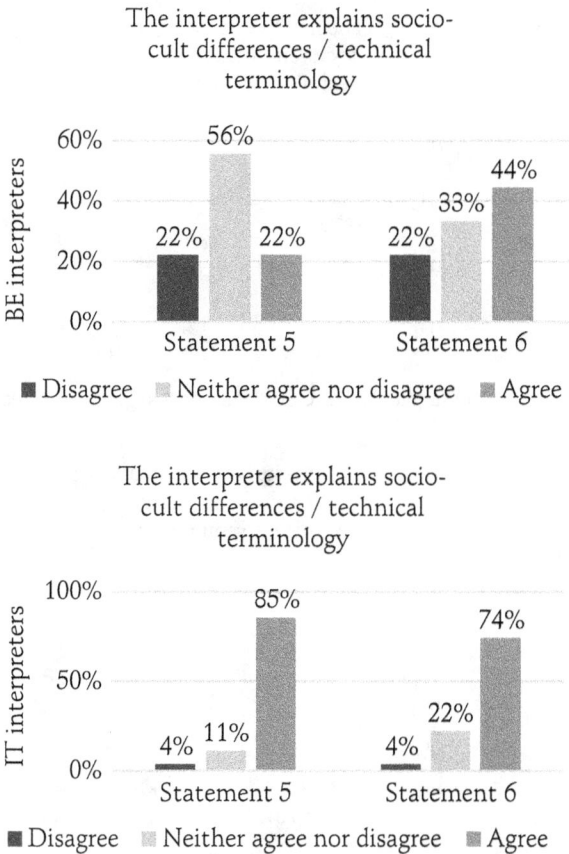

The interpreter explains socio-cult differences / technical terminology

The interpreter explains socio-cult differences / technical terminology

Figure 8.4 Chart 6: Statements 5 and 6 interpreters (BE). Chart 7: Statements 5 and 6 interpreters (IT)

When analysing the responses of the legal professionals (Charts 8 and 9), we observed that the expectations of the Italian legal professionals exactly mirror those of the Italian legal interpreters. They all agree almost unanimously on whether the interpreter should explain sociocultural differences and technical terminology. On the contrary, the expectations of the Belgian legal professionals do not match the 'undecided' attitude of the Belgian interpreters, which can be explained by the way in which legal professionals define the interpreter's role boundaries as limited and not too intrusive as we can see in the overall results. Literal interpreting (seen as 'translating and nothing else') is appreciated by not less than 69% of the respondents (Balogh & Salaets, 2015a: 193) (Figure 8.5).

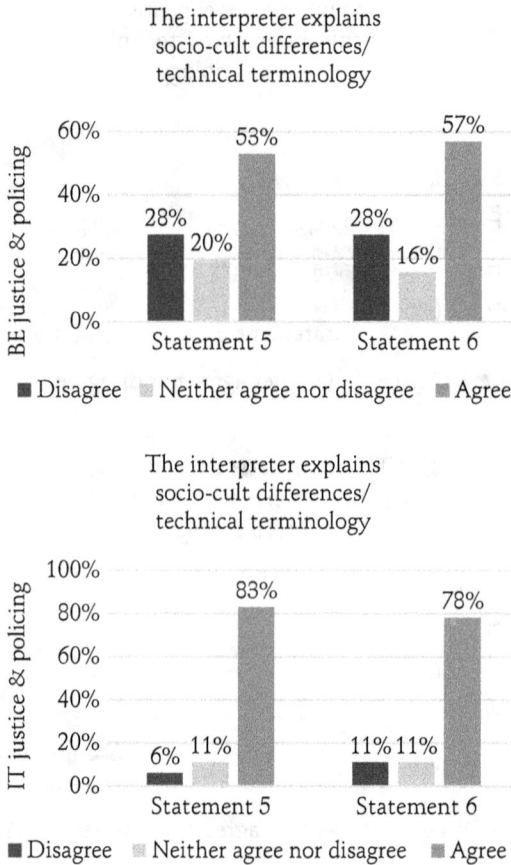

Figure 8.5 Chart 8: Statements 5 and 6 justice/police respondents (BE). Chart 9: Statements 5 and 6 justice/police respondents (IT)

It is clear that the responses across all the Italian professional groups show a similar approach: furthermore, the CSW seem to put a lot of additional weight on the shoulders of the interpreters (Figure 8.6).

The interpreter explains socio-cult differences/technical terminology

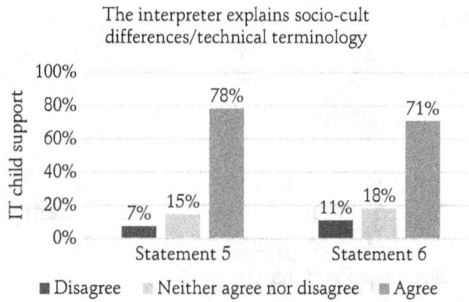

Figure 8.6 Chart 10: Statements 5 and 6 CSW (IT)

Statement 7, 8 and 9

Here, we can see a clear discrepancy between the attitude of the Belgian and the Italian legal interpreters. If we look at the results one by one, we can observe the following differences: for the Belgian interpreters, the initiatives listed (e.g. adjust language, put minor at ease, keep communication flowing) are not considered part of the interpreter's responsibility. By contrast, not a single Italian interpreter considers them beyond his/her remit (Figure 8.7).

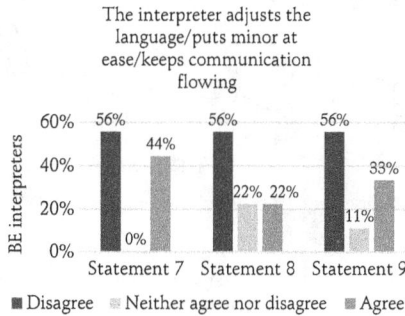

The interpreter adjusts the language/puts minor at ease/keeps communication flowing

The interpreter adjusts the language/puts minor at ease/keeps communication flowing

Figure 8.7 Chart 11: Statements 7, 8 and 9 interpreters (BE). Chart 12: Statements 7, 8 and 9 interpreters (IT)

The analysis of the answers given by the Belgian and Italian respondents from the justice and police services to the same three statements (7, 8 and 9) show us the following (Charts 13 and 14): the responses of the Belgian legal professionals do not mirror the attitude of the Belgian interpreters and only the responses of Belgian legal professionals to statement 9 (keep communication flowing) correspond more or less to the Belgian interpreters' responses. Interestingly, the level of agreement on this last statement among the legal actors (12%) is much lower compared to that of the interpreters (33 %). On analysing the Italian responses to these statements, we could conclude that the views of the Italian legal professionals mirror those of the legal interpreters in the sense that they are convinced that it is the interpreter's responsibility to take certain initiatives. The crucial question – and one that we cannot answer with pure quantitative data – concerns the extent to which they are aware of the impact such initiatives can have on the interview (Figure 8.8).

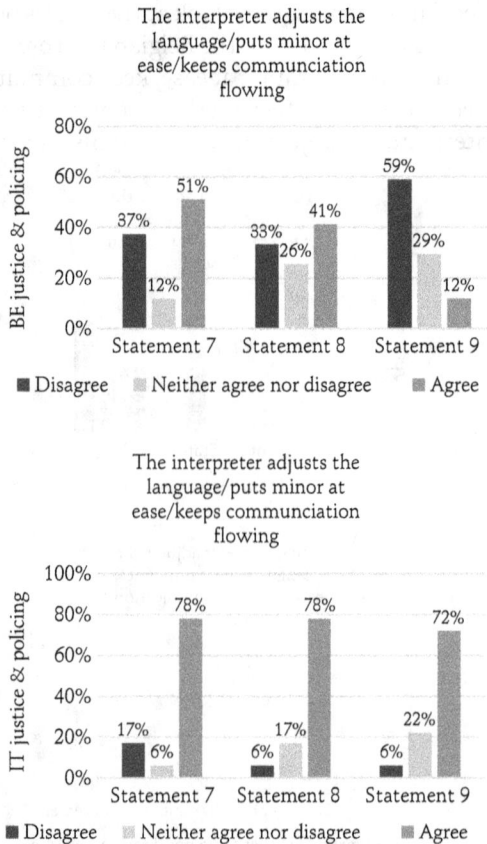

Figure 8.8 Chart 13: Statements 7, 8 and 9 justice /police respondents (BE). Chart 14: Statements 7, 8 and 9 justice/police respondents (IT)

The responses of the Italian CSW confirm our earlier observation about role boundaries and expectations for legal interpreters during an ImQM, as expressed by the Italian legal interpreters themselves and the Italian legal professionals. Not only do the responses of the CSW mirror the opinion of the interpreters and legal professionals, but the distribution of their answers is also relatively similar, meaning that they also transfer a lot of responsibility to the interpreter (Figure 8.9).

The interpreter adjusts the language/puts minor at ease/keeps communication flowing

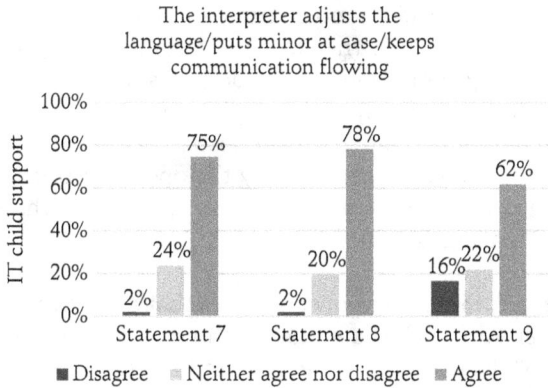

Figure 8.9 Chart 15: Statements 7, 8 and 9 CSW (IT)

Discussion

The answers to the statements discussed above show a diverse and sometimes even inconsistent picture. On the one hand, the results of the Belgian participants are divergent: the answers of the various professional groups reveal different tendencies. This creates the impression that each professional works individually and not as a member of a team. When we return to the introductory question about training, we can observe that the majority of the legal interpreters and the legal professionals did participate in professional training but when respondents indicated that they had 'received training', the researchers did not receive (or rarely received) additional information about the exact content or degree of specialisation of these training sessions (although information was requested). Nobody explicitly mentioned training with other professionals (e.g. training of interpreters with legal actors/police officers or training of CSW with interpreters). This probably explains one aspect of the divergent answers. Another aspect to take into account concerns the limitations of questionnaires, which we highlighted in the Methodology section. There are other possible drawbacks: in analysing a questionnaire you cannot exclude the fact that people give 'socially' acceptable answers or answer in relation to the way they think they act(ed) or will act, but not the way they actually did. Moreover, the concept of 'minor' itself is very broad and ranges from zero to 18-years-old, which can lead to different interpretations, e.g. some respondents mostly work with young children, others mostly work with teenagers. We are aware of the kind of limitations a questionnaire entails and explain it as follows:

> Extensive explanations cannot be added to the survey, because it would make the reading more tiring and increase the risk that people quit. Questions should, therefore, be formulated in a short, clear and structured way, which we tried to do (the survey was also piloted) but the individual personality of the respondents and the way in which they are going to interpret a particular question can never be evaluated. This limitation is somehow balanced by the open questions, the possibility of adding comments or selecting (and specifying) the option 'other'. (Balogh & Salaets, 2015a: 224)

As was expected, most of the uncertainties that arose concerned the role of the interpreter. Although the literature shows that since Wadensjö (1998), the concept of the completely 'neutral' and invisible subtitling interpreter does not exist, some users of interpreting services still seem to expect this. Others do the opposite and confer too much responsibility on the interpreter. An example of the former is that according to some users, an interpreter should 'translate literally'; an example of the latter is that the interpreter is supposed to explain difficult terminology. This shows how, despite research and training (see the first section), professional groups are seldom made aware of how to work together as a team. In spite of the fact that interdisciplinarity is recommended and increasingly applied in research, it still isn't the case in the workplace. Professional training is often offered to one group of professionals (the interpreter OR the legal actor OR the psychologist OR the child support worker). When these professionals have to work together (like for instance in the ImQM), they don't know anything about the professional way of working of their peers.

This problem is sometimes reflected in the narratives. For instance, one Belgian respondent from the justice and police group seems to impose his way of working and his idea of what interpreting should be on the interpreter, without prior consultation. A Belgian interpreter describes from his point of view the gap between theory (deontological code) and practice (daily life).

> An interpreter is there to enable communication between the interviewer and the minor. He can give me some explanations on socio-cultural aspects in the context of the investigation but NOT during the interview, he can do that before. The interpreter must translate literally

what I say and what the minor says without interpretations, etc. The interviewer should build rapport with the minor, not the interpreter. (Legal Actor, B)

Regarding the initiative to explain socio-cultural differences: even though this is not allowed, in practice it is sometimes different. Without further explanation, communication is simply impossible! If the interviewer does not have a clue about what to expect from a child from another culture or how to talk to a child from another culture, a conversation would not be possible without any explanation! (Interpreter, B)

These answers also show that briefing and joint consultation before the actual interview starts are very useful and helpful when it comes to discussing common goals, methods and strategies that are designed to cope with issues related to the language level of the child, rapport building, cultural differences or difficult terminology. When we consider the legal actor's comments above, we can conclude that it is still necessary to explain to those using interpreter services that a 'literal' ('word-for-word') translation does not exist, whereas a 'faithful' translation – meaning 'true to the original, not necessarily with the same exact (amount of) words' – remains feasible.

When we compare these observations to the Italian responses, a different line of thinking emerges across all three professional groups. The legal professionals and CSW have the same expectations about what an interpreter should (not) do and the interpreters seem to try to meet these requirements. Within the interview team, all members seem to share the same views about the role of the interpreter and, consequently, seek to cooperate more closely. This cooperation results in a conceptualisation of the role of the interpreter as an active participant (Wadensjö, 1998). But in some cases, the interpreter risks having too much responsibility, including taking on roles that are not related to the profession, such as a mediator, 'colleague' of or 'assistant' to the interviewer. Thus, role boundaries are particularly fuzzy: it is no longer entirely clear who takes the lead during an ImQM encounter and this entails a potentially problematic shift. If the interpreter is defined as an active third participant in the triad, this doesn't mean that he/she can take over the lead. We believe that this can be linked to the previous explanation (see the first section) regarding the difference in historical development in Italy and resulting views on what an interpreter/intercultural mediator should (not) do. It is also a rather 'risky' view regarding the competencies required of the interpreter, which automatically raises the question: are interpreters trained to adapt the language to the level of the child? Are they capable of explaining technical terminology from different professional fields: justice, pedagogy or developmental psychology, just to name a few? Explaining terminology is of course not the same as knowing or finding the corresponding technical terms in the target language. Are interpreters as well trained as CSW in putting minors at ease and detecting their doubts, anxieties and traumas? And what about identifying specific problems in highly vulnerable children with physical or mental impairment(s) or behavioural disorders?

These questions suggest the importance of setting clear parameters when considering possible initiatives to be taken by the interpreter/mediator, as this Italian legal actor explains:

> I completely agree with initiatives taken by the mediator, on the condition that all the interlocutors are made aware of it, so that this does not result in a private conversation between the interpreter and the minor. Usually, all professionals want the minor to feel at ease during the interview.

Again, it is important to note that in the Italian context both terms – mediator and interpreter – are used as if they were synonyms, which means that there is no strict separation of roles and no awareness of what these different roles entail.

Conclusion

Drawing on the Co-Minor-IN/QUEST survey results, we compared the perceptions of the role of the interpreter as expressed by the interpreters themselves and the legal actors in a northern European country (Belgium) and a southern European country (Italy). To these we added the views of Italian CSW. We have outlined the weaknesses and drawbacks of our methodological approach. Although we cannot draw sound country-specific conclusions because of the small sample size, we would cautiously put forward that the professionals involved in an ImQM in Belgium are not always aware of each other's role and try to impose – or at least make known – their opinion on how the other professionals in the encounter should act on the basis of their own professional reference framework.

In Italy, on the other hand, professionals and interpreters/mediators seem to share the same opinions about the interpreter's role, according to which interpreters/mediators should possess various interpersonal and intercultural competencies in addition to interpreting skills. This most likely stems from historical differences, which have shaped the role and tasks of interpreters/mediators. Even though all participants in an ImQM seem to agree on the functions attributed to the interpreter, their assumptions – such as interpreters are supposed to undertake many tasks for which they are not trained – are not always correct.

If we add to this, albeit briefly for reasons of space, that the needs expressed by all professionals from all participating countries (including the Belgian and Italian samples) concern the demand for more time and for briefing beforehand, but also closer teamwork and better training for all parties involved (Salaets & Balogh, 2015a: 222–224), this could eventually account for the divergent responses regarding the role of the interpreter in the study. Specifically, with regard to the North–South (Belgian–Italian) research sample where the role of the interpreter/*mediatore linguistico-culturale* is articulated in different ways following different historical developments, we can conclude that specialised training on the specific skills needed during an ImQM would be a necessary requirement for all the professional groups involved in Belgium and Italy.

To draw further conclusions more research is clearly needed. In our opinion, future research would ideally encompass in-depth research by way of focus groups with all participants involved in an ImQM, which, among other things, would help to address questions about terminology and concepts (the 'role' of the interpreter, a minor from 0 to 18, etc.) and provide an opportunity for constructive discussions on the nature of teamwork between all parties in an ImQM. Secondly, the results from focus-group research would usefully feed into the development of a joint interprofessional training model.

A joint training approach has been developed – by way of tentative recommendations – by Van Der Mussele *et al.* (2014: 313–326) and will form part of the follow-up research in the Co-Minor-IN/QUEST II-project (2016–2018). The work will involve piloting different models and developing training materials such as instruction videos for awareness raising and didactic materials that are multidisciplinary in content. This joint interprofessional training model would allow us both to eradicate false beliefs and expectations on the role of the interpreter and to highlight the importance of close cooperation and teamwork.

Notes

(1) See: http://www.ejjc.org/news/adoption-new-eu-directive-procedural-safeguards-children-criminal-proceedings and for the full text of Directive (EU) 2016/800 of 11 May 2016: http://db.eurocrim.org/db/en/doc/2500.pdf.

(2) 'This Directive applies to children who were not initially suspects or accused persons but become suspects or accused persons in the course of questioning by the police or by another law enforcement authority' (Article 2 Scope (4)).

(3) For a more extensive explanation on the role of the interpreter see also an earlier publication on Co-Minor-IN/QUEST, namely, Salaets and Balogh (2015b).

(4) Planning and preparation, Engage and explain, Account clarification and challenge, Closure, Evaluation. See https://www.app.college.police.uk/app-content/investigations/investigative-interviewing/ (accessed 1 February 2016).

(5) https://aupiu.wordpress.com/2013/11/30/interprete-e-traduttore-mediatore-linguistico-culturale-e-interculturale/.

(6) For Belgium this means that the respondents did not participate in the CBTI/BKVT training, or in the KU Leuven, Antwerp campus training, since these are the only two available training courses as described before.

References

Achieving Best Evidence in Criminal Proceedings (2011) *Guidance on Interviewing Victims and Witnesses, and Guidance on using Special Measures.* London: Ministry of Justice. See https://www.cps.gov.uk/publications/docs/best_evidence_in_criminal_proceedings.pdf (accessed 31 October 2016).

Amato, A. and Garwood, C. (2011) Cultural mediators in Italy: A new breed of linguists. *inTRAlinea: Online Translation Journal* 13. See http://www.intralinea.org/archive/article/Cultural_mediators_in_Italy_a_new_breed_of_linguists#n12 (accessed 31 October 2016).

Amato, A. and Mack, G. (2015) Briefing, debriefing and support. In K. Balogh and H. Salaets (eds) *Children and Justice: Overcoming Language Barriers. Cooperation in Interpreter-Mediated Questioning of Minors* (pp. 247–280). Antwerp/Oxford/Portland, OR: Intersentia.

Baigorri-Jalón, J. (2014) *From Paris to Nuremberg. The Birth of Conference Interpreting.* Amsterdam/Philadelphia, PA: John Benjamins.

Balogh, K. and Salaets, H. (eds) (2015) *Children and Justice: Overcoming Language Barriers. Cooperation in Interpreter-Mediated Questioning of Minors.* Antwerp/Oxford/Portland, OR: Intersentia.

Berk-Seligson, S. (1990) *The Bilingual Courtroom: Court Interpreters in the Judicial Process.* Chicago, IL: University of Chicago Press.

Berk-Seligson, S. (2009) *Coerced Confessions: The Discourse of Bilingual Police Interrogations.* New York: Mouton de Gruyter.

Bettin, G. and Cela, E. (2014) The evolution of migration flows in Europe and Italy. *Economia Marche Journal of Applied Economics* XXXIII (1), 37–63. See https://www.google.be/search?q=Bettin%2C+G.+and+Cela%2C+E.+(2014)+The+evolution+of+migration+flows+in+Europe+and+Italy.+Economia+Marche+Journal+of+Applied+Economics+XXXIII+(1)%2C+37%E2%80%9363.+&ie=utf-8&oe=utf-8&client=firefox-b&gfe_rd=cr&ei=_dcYWNO0Ns3S8Afk7oHYDw (accessed 31 October 2016).

Böser, U. (2013) So tell me what happened! Interpreting the free recall segment of the investigative interview. *Translation and Interpreting Studies* 8 (1), 112–136.

Cokely, D. (2005) Shifting positionality: A critical examination of the turning point in the relationship of interpreters and the deaf community. In M. Marschark, R. Peterson and E.A. Winston (eds) *Sign Language Interpreting and Interpreter Education: Directions for Research and Practice* (pp. 3–28). New York: Oxford University Press.

Davies, G.M. and Westcott, H.L. (1999) *Interviewing Child Witnesses under the 'Memorandum of Good Practice': A Research Review.* London: Barry Webb Home Office. See http://lx.iriss.org.uk/sites/default/files/resources/040.%20Research%20Review%20of%20the%20Memorandum%20of%20Good%20Practice.pdf (accessed 31 October 2016).

Hale, S. and Napier, J. (2013) *Research Methods in Interpreting. A Practical Resource.* London/New York: Bloomsbury.

Hertog, E. (2010) Community interpreting. In Y. Gambier and L. Van Doorslaer (eds) *Handbook of Translation Studies, Volume 1* (pp. 49–54). Amsterdam/Philadelphia, PA: John Benjamins.

Kent, S.J. (2009) A discourse of danger and loss. Interpreters on interpreting for the European Parliament. In S. Hale, U. Ozolins and L. Stern (eds) *Critical Link 5: Quality in Interpreting – A Shared Responsibility* (pp. 55–70). Amsterdam/Philadelphia, PA: John Benjamins.

Lamb, M.D., Herschkowitz, I., Orbach, Y. and Esplin, P.W. (2008) *Tell Me What Happened: Structured Investigative Interviews of Child Victims and Witnesses.* Chichester: Wiley.

La Rooy, D.J., Ahern, E.C. and Andrews, S.J. (2015) Developmentally appropriate interviewing of highly vulnerable children: A developmental psychology perspective.

In K. Balogh and H. Salaets (eds) *Children and Justice: Overcoming Language Barriers. Cooperation in Interpreter-Mediated Questioning of Minors* (pp. 113–131). Antwerp/Oxford/Portland, OR: Intersentia.

Llewellyn-Jones, P. and Lee, R.G. (2014) *Defining the Role of the Community Interpreter: The Concept of 'Role-Space'*. Lincoln: SLI Ltd.

Mason, I. (2009) Role, positioning and discourse in face-to-face interpreting. In R. de Pedro Ricoy, I.A. Perez and C.W.L. Wilson (eds) *Interpreting and Translating in Public Service Settings. Policy, Practice, Pedagogy* (pp. 52–73). Manchester/Kinderhook, NY: St. Jerome Publishing.

Nakane, I. (2014) *Interpreter-Mediated Police Interviews*. Basingstoke: Palgrave Macmillan.

Nilsen, A.B. (2013) Exploring interpreting for young children. *The International Journal of Translation & Interpreting Research* 5 (2), 14–29.

Perez, I.A. and Wilson, C.W.L. (2007) Interpreter-mediated police interviews: Working as a professional team. In C. Wadensjö, B. Englund Dimitrova and A.-L. Nilsson (eds) *The Critical Link 4/Professionalisation of Interpreting in the Community. Selected Papers from the 4th International Conference on Interpreting in Legal, Health and Social Service Settings (Stockholm 20–23 May 2004)* (pp. 79–93). Amsterdam/Philadelphia, PA: John Benjamins.

Pöchhacker, F. (2004) *Introducing Interpreting Studies*. London/New York: Routledge.

Roy, C.B. (2000) *Interpreting as a Discourse Process*. New York/Oxford: Oxford University Press.

Rudvin, M. and Tomassini, E. (2008) Migration, ideology and the interpreter-mediator: The role of the language mediator in educational and medical settings in Italy. In C. Valero-Garcés and A. Martin (eds) *Crossing Borders in Community Interpreting. Definitions and Dilemmas.* (pp. 245–266). Amsterdam/Philadelphia, PA: John Benjamins.

Russel, S. (2002) Three's a crowd: Shifting dynamics in the interpreted interview. In J. Cotterill (ed.) *Language in the Legal Process* (pp. 111–126). Basingstoke: Palgrave Macmillan.

Salaets, H. and Balogh, K. (2015a) Co-Minor-IN/QUEST: Research findings. In K. Balogh and H. Salaets (eds) *Children and Justice: Overcoming Language Barriers. Cooperation in Interpreter-Mediated Questioning of Minors* (pp. 175–227). Antwerp/Oxford/Portland, OR: Intersentia.

Salaets, H. and Balogh, K. (2015b) Improving interpreter-mediated pre-trial interviews with minors. *TRANS: Revista de Traductologia* 19 (2), 57–76.

Shepherd, E. (2007) *Investigative Interviewing: The Conversation Management Approach*. Oxford: Oxford University Press.

Solem, L. (2015) Interpreting techniques. In K. Balogh and H. Salaets (eds) *Children and Justice: Overcoming Language Barriers. Cooperation in Interpreter-Mediated Questioning of Minors* (pp. 281–312). Antwerp/Oxford/Portland, OR: Intersentia.

Valero-Garcés, C. and Martin, A. (eds) (2008) *Crossing Borders in Community Interpreting. Definitions and Dilemmas*. Amsterdam/Philadelphia, PA: John Benjamins.

Van der Mussele, E., Virág, G. and Driesen, C. (2014) Joint training. In K. Balogh and H. Salaets (eds) *Children and Justice: Overcoming Language Barriers. Cooperation in Interpreter-Mediated Questioning of Minors* (pp. 313–326). Antwerp/Oxford/Portland, OR: Intersentia.

Verrept, H. (2008) Intercultural mediation: An answer to health care disparities? In C. Valero-Garcés and A. Martin (eds) *Crossing Borders in Community Interpreting. Definitions and Dilemmas* (pp. 187–201). Amsterdam/Philadelphia, PA: John Benjamins.

Wadensjö, C. (1998) *Interpreting as Interaction*. London: Longman.

Wilcox, S. and Shaffer, B. (2005) Towards a cognitive model of interpreting. In T. Janzen (ed.) *Topics in Signed Language Interpreting* (pp. 27–50). Amsterdam/Philadelphia, PA: John Benjamins.

Websites

Belgian Chamber of Translators and Interpreters (CBTI/BKVT): http://www.cbti-bkvt. org/en/about-us/cbti-bkvt

Belgian Law of 10-4-2014 on a National Register for legal experts, translators and interpreters: http://www.ejustice.just.fgov.be/cgi_loi/loi_a.pl?N=&=&sql=%28text+contains+ %28%27%27%29%29&rech=1&language=nl&tri=dd+AS+RANK&numero=1&t able_name=wet&cn=2014041090&caller=image_a1&fromtab=wet&la=N&pdf_ page=9&pdf_file=http://www.ejustice.just.fgov.be/mopdf/2014/12/19_2.pdf

Directive 2010/64/EU: http://eur-lex.europa.eu/LexUriServ/LexUriServ.do?uri=OJ:L:201 0:280:0001:0007:en:PDF

Directive 2012/29/EU: http://eur-lex.europa.eu/legal-content/EN/TXT/PDF/?uri=CEL EX:32012L0029&from=NL

Directive 2016/800/EU: http://db.eurocrim.org/db/en/doc/2500.pdf (accessed 31 October 2016).

Flemish Decree of 30 April 2009 on Integration: http://www.codex.vlaanderen.be/ Zoeken/Document.aspx?DID=1006181&param=inhoud&AID=1025769

ImPLI report: http://www.isit-paris.fr/wp-content/uploads/2014/11/IMPLI_Final_ Report.pdf

LIT course at KU Leuven, Antwerp campus (only available in Dutch): https:// www.arts.kuleuven.be/home/opleidingen/manamas/gerechtsvertalen_tolken/ programmema-2 (accessed 31 October 2016).

PEACE method for Investigative Interviewing: https://www.app.college.police.uk/ app-content/investigations/investigative-interviewing/

Project website (Co-Minor-IN/QUEST): https://www.arts.kuleuven.be/english/ rg_interpreting_studies/research-projects/co_minor_in_quest

SERV (Sociaal-Economische Raad van Vlaanderen): http://www.serv.be/sites/default/ files/STSociaalTolkDEF.pdf (accessed 31 October 2016).

UNCRC (United Nations Convention on the Rights of the Child): http://ec.europa.eu/ smart-regulation/impact/ia_carried_out/docs/ia_2013/com_2013_0822_en.pdf

9 Conflict. Tension. Aggression. Ethical Issues in Interpreted Asylum Hearings at the Office for Foreigners in Warsaw

Małgorzata Tryuk

Introduction

Early accounts of the community interpreter's participative role in a communicative event (e.g. Anderson, 1976; Lang, 1978) as well as later studies (e.g. Pöllabauer, 2004; Tryuk, 2004; Wadensjö, 1998) clearly indicate that interpreters, whether professional or non-professional, deviate from role prescriptions formulated in the majority of codes of ethics and professional standards. These recommend, among others, emotional detachment and faithfulness of translation, the latter implying the use of the first-person singular in interpretation and the need to refrain from making any additional comments. Nevertheless, the principles of neutrality and invisibility promoted by such role prescriptions have been called into question since the interpreter has been observed to actively engage in interpreted events in order to prevent and mitigate conflicts or communication breakdowns (e.g. Barsky, 1996; Pöllabauer, 2004; Wadensjö, 1998). If the interpreter assumes the role of a passive or neutral 'translating machine', this can lead to the negative outcome of interpreted events. It also suggests that the interpreter who assumes such a role will automatically fail to meet the provisions of respective codes and standards, which prohibit his/her extensive involvement in interpreted communication.

Prescriptive approaches to the role of the interpreter derive from a commonly held conviction that the communication that takes place through the interpreter does not differ in any way from direct communication (e.g. Gentile *et al.*, 1996). Yet, research findings (e.g. Valero-Garcés, 2005a) have shown that the interpreter's presence affects the way the speakers representing different language systems and cultures communicate in various institutional contexts. Interpreter-mediated communication changes qualitatively irrespective of the situation that demands the intervention of an interpreter. For instance, Meyer (2012: 111) argues that in medical settings 'doctors and patients accommodate less to each other when a trained interpreter is present', which means that a significant amount of responsibility for effective communication between the parties rests with the interpreter and suggests that the interpreter's role is highly multifaceted. By investigating situations in which interpersonal conflicts arise between interlocutors in interpreted events, the many facets of the interpreter's role can be illuminated.

This chapter focuses on immigration officers' perceptions of the interpreter's role in refugee hearings in the Office for Foreigners in Warsaw (pol. *Urząd ds Cudzoziemców*). The Office is the Polish authority that provides a comprehensive and professional service to legalise the stay of foreigners and offers protection to refugees in the territory of the Republic of Poland. Firstly, I briefly discuss public service interpreting during a refugee hearing and the current situation in this particular field with respect to immigration in Poland. Secondly, I explore how an interpreter can (partly) overcome conflicts, tensions, emotions and verbal aggression between the officers and the refugee applicants during an interpreter-mediated interaction. The chapter presents the results of a survey conducted in the Office for Foreigners, which consisted of a questionnaire and a series of interviews with officers.

Research on Interpreting During Asylum and Refugee Hearings

Research on interpreting for the needs of refugees and asylum seekers has focused on issues such as the micro-interactional dynamics of interpreter-mediated communication (e.g. Pöchhacker, 2000, 2008; Pöllabauer, 2004; Tryuk, 2004, 2007; Wadensjö, 1998), the development and status of narratives in interviews (e.g. Barsky, 1996; Maryns, 2006), the position of the interpreter in the asylum system (e.g. Inghilleri, 2003) and the role of interpreters in interpreter-mediated psychotherapeutic sessions for traumatised refugees and asylum seekers (e.g. Bot, 2003).

Studies of interpreter-mediated asylum and refugee hearings incorporate a number of methodological tools and theoretical assumptions, in particular interactional sociolinguistics, conversational analysis and critical discourse analysis. Researchers have been primarily concerned with such issues as the way in which utterances are controlled and coordinated in the course of an interaction, how interview participants align, as well as power relations, face-saving strategies and the interpreter's identity. Research has problematised the interpreter's visibility and illuminated the complexity of his/her role from the perspective of the needs and expectations of participants in the interaction. The problems of the interpreter's actual performance have been examined in relation to the existing role prescriptions set out in codes of ethics.

As shown by the above-mentioned research, in the immigration setting, the interpreter's role cannot be conceived as clear-cut and predetermined. It seems that there has been little agreement on what exactly lies within the scope of the interpreter's responsibilities in the refugee context, which may have been conditioned by conflicting expectations of the interpreter's clients and the multiplicity of the tasks that he/she often undertakes. The interpreter affects the course of interaction by compensating for gaps in power distribution and bridging linguistic and cultural barriers. At the same time, research shows that the interpreter rarely acts as a detached or neutral 'translating machine' as prescribed in many codes of ethics. This may be due to the complexity of his/her role but also to his/her exposure to accounts of violence and brutality during refugee hearings in which the interpreter is unlikely to remain emotionally detached and neutral.

The delimitation of the interpreter's role in asylum and refugee hearings has critical importance for the professionalisation of public service interpreting and translation (PSIT). Existing codes of ethics and professional standards should facilitate such a definition, but they are not commonly written from a setting-specific perspective. By providing guidelines concerning the interpreter's involvement in interpreter-mediated interaction, such codes could enhance understanding of the interpreter's position in immigration-related events and improve the nature of cooperation with other professionals (e.g. lawyers, healthcare providers, public service officers and immigration officers). They could also articulate in clearer terms how an interpreter's impartiality or invisibility during interpreter-mediated interaction can be understood.

Public Service Interpreting and Translation in Poland

In Poland, PSIT is still at a pre-professional stage, which is characterised, among others, by a lack of recognition of the profession and a very low level of knowledge about the features of the job by officials and clients (e.g. Tryuk, 2008). The only exception concerns the domain of legal translation and interpretation, which has constituted a separate profession since the adoption of the Act on the Profession of the Sworn Translator and Interpreter of 25 November 2004 (pol. *Ustawa z dnia 25 listopada 2004 r. o zawodzie tłumacza przysięgłego*). In all other domains and settings, the mechanisms of professionalisation are absent. As a consequence, the recruitment of (professional) translators and interpreters is rare, and *ad hoc* solutions are the order of the day. Public institutions lack awareness of the specificity of PSIT. Paradoxically, their personnel are frequently assigned to act as translators and interpreters and, if the institutions recruit anyone, they tend to prefer bilingual clerks who double as translators and interpreters. In Poland, there are still neither certification nor accreditation procedures for professional translators and interpreters and, in general, there is a lack of academic training for PSIT, with the exception of specialised training of legal translators and interpreters (e.g. Tryuk, 2008).

The issue of professionalism has been a focus of research from the very early phases of the study of the theory and practice of interpreting for public services (e.g. Angelelli, 2004; Gentile *et al.*, 1996; Kadrić, 2000; Pöchhacker & Kadrić, 1999; Tryuk, 2004, 2008; Valero-Garcés, 2005b, Valero-Garcés & Martin, 2008; Wadensjö *et al.*, 2007). It is commonly believed that a high degree of professionalism in translating and interpreting can be achieved through strict adherence to the rules and norms which are generally presented as a set of recommendations or codes (e.g. Hale, 2007). The Polish *Code of Sworn Translators and Interpreters* (pol. *Kodeks Tłumacza Przysięgłego*, 2005, hereinafter referred to as the *Code*) can be considered as such a prescriptive tool. This document was drafted by the Polish Society of Sworn and Specialised Translators (TEPIS) as a set of best practice recommendations after the Act of 2004 entered into force. The *Code* stipulates that there are three main norms in legal translation and interpreting: accuracy, impartiality and confidentiality. These three norms constitute the pillars of professionalism and underpin the high quality of the performance of the (public service) translator and/or interpreter.

The professionalism of public service interpreters and translators can be measured on the one hand by the level of compliance with the codes and also through observations, surveys or analysis of different settings, parameters, agents and conditions in which the translator and/or interpreter participates as an important mediator. Empirical research on different issues in PSIT such as the assessment of performance quality, profiles of translators and interpreters or recipients' expectations concerning the job has not been carried out on a large scale in Poland to date. Nevertheless, such research is of particular importance if translators and interpreters are to reconcile their vision of professional translation and interpreting with their actual practice; at best this is currently based on their knowledge of the *Code* and at worst, on their intuition about their vision and the expectations of recipients, among whom the employer (e.g. the immigration officer, the healthcare provider, public service provider or the lawyer) is the most important. The research that I carried out with my MA students at the Institute of Applied Linguistics, University of Warsaw, analyses the perception of the role of the interpreter by three groups of professionals: lawyers, healthcare service providers and immigration officers at the Office for Foreigners in Warsaw. The study explores opinions on the status, place and role of community interpreters with regard to their knowledge and level of compliance with the norms as proposed by the *Code*. The study employed a mixed methods approach: questionnaires, interviews and observations of real situations in which professionals work with interpreters. The results of the research were presented in an article in Polish (Tryuk, 2010), while selected issues concerning the study were discussed in an article published in English (Tryuk, 2012). This chapter concerns exclusively the findings of the study carried out in the immigration setting.

Immigration in Poland

Polish society is neither multilingual nor multicultural. The number of immigrants is scarce and constitutes as little as 0.2% of the total number of inhabitants. Even taking into account the highest estimated data concerning undocumented (i.e. illegal) immigration, the number of immigrants would not exceed half a million which would amount to a little over 1.3% of the population. In other European countries, the proportion of immigrants is as high as 12.2% of the total registered population, as it was in the case of Spain in 2010 (Rubio Malinowski, 2013). In this context it is worth considering the issue of refugees and asylum seekers in Poland as well as the need for linguistic and cultural mediation during the asylum procedure.

Seeking asylum is an inviolable right, which was internationally laid down by the United Nations through the Geneva Convention of 1951. In Poland, current procedures for granting refugee status are set out in the following acts: the Act of 13 June 2003 on Granting Protection to Foreigners in the Territory of the Republic of Poland (*Ustawa z dnia 13 czerwca 2003 o udzieleniu pomocy cudzoziemcom ochrony na terytorium Rzeczypospolitej Polskiej*), the Act of 12 December 2013 on Foreigners (pol. *Ustawa z dn. 12 grudnia 2013 r. o cudzoziemcach*) and the Act of 10 September 2015 on the Amendment to the Act on Granting Protection to Foreigners in the Territory of the Republic of Poland, among others (pol. *Ustawa z dnia 10 września 2015 r. o zmianie ustawy o udzielaniu cudzoziemcom ochrony na terytorium Rzeczypospolitej Polskiej oraz niektórych innych ustaw*). According to these Acts, the Polish state can grant protection to foreigners remaining in the territory of the Republic of Poland that can take one of the following forms: refugee status, supplementary protection, asylum, permit for tolerated stay and temporary protection. Refugee status is granted to a foreigner who, owing to a well-founded fear of being persecuted for reasons of race, religion, nationality, membership of a particular group or political opinion, is outside the country of his/her nationality and is unable or unwilling to avail himself/herself of the protection of that country. If a foreigner is refused a refugee status, he/she may be granted any of the remaining forms of protection or, alternatively, be deported from the territory of Poland (see www.udsc.gov.pl/en/prawo, accessed 1 February 2016).

In the years 1992–2007, the largest group of applicants consisted of Russians, mainly Chechens, the second largest group being applicants from Armenia. In 2014, 6621 foreigners applied for international protection in

Poland, most of whom were of Russian origin, followed by Ukrainians, Georgians, Armenians and Syrians. Out of 8193 applicants, refugee status was granted to Syrians (115 persons), Afghanis (27), Kazakhs (22), Belarusians (14) and Russians (13). Twenty-two persons did not indicate any citizenship in their refugee applications (see http://udsc.gov.pl/statystyki/raporty-okresowe/zestawienia-roczne accessed 1 February 2016).

This situation is subject to change as a result of the refugee crisis in Europe at the time of writing (Spring 2015) and plans to relocate refugees and asylum seekers from the Middle East and Africa to member states in the European Union. According to the plans put forward by EU ministers, Poland is to receive approximately 7000 refugees in the months and years to come. The figures show clearly that Poland is in a privileged situation to implement a proactive policy relating to immigration, which, in turn, is not only unavoidable but also desired from the point of view of the Polish economy and its demography (Rubio Malinowski, 2013: 297–298). There is already a social need to carry out research and to train specialists in intercultural communication, including public service interpreters and translators. Increasing pressure from immigration offices, the immigrants' expectations and concerns of public opinion highlighted in the press which reports a lack of access to interpreting and translation services are a sufficient incentive to start working on a more comprehensive approach to PSIT provision.

Data and Methodology

The survey presented in this section was conducted at the Office for Foreigners in Warsaw between November 2008 and March 2009 (e.g. Springer, 2009, 2010; Tryuk, 2010, 2012). It was a two-phase study, which consisted of a questionnaire and a series of interviews with immigration officers. The questionnaire comprised 29 questions concerning the interpreters' roles as perceived by the officers during a refugee hearing and was completed by 16 office employees. The majority of questions were closed multiple-choice questions or 'yes–no' questions. The first six questions referred to the professional profile of the officer (his/her education, experience and working languages, if any). The remaining questions concerned the officer's perception of the interpreter's role, the prescriptive norms of interpreting during the hearings in the Office, cooperation between the officers and the interpreters, as well as questions on the professionalisation of PSIT.

The second phase of the study involved a series of interviews held at the Office with 10 officers who usually work with interpreters. Each interview lasted approximately 45 minutes, and was recorded, transcribed and translated into English for the purpose of this discussion. The interviews were semi-structured and based on a list of questions but asked in varying order depending on the interviewee. Each interview began with a general question concerning the officer's experience in conducting hearings with the participation of an interpreter. The remaining questions related to the officer's expectations of the interpreter as well as his/her observations concerning the interpreter's actual performance. One of the questions was also intended to cover the officer's view on improving cooperation with interpreters by means of adequate training. The questionnaire and the interviews covered the following main issues: views concerning the general role of the interpreter during hearings; the use of the first- and third-person singular in the renditions; the neutrality and invisibility of the interpreter in the hearings; impartiality; and, finally, other additional roles of an interpreter during the hearings.

Survey

The first part of the study consisted of a questionnaire that elicited officers' perceptions of the interpreters' roles during a refugee hearing. The findings show that the majority of officers surveyed were aware of the prescriptive nature of the norms set out in the *Code*. According to the officers, the interpreter's overall task is to interpret only, to interpret everything (even literally) and to interfere as little as possible in the foreigner's utterances. However, in their answers to the question concerning the actual performance of an interpreter, the officers responded that the interpreter should do more than 'just interpret': he/she should clarify technical or legal terminology, explain cultural differences, ask additional questions or simplify the utterances, as well as help foreigners to complete forms. Some officers felt that the interpreter should also counteract misunderstanding and coordinate the flow of interaction. The overwhelming majority of officers underlined the impartiality and 'transparency' or invisibility of an interpreter as well as his/her non-involvement in the hearing. They also stressed that the interpretation must be comprehensible and accurate. Lastly, the responses show that the officers believe that recommendations of impartiality and fidelity as defined in the *Code* should be strictly observed by interpreters.

During the interviews with the immigration officers that followed the questionnaire, the introductory comments on the interpreter's general task in asylum hearings clearly show that they conceive of it mainly in terms of invisibility, neutrality, impartiality and accuracy as set out in the Polish *Code*. The officers reject the idea of the interpreter as a ratified participant in the overall process of interpreted communication by presenting him/her as a mere tool for transferring messages between representatives of two different linguistic and cultural systems, that is, they tend to conceive of the interpreter's task as *just translating*. The concept of the interpreter as a mediator does not feature at all in their considerations. Nevertheless, the immigration officers' accounts referred to situations in which it was unlikely for the interpreter to remain neutral or impartial. One of the officers even claimed that it is not possible for the interpreter to abstain from interfering in the communication when a foreigner shows emotion, e.g. when he/she begins to cry. When describing situations of high tension, for example during a long and exhausting interview, officers believe that the interpreter should take control over the course of the events if the foreigner behaves in an aggressive way. One officer, for instance, asserted that it is the task of the interpreter to release the tension by taking action, without waiting for the officer's permission:

Extract 1

Question (Q): [...]how can an interpreter help [in a conflict situation]?
Answer by a female Immigration Officer (IO): [...] in conflict situations s/he [the interpreter] may sometimes react... if for example the foreigner who is interrogated, is aggressive. May be s/he doesn't have to wait as he, the foreigner, produces a knife, but sometimes s/he may react and say something her/himself and take control in such emergency situations.

However, the officer does not specify what measures should be taken by the interpreter if such a situation emerges. In general, the responses reveal that the officers expect help from the interpreter to conduct an interview and to maintain order during the hearing. According to some officers, the interpreter should even 'get close' to the foreigner so that the officer can achieve his/her goal, as reported by the same officer as above:

Extract 2

IO: [...] there are situations when an interpreter is trying to get closer to the person being interrogated and fraternize with him.

In the view of some officers, the interpreter may comfort, cheer, help the interviewees, as one reports:

Extract 3

IO: When I conducted the hearing with the assistance of the Chechen interpreter, we interviewed one lady who was old and seriously ill. What's more, she was really nervous and I had the impression that she was going to die there and then. The interpreter then cuddled her, which amused me a bit, but in fact it worked well with the immigrant.
Q: So the interpreter managed to release the tension somehow, right?

IO: Yes, the interpreter held her hand, sat by her and calmed her down.

For some of the officers, any corporal contact is prohibited *'because of the possibility of infections'*, but the interpreter is considered a helper and sometimes also a friend, meaning that such contact is not necessarily unwelcome. The interpreter is also perceived by most of the officers as an experienced expert not only in cultural issues, but also in interpersonal mediation, as one of them explains:

Extract 4

IO: Once I remember, I asked a question, because the foreigner had travelled in different countries and then he came to Poland, so I asked a question, but the interpreter told me: 'Don't ask this question, he will be upset'.

Q: She told you so, because it was a question of a cultural difference, a sort of taboo?

IO: I don't think I could upset him […] but she told me that he could take offense at it.

Another immigration officer remembers that the interpreter reprimanded her when she wanted to ask about the persecutions that the Chechen immigrant was a victim of. The interpreter would tell her:

Extract 5

Don't ask about it, it is a silly question.

For the interpreter, a question about Chechnya, a region where the citizens are constantly persecuted, would be needless. As he explained to the officer, in this particular situation the meaning of persecution could be differently perceived by the interviewer and the interviewee and could lead to serious misunderstanding between the participants of the hearing. The officers often reported a belief that each refugee hearing was the responsibility of the officer–interpreter team, as in this example:

Extract 6

IO: They [e.g. the immigrants] perceive us as one unit.

Q: As the Office's representatives?

IO: As one unit […] so if the foreigner is angry or annoyed, expresses sorrow, anger, the anger or annoyance is also addressed at the interpreter.

Q: I see. And does the interpreter try to release the tension, which may arise then?

IO: Yes. If he can use the foreigner's language with ease, releasing tension help us all in the task.

In the case of intense aggression, it is usually the interpreter who is addressed by the applicant, as declares one officer:

Extract 7

IO: The aggression is towards the interpreter [...]. The interpreter must remain calm, and after that he must continue his job.

The officers' responses suggest a degree of ambiguity in relation to the interpreter's role. For instance, some officers assert that the interpreter represents the Office and is considered as an institutional agent who is responsible for the outcome of the hearings, just like the officers themselves. By contrast, others assert that any conflict situations that arise during the hearing must be resolved solely by the officers:

Extract 8

IO: In a conflict situation, I wouldn't allow the interpreter to solve the problem. This is my entire responsibility. It means it should never occur.

Q: But you mentioned before that the interpreter is a sort of a buffer.

IO: In a way, yes. In general, there are two of us to solve the problem. I can count on him in a difficult situation.

Q: It means that when an interviewee becomes aggressive, you are two.

IO: We are two to share it [...] It is easier to be with an interpreter.

Another officer confirms:

Extract 9

IO: If there is some verbal aggression, if it occurs, the interpreter is of great help. He would speak in a more categorical way.

This extract reveals that the support provided by interpreters in relieving tension is sometimes valued, based on a view of interpreters as mediators capable of resolving any potential conflicts thanks to their command of the foreigner's language. Therefore, some view the interpreter's task as involving reacting to aggressive remarks, reprimanding foreigners and summarising utterances, as one officer explains:

Extract 10

Q: How would you handle the tensions?

IO: I could imagine what I would do if it happened to me. I would ask the interpreter to reassure [the foreigner] in his native language. And tell the interpreter what he should say...

It often happens that the officers are the cause of the tension or aggression. In such a case, the interpreter's task is to calm down the officers. One officer remembers that during an interview the applicant began to cry. The officer who was in charge of the hearing showed no reaction and didn't even try to reassure the applicant or suggest a break be taken, and instead shouted: *'Why are you crying? Calm down, you are lying'*. It was an intensively emotional interaction and the officer asserted that in this situation the task of the interpreter was to ease the tension between the two participants. If such a situation occurs, Wadensjö (1998: 194–195) claims that interpreters need to learn 'how to support the establishment of communicative interaction between quarrelling antagonists, and how to perform as an interpreter without denying the parties to be (and their responsibility for being) angry with one another'. The officers believe that the interpreter must be prepared to anticipate the possibility of stepping aside, waiting or walking out if the interview conditions make it impossible for him/her to proceed. It means that the interpreter has the right to refrain (temporarily) from continuing his/her task. It also happens during the hearings in the Office for Foreigners in Warsaw as reported by one of the officers:

Extract 11

IO: When the interviewing IO urged the interpreter to continue to translate the hearing in spite of the fact that the lady was crying and was unable to answer, the interpreter refused to translate and asked the officer to wait for a while to let her calm down as any further questioning was pointless.

According to the officers, the interpreter's role in conflict situations consists of helping mainly the officer, and also conducting the refugee hearing along with the officer. They also believe that the tasks of an interpreter include rebuking and calming down the officer, and, sometimes, getting close to the foreigner. The officers view interpreters as individuals capable of resolving any potential conflicts by virtue of their command of the foreigner's language. Therefore, they expect the interpreters to react in an emergency situation and act upon the requests to help calm a foreigner or even intervene without a formal request or order. In addition, some officers reported that if the need arises, they would ask the interpreter to evaluate the foreigner's credibility on the basis of his/her linguistic as well as cultural evidence. Notwithstanding such requests, the officers also reported situations of misunderstanding resulting from the interpreter's limited competence. One of them recounts the case of a Chechen applicant where a potential conflict was avoided thanks to the officer's knowledge of the local conditions:

Extract 12

IO: There was a situation when the interpreter didn't really understand the meaning of the foreigner's words. It related to... he, the foreigner said it in the way... the most delicate way he could say so, he said that 'ja poteral vsëo svoû muzskoe dostoinstva'. The interpreter translated it literally as 'He was deprived of his male pride.' So I said that from what I understand, it does not relate to depriving him of his male pride but to the fact that he was raped. So, [...], to ask him a question what he means by saying that 'he was deprived of his male pride or dignity' and then it actually came out that nobody, I don't know, insulted him or slapped in his face but there was an attempt of rape.

Q: You would rather expect [...] the interpreter to say offhand, that he meant a rape. In other words, the interpreter made a mistake, as he did not understand the foreigner's utterance?

IO: Yes, the interpreter made a mistake, translated literally what the foreigner had said. Although, I repeat, in spite of the literal translation, it would come to light because the officer conducting the hearing probed the matter, in what way he was humiliated and deprived of his male dignity... it would come out into the open.

Discussion

The qualitative analysis of the questionnaire and the interviews shows that Polish immigration officers perceive interpreters as machines whose only task is referred to in terms of *'just interpreting'*. This view is reflected in the officers' opinions concerning the interpreters' general role in refugee hearings. They frequently describe the interpreters' tasks using such metaphors as *'link'*, *'white sheet of paper'*, *'tool'*, *'voice'* and as someone whose presence should be little felt. The mechanistic depiction of the interpreter is also confirmed by the officers' more detailed comments on the interpreters' use of the first- or third-person singular, as well as their expectations towards the preservation of faithfulness and accuracy, without omitting or adding anything, as well as towards their neutrality and impartiality at all times. Such behaviour is to ensure optimum communication between the officer and the foreigner. In reality, the officers' actual expectations of interpreters in asylum hearings clearly contradict the idealistic image of the interpreter initially reported by them in the questionnaire.

In fact, immigration officers expect the interpreter to carry out a number of additional tasks in relation to his/her principal activity. As a consequence, interpreters in refugee hearings are regularly in breach of the principle of invisibility, impartiality, neutrality and faithfulness and this is conditioned by a number of factors. Firstly, the interpreter usually sits next to the immigration officer. It is commonly perceived as an ideal position for an interpreter during the interview. However, with such positioning, the task for him/her not to 'align with' the immigration officer, to remain neutral seems unrealistic. Secondly, the interpreter is expected by the officers to openly intervene when verbal aggression or conflicts arise. Thirdly, the fact that some of the interpreters are of the same nationality as the foreigners being interviewed automatically makes the former more inclined to establish a closer contact with the foreigner ('to fraternise' as they say) rather than the immigration officer. Lastly, interpreters are required by some immigration officers to modify the immigrant's discourse, which eliminates the principle of faithfulness, or regard themselves as the Office's representatives. The interpreters in refugee hearings in Poland assume a variety of roles which prevent them from staying neutral or invisible: they gauge foreigners' credibility, reprimand foreigners on different occasions, resolve conflicts, release tension, explain cultural differences and help the officers in drafting the minutes of the hearing, to name but a few. The officers admit that the interpreters are not prepared for assuming such additional roles, nor are they prepared for dealing with conflicts or aggression. According to the officers, there are also situations in which the interpreters' involvement is objectively too extensive, for instance when they begin interviewing the foreigner on their own.

Conclusion

For the immigration officers, in situations when conflicts or verbal aggression occur, the presence of the third person, i.e. the interpreter, can and even must relieve rising tension. As was shown in the above examples, during the hearings at the Office for Foreigners in Warsaw the interpreter can take over an initiative, calm down or rebuke an aggressive party to the interaction, whether this be the interviewing officer or the interviewee (see also Nakane, 2014). At the same time, the interpreter is situated 'in the first line of fire' as stated by one officer. Sometimes, he/she is helpless with respect to the verbal aggression of speakers. As one of the officers admits: 'If there is the case where verbal aggression takes place, it will really hit the interpreter first'. Baraldi and Gavioli (2012a: 11–12) stress that the role of the interpreter or translator in a public service setting is that of a mediator, i.e. a person who intervenes when tensions, aggression and conflicts appear. His/her role is also to coordinate interlingual and intercultural interaction when parties have different preferences or goals to achieve. The role of an interpreter is to help the parties to communicate, to improve relationships and ultimately to find solutions to the problem of the participants. Baraldi and Gavioli (2012) affirm that:

> [T]he need for intercultural mediation on the part of interpreters comes from a possible lack of fit between institutional and clients' perspectives. Interpreting as intercultural mediation is important because, while institutional cultural forms are well-established, new cultural forms which are not known or accepted by the institution can create serious problems in the interaction (Baraldi & Gavioli, 2012: 13).

For this reason, it is necessary to carry out further work concerning the intercultural dimension of PSIT taking into account specific aspects of the interpreter-mediated communication such as all parties' perceptions of the interpreters' role, the level of expertise and knowledge of the interpreters of their tasks and understanding of the purposes of the interaction, as well as the communicative needs of the officers and the foreigners. It will enhance understanding of the interpreters' social and communicative roles as mediators in public service institutions, and thus, help them to better prepare for the work involved. In the future, such research will help support the development of new guidelines or standards for the community interpreter's work in the immigration setting.

References

Anderson, R.B.W. (1976) Perspectives on the role of the interpreter. In R.W. Brislin (ed.) *Translation: Application and Research* (pp. 208–228). New York: Gardner Press. Reprinted in Pöchhacker, F. and Shlesinger, M. (eds) (2002) *The Interpreting Studies Reader* (pp. 209–217). London/New York: Routledge.

Angelelli, C. (2004) *Revisiting the Interpreter's Role. A Study of Conference, Court, and Medical Interpreters in Canada, Mexico and the United States*. Amsterdam/Philadelphia, PA: John Benjamins.

Baraldi, C. and Gavioli L. (2012) Understanding coordination in interpreter-mediated interaction. In C. Baraldi and L. Gavioli (eds) *Coordinating Participation in Dialogue Interpreting* (pp. 1-21). Amsterdam/Philadelphia, PA: John Benjamins.

Barsky, R.F. (1996) The interpreter as intercultural agent in Convention refugee hearings. *The Translator* 2 (10), 45–63.

Bot, H. (2003) The myth of the uninvolved interpreter interpreting in mental health and the development of a three-person psychology. In L. Brunette, G.L. Bastin, I. Hemlin and H. Clarke (eds) *The Critical Link 3. Interpreters in the Community* (pp. 27–35). Amsterdam/Philadelphia, PA: John Benjamins.

Gentile, A., Ozolins, U. and Vasilakakos, M. (1996) *Liaison Interpreting*. Melbourne: Melbourne University Press.

Hale, S. (2007) *Community Interpreting*. Basingstoke: Palgrave Macmillan.

Inghilleri, M. (2003) Habitus, field and discourse: Interpreting as a socially situated activity. *Target* 15 (2), 243–268.

Kadrić, M. (2000) Interpreting in the Austrian courtroom. In R.P. Roberts, S.E. Carr and A. Dufour (eds) *The Critical Link 2: Interpreters in the Community* (pp. 153–164). Amsterdam/Philadelphia, PA: John Benjamins.

Kodeks Tłumacza Przysięgłego z komentarzem [Code of Sworn Translators and Interpreters] (2005). Warszawa: Wyd. TEPIS.

Lang, R. (1978) Behavioral aspects of liaison interpreters in Papua New Guinea: Some preliminary observations. In D. Gerver and H. Wallace Sinaiko (eds) *Language Interpretation and Communication* (pp. 231–244). New York/London: Plenum Press.

Maryns, K. (2006) *The Asylum Speaker. Language in the Belgian Asylum Procedure.* Manchester: St. Jerome.

Meyer, B. (2012) *Ad hoc* interpreting for partially language-proficient patients: Participation in multilingual constellations. In C. Baraldi and L. Gavioli (eds) *Coordinating Participation in Dialogue Interpreting* (pp. 99–113). Amsterdam/ Philadelphia, PA: John Benjamins.

Nakane, I. (2014) *Interpreter-Mediated Police Interviews. A Discourse-Pragmatic Approach.* London: Palgrave Macmillan.

Pöchhacker, F. (2000) The community interpreter's task: Self-perception and provider views. In R.P. Roberts, S.E. Carr and A. Dufour (eds) *The Critical Link 2: Interpreters in the Community* (pp. 49–65). Amsterdam/Philadelphia, PA: John Benjamins.

Pöchhacker, F. (2008) Interpreting as mediation. In C. Valero-Garcés and A. Martin (eds) *Crossing Borders in Community Interpreting* (pp. 9–26). Amsterdam/Philadelphia, PA: John Benjamins.

Pöchhacker, F. and Kadrić, M. (1999) The hospital cleaner as healthcare interpreter. A case study. *The Translator, Secial Issue on Dialogue Interpreting* 5 (2), 161–178.

Pöllabauer, S. (2004) Interpreting in asylum hearings. Issues of role, responsibility and power. *Interpreting* 6 (2), 143–175.

Rubio Malinowski, M.P. (2013) *Imigranci a komunikacja międzykulturowa w sferze usług publicznych w Polsce.* Kraków: Nomos.

Springer, R. (2009) The role(s) of a community interpreter versus professional standards and ethics. Unpublished MA thesis, University of Warsaw.

Springer, R. (2010) Rola(e) tłumacza środowiskowego w kontekście azylanckim i uchodźczym a etyka, standardy zawodowe i oczekiwania pracowników urzędu imigracyjnego. In M. Tryuk (ed.) *O tłumaczach, prawnikach, lekarzach i urzędnikach. Teoria i praktyka przekładu środowiskowego w Polsce* (pp. 157–216). Warszawa: Wyd. Bel.

Tryuk, M. (2004) *L'interprétation communautaire. Des normes et des rôles dans l'interprétation.* Warszawa: Wyd. TEPIS.

Tryuk, M. (2007) Community Interpreting in Poland. In C. Wadensjö, B. Englund Dimitrova and A.-L. Nilsson (eds) *The Critical Link 4. Professionalisation of Interpreting in the Community* (pp. 95–105). Amsterdam/Philadelphia, PA: John Benjamins.

Tryuk, M. (2008) Five years later. Picture of community interpreting in Poland. In C. Valero-Garcés and A. Martin (eds) *Crossing Borders in Community Interpreting* (pp. 87–101). Amsterdam/Philadelphia, PA: John Benjamins.

Tryuk, M. (ed.) (2010) *O tłumaczach, prawnikach, lekarzach i urzędnikach.Teoria i praktyka przekładu środowiskowego w Polsce.* Warszawa: Wyd. Bel.

Tryuk, M. (2012) The judge, the doctor, the immigration officer and the interpreters. Community interpreter's role perception – a Polish perspective. *Interpreters' Newsletter* 17, 117–138.

Ustawa z dnia 25 listopada 2004 r. o zawodzie tłumacza przysięgłego [Act on the Profession of the Sworn Translator and Interpreter of 25 November 2004], Dz. U. 2004 nr 273, poz. 2702 (Journal of Laws 2004 no. 273, item 2702).

Valero-Garcés, C. (2005a) Doctor-patient consultations in dyadic and triadic exchanges. *Interpreting* 7 (2), 193–210.

Valero-Garcés, C. (ed.) (2005b) *Traducción como mediación entre lenguas y culturas/Translation as Mediation or How to Bridge Linguistic and Cultural Gaps.* Alcalá de Henares: Servicios de Publicaciones, Universidad de Alcalá.

Valero-Garcés, C. and Martin, A. (eds) (2008) *Crossing Borders in Community Interpreting.* Amsterdam/Philadelphia, PA: John Benjamins.

Valero-Garcés, C, Pena Díaz, C. and Lázaro Gutiérrez, R. (eds) (2008) *Investigación y práctica en traducción e interpretación en los servicios públicos. Desafíos y alianzas/Research and Practice in Public Service Interpreting and Translation. Challenges and Alliances.* Alcalá de Henares: Servicios de Publicaciones, Universidad de Alcalá.

Wadensjö, C. (1998) *Interpreting as Interaction.* London/New York: Longman.

Wadensjö, C., Englund Dimitrova, B. and Nilsson, A.-L. (eds) (2007) *The Critical Link 4. Professionalisation of Interpreting in the Community.* Amsterdam/Philadelphia, PA: John Benjamins.

10 The Voice of Compassion: Exploring Trauma-Informed Interpreting

Marjory A. Bancroft

Introduction

> When a client explains themselves very well the way it should be, and the provider is very [willing] to hear everything, things become very smooth. So you feel very happy, very good about yourself. – A refugee. (Bambarén-Call *et al.*, 2012: 17)
> I did not feel the interpreter was saying everything.... The man was just like a machine: the tone was not being conveyed. – An Iraqi war trauma survivor. (Bambarén-Call *et al.*, 2012: 11)

This chapter introduces a young yet vital specialisation: trauma-informed interpreting (TII), defined here as a specialisation of interpreting that integrates research on trauma into the professional practice of interpreters. TII involves interpreting for survivors of any violent crime or traumatic event, such as child abuse, gender-based violence, trafficking, torture, war trauma and mass disasters. It takes place in community settings that cross other interpreting specialisations within public service interpreting (PSI), including legal, medical, social services, educational and mental health interpreting.

Interpreting for trauma survivors is typically more intense and complex than general community interpreting (the more common international term for PSI, cf, ISO, 2014). This chapter explores needs assessment and training that was undertaken in the United States between 2011 and 2015 to support the development of TII. The needs assessment included preliminary literature reviews; two national surveys; 15 focus groups held across the country; 20 in-depth interviews with service providers and interpreters; and several pilot sessions of a five-day training programme for refugee interpreting and a four-day training programme for victim services interpreting.

The purpose of the chapter is threefold: to introduce the historical background of TII; to explore the needs assessment data that formed the basis of two specialised training programmes for TII; and finally, to discuss the two training programmes, including examples of specific techniques taught to interpreters to support survivor autonomy and reduce interpreter vicarious trauma (VT). First, a note on two key terms in this field: *victim* and *survivor*. These terms have engendered debate. The United Nations provides this definition of *victim*:

> 'Victims' means persons who, individually or collectively, have suffered harm, including physical or mental injury, emotional suffering, economic loss or substantial impairment of their fundamental rights, through acts or omissions that are in violation of criminal laws. (United Nations, 1985)

There is no internationally accepted definition of *survivor*, in part because the linguistic distinction between *victim* and *survivor* does not easily cross languages. However, in services to trauma survivors the distinction between these terms has become paramount to many, especially those who consider the term *survivor* more empowering than *victim*:

> 'Survivor' is a term used by many in the services field to recognize the strength it takes to continue on a journey toward healing in the aftermath of a traumatic experience. (President's Interagency Task Force [United States], 2013: 8)

Often, the term *victim* is preferred in the justice system and *survivor* in direct services provided to victims of crime. In this chapter, the two terms will be used interchangeably, but most often the term *survivor* is preferred.

Historical Background on Trauma-Informed Interpreting

> **Trauma** is an emotional response to a terrible event like an accident, rape or natural disaster. Immediately after the event, shock and denial are typical. Longer term reactions include unpredictable emotions, flashbacks, strained relationships and even physical symptoms like headaches or nausea. While these feelings are normal, some people have difficulty moving on with their lives. Psychologists can help these individuals find constructive ways of managing their emotions. (American Psychological Association, http://www.apa.org/topics/trauma/)

> Psychological trauma is an affiliation of the powerless. At the moment of trauma, the victim is rendered helpless by overwhelming force. ... Traumatic events overwhelm the ordinary systems of care that give people a sense of control, connection, and meaning... Traumatic events are extraordinary, not because they occur rarely, but rather because they overwhelm the ordinary human adaptations to life. (Herman, 1997: 33)

Everyone experiences trauma. Few of us stop to define it or reflect on it. While trauma is universal, a clear understanding of its impact is not well understood, even by many providers who offer services to trauma survivors, far less by interpreters. There is no universally accepted definition of *trauma*. For the purposes of this discussion, it can be viewed as a unique response by an individual to an event or series of events that cause physical or emotional harm. Trauma is not the result of a bad day at the office. Traumatic events can affect and overwhelm every part of any individual's body, mind, work, relationships, beliefs and values.

Decades of research have shown that trauma can have a small impact or a deep one that lasts briefly or goes on for decades (Herman, 1997). There is no way to predict the impact of trauma because it varies so much by individual (van der Kolk, 2015), but differences of language and culture can add complexity to the experience. The impact of violence on each victim is unique and can lead to many emotional and physical problems. The nature of trauma-informed work is described as:

> A programme, organization, or system that is trauma-informed realizes the widespread impact of trauma and understands potential paths for healing; recognizes the signs and symptoms of trauma in staff, clients, and others involved with the system; and responds by fully integrating knowledge about trauma into policies, procedures, practices, and settings. (SAMHSA, 2012: 4)

TII, therefore, is a part of the larger field of 'trauma-informed services' (TIS) – a relatively young domain that appears to have emerged first in the United States. The publication there in 1992 of Judith Herman's groundbreaking *Trauma and Recovery* (Herman, 1992, revised in 1997, reissued in 2015) marked a watershed in trauma studies. Herman developed a research-based three-stage model for trauma recovery: (1) safety; (2) remembrance and mourning; and (3) reconnection (she did not imply that these occur in a linear progression). Her emphasis on safety and reconnection are particularly important for communication and interpreting.

Although services to trauma survivors had been provided for decades, if not centuries, a new focus emerged on the question of how best to promote meaningful recovery for trauma survivors. The response was the development of trauma-informed care (TIC), a discipline that emerged widely in the early 2000s, initially in mental health services. TIC is 'an overarching framework that emphasizes the impact of trauma and guides the general organisation and behaviour of an entire system' including specific TIS that can be provided within a trauma-informed programme (Hopper *et al.*, 2010: 81). The evolution of TIC stems from the intersection of a number of cross-disciplinary paradigms that focus on enhancing the quality of services to trauma survivors. TIC differentiates itself from other services by its focus on power and control (empowering the survivor); the responsibility of providers to educate survivors about trauma and recovery; and a systematic use of language. For example, 'Choice of language should convey that staff view consumers as human beings, not as impaired cases' and avoid jargon and specific terms and phrases that could be retraumatising while also being respectful and welcoming (Hodas, 2006: 35).

Parallel to the evolution of TIC was the US crime victim movement. Its origins date back to the 1960s, emerging as part of deep social changes fomenting in the United States and elsewhere. These social changes resulted in the development of a field called victimology, the introduction of state victim compensation movements, the rise of the women's movement, the rise in crime and the subsequent growth of victim activism (Young & Stein, 2004: 4). The result for crime victims was intense nationwide efforts by federal, state and charitable agencies to 'reach out with a compassionate, skilled and effective response to victims who have suffered physical, sexual, emotional, and financial harm as a result of crime' (US Office for Victims of Crime, 2010).

The initial focus of the crime victims' movement was counselling and access to justice; the initial focus of TIC was counselling and mental health. Yet almost at once, the concern for survivor recovery expanded to include a broad array of services and settings that support survivors (see e.g. Elliott *et al.*, 2005; Ko *et al.*, 2008). Today, TIC/TIS is an established field of service in the United States in numerous domains such as education, juvenile justice, services for the homeless and substance abuse, to name only a few.

To avoid adding to the suffering of survivors, service providers need to become well informed about trauma, which requires specialised training and education (education is defined here as programmes housed within institutions of higher education, whereas training refers to programmes offered outside such institutions). A growing number of services offer exactly these specialised paths for education and training, for example, for health professionals (sexual assault forensic examiners, doctors who perform forensic medical exams for asylum applications and forensic nurse examiners); social service providers (such as social workers and advocates); clinicians (trauma-informed therapists, including psychologists, psychiatrists, licensed professional counsellors and certified clinical social workers); and even lawyers (particularly those who specialise in victim services and immigration).

The research, discourse, practice and 'spirit' of the field converged in the 2000s on several core issues. The two that are most relevant for PSI are the need for practitioners to incorporate evidence-based research on trauma into practice and a concomitant need to support the autonomy of the survivor. Hence the need for training and education: trauma-informed service providers incorporate an understanding of trauma into every aspect of their work and are particularly concerned with supporting recovery and avoiding retraumatising the survivor.

Contributions to the field from many disciplines, such as feminist studies (e.g. Burstow, 2003), trauma theory and relational theory (Elliott *et al.*, 2005) and community intervention approaches (such as the 'ecology model', see Harvey, 1996) among others tend to agree on a fundamental principle: recovery involves restoring *agency* to the trauma survivor, who typically has lost it during the event(s) that caused the trauma. Historically, service systems have often failed to support survivor agency, autonomy or recovery. In fact, as many rape survivors can attest, seeking help after an assault can add on an extra layer of trauma, particularly within the justice system.

Survivors and their service providers in TIC and TIS work together to support the survivor on his/her path to recovery. These services are designed to be welcoming and warm. Providers listen, empathise and create a 'safe space' where the trauma survivor can share his/her story, a critical part of recovery. In doing so, TIS are particularly designed to avoid dynamics, situations, settings and actions that might be 'triggering' for survivors.

So far, the bulk of the research literature, discourse and practice has historically neglected the interpreter. Yet, in this age of international migration, interpreters are very often needed in TIS. The United Nations (2015), for example, reports that international migration reached 244 million in 2015: an increase of 41%. As more comprehensive evidence-based research becomes available (e.g. Morrisey *et al.*, 2005) to confirm anecdotal reports, it also appears that counselling for survivors of major trauma is still considered an often crucial component of healing. Many – and perhaps most – survivors need to find a safe place to share their story. Here, the impact of the interpreter on the encounter is especially crucial.

Yet a scan of the research literature on TIC, TIS and interpreting yields little. The scant research tends to focus more on the risks of interpreter VT (e.g. Lor, 2012; Macdonald, 2015) than on how interpreters can impede or support TIS and survivor recovery. Yet, such research is sorely needed. As this chapter makes clear, service providers in TIS make every effort to avoid retraumatising the survivor, yet interpreters can and sometimes do actively undermine their efforts. For example, most interpreters are not even aware what retraumatising a survivor means, far less how to avoid it. Trauma-informed providers typically receive specialised training in TIS; most interpreters do not.

Trauma-informed providers seek above all to help the survivor feel respected, safe and empowered to make decisions. The interpreter untrained in TIS, even with good intentions, can inadvertently make the survivor feel ashamed, unsafe and disempowered, issues that this chapter will address in more depth. For all these reasons and more, there is an urgent need for research that can help the interpreter to explore and establish training paths for TII. In the absence of such research, the information discussed here may help to guide future studies.

Trauma-Informed Interpreting: An Emerging Specialisation

> **Social worker** (Washington, DC): It is really important to have that trauma-informed perspective, because there are many things that can be triggering, and so many things in sexual assault and domestic violence are related to power and control... Any sort of issue can retrigger a client into falling back into the same feelings that they had. An interpreter can trigger those feelings again because there is a control issue. The interpreter has control over the clients' words and how they are conveyed and has control over the service provider's words and how they are portrayed to the client. So establishing trust is important both in terms of confidentiality and in terms of obvious nonverbal ways of communicating that [show] you're being an honest communicator.
>
> **Lawyer**: That's really interesting! Have you witnessed where an interpreter was not being sensitive enough to the power dynamic and the client felt a sense of loss of control or powerlessness?
>
> **Social worker**: I haven't seen a client put words around that, but ... [i]n situations where the interpreter is not doing a good job, I see the client shut down. They no longer trust that person to convey the meaning, so they shut down. So I can't provide the services: [survivors] are going to protect themselves by not giving the interpreter control.... (Bancroft et al., 2016a)

'Trauma-informed interpreter' is a new term. It is not yet widely used or cited in the research literature, unlike terms such as 'trauma-informed clinician' or 'trauma-informed therapist'. Yet, this new term has tremendous power and practical application to describe interpreters who are trained to work with survivors of major trauma and their service providers. TII explicitly supports TIS by *allowing the service provider and the survivor to communicate clearly and transparently without undermining the provider–survivor relationship.*

In doing so, the interpreter should avoid engaging in any act or utterance that might harm the survivor or jeopardise recovery.

Above all, trauma-informed interpreters 'give voice'. The term 'giving voice' is used here specifically to refer to the supporting ethical requirements governing accuracy, impartiality, professional boundaries/scope of practice and professionalism. These requirements usually specify that interpreters should not add to, change or omit anything in the communications between a service provider and a service user, nor otherwise interfere with their communication. In this capacity, even when interpreting the most horrific material, the interpreter resists the temptation to cross professional boundaries, honours the message and does not explain it, but instead makes sure it is clearly understood (except in court, where typically the interpreter has a more restricted role). Trauma-informed interpreters ideally respect role boundaries while still intervening – though only when necessary and permissible – to ensure clear communication.

A more technical term for 'giving voice' would be the concept of *communicative autonomy*. As defined here and applied to interpreting for service users and providers, the concept refers to their 'capacity to be in control of, and responsible for, [their] own communication' (Bancroft *et al.*, 2015: viii). When the interpreter works effectively, communication flows nearly as if the provider and service user share a common language. This concept of communicative autonomy echoes the concern of providers in TIS for the self-determination of the survivor because control has been taken away from victims of crime and one goal of TIS involves restoring the survivor's ability to impact the world. Thus, interpreters who get involved, give advice, explain cultural issues or tell survivors or service providers what to do out of an emotional desire to 'help out' are in fact taking control of that victim's life at a vulnerable moment.

Developing techniques that support communicative autonomy even when the interpreter is interpreting traumatic content lies at the heart of TII. However, TII as a term and concept is so new that in 2015, an online search using the words *trauma-informed interpreters* revealed few references (compared with a search for the term *trauma-informed clinician*). Today, the same search turns up thousands of websites, many of them relevant if mostly US based. This rapid online evolution is a snapshot of an emerging specialisation. Unfortunately, the specialisation is evolving without rigorous research to support it.

Trauma survivors and interpreters

[A]nyone who's been a victim has been taken over and controlled in some way. So allowing them to make decisions even if you don't agree with them [is critical] because it's giving them a safe place to make decisions. When they come to a safe place, it's important for interpreters to understand that their piece and their role, the way they inflect and control what they say, can make the client feel safe or stable [or the opposite]. – Clinical social worker. (Bancroft *et al.*, 2016a)

Survivors of major trauma navigate unfamiliar complex service systems that often seem bewildering and bizarre. At each stage, the survivor might need to retell the story – many times. During each telling, he/she can relive the crime or horrific event. Simply telling the story often triggers the same emotions experienced during the event itself, such as helplessness, shame, terror, guilt or anguish. An initial trauma can be aggravated over and over as crime victims move through the legal and social service system that was designed to help them.

The risk for interpreters of retraumatising the survivor unintentionally throughout this process cannot be overstated. Common examples that trauma-informed providers have mentioned (Bancroft *et al.*, in press) include interpreters who touch or hug survivors; show judgment in their face or body language; explain concepts like domestic violence (in one case, an interpreter gave a 40-minute lecture on this topic to a patient hospitalised for her injuries, in Mandarin, in front of a puzzled clinical social worker); or telling the survivor things like 'everything will be all right', 'don't cry' or 'tell the therapist about that nightmare you told the attorney'. Many more examples will be explored here.

Needs Assessment for Two US TII Programmes

Background on healing voices and breaking silence

Until recently, few short training programmes for TII existed in North America, and they typically have taken place at conferences for PSI such as Critical Link, refugee resettlement programmes or community (two-year) colleges with interpreting certificate programmes. Typically only a half-day or shorter, such programmes in the author's anecdotal observations of either attending them, speaking to their creators or viewing slide presentations of these sessions, have focused on VT for the interpreter and not the impact of interpreting on the survivor. Anecdotally, these short sessions also appear somewhat more commonly offered for sign language than for spoken language interpreters.

This section explores the needs assessment for and piloting of two training programmes of five and four days, respectively. The lessons learned from both programmes are critical. The two programmes are most easily distinguished by their titles, *Healing Voices* and *Breaking Silence*:

• *Healing Voices: Interpreting for Survivors of Torture, War Trauma and Sexual Violence*, a five-day training programme, was developed by a registered charity in the United States called The Voice of Love (Bancroft *et al.*, in press), founded and directed by the author of this chapter. The programme, developed entirely by a national corps of specialist volunteers, focuses on refugee interpreting. Authors of this programme included a psychiatrist and a PhD psychologist running torture treatment programmes; a PhD professor of clinical social work; a licensed clinical social worker and medical interpreter trainer; legal, medical and mental health interpreters; several national interpreting curriculum specialists; an authority on remote interpreting; two attorneys directing a legal interpreter service.

- *Breaking Silence: Interpreting for Victim Services* is a four-day training programme about how to interpret for victims of any violent crime. Commissioned by the Office of Victim Services of Washington, DC, it was developed on contract for Ayuda, a registered charity in Washington, DC, by a training agency directed by the author of this chapter. The four US authors of the training manual and workbook (Bancroft *et al.*, 2016a, 2016b) included a lawyer who is a national legal interpreting specialist and three national interpreting curriculum specialists with expertise in gender-based violence and legal, medical, community and mental health interpreting.

Both programmes focus more on spoken language interpreting. However, one of them, *Breaking Silence*, has been piloted with a number of sign language interpreters, including certified deaf interpreters; it was also reviewed by a sign language interpreter and trainer who is a licensed trauma-informed therapist and who provided input for revisions. Both programmes are based on clinical research introduced to interpreter trainers by TIC clinicians and national and local collaboration with refugee mental health services, torture treatment programmes and victim service networks.

The 300+ page training manuals for each of these programmes, are unique. While other training programmes in various countries address interpreting in specialised areas for victims of crime, such as interpreting for victims of gender-based violence (e.g. Toledano Buendía & Del Pozo Triviño, 2015), these two programmes specifically focus on training techniques for TII to support trauma survivors, TIS service providers and interpreters themselves as they all navigate the survivor's journey to recovery.

The needs assessment carried out for these programmes was somewhat extensive but not a formal study. For *Healing Voices*, however, data results from surveys and focus groups were formally collated and analysed by a specialist at Common Sense Advisory (the leading US market research firm for language services) in collaboration with the project's clinical researchers, interpreters and interpreter instructors and trainers in both academic and private settings, all project volunteers. Their work resulted in a detailed, published report (Bambarén-Call *et al.*, 2012) and a training manual (Bancroft *et al.*, in press).

For *Breaking Silence*, the needs assessment informed both a training manual and a workbook of role plays and exercises (Bancroft *et al.*, 2016a & b) but data results were not collated or reported on. The data from both needs assessment processes were used to shape their respective programme curricula and have to some degree influenced each other though they address somewhat different audiences (refugee interpreting vs. interpreting for victims of violent crime).

The *Healing Voices* needs assessment focused on three key areas: torture treatment services, mental health services and refugee resettlement. In 2011, 15 focus groups were held in 10 cities across the country for providers (seven groups), interpreters (six groups) and survivors (two groups) in these services. In addition, two national cross-sectional electronic surveys for interpreters and service providers on the three areas mentioned above were made accessible on the internet and distributed through social and professional networks via listservs, e-newsletters, electronic mail blasts and communications from interpreter associations and refugee resettlement organisations. In all, 75 service providers completed a 27-question survey, and 169 interpreters responded to 44-question surveys. Many questions in each were open-ended, yielding strikingly rich qualitative data.

The needs assessment for *Breaking Silence*, in addition to a literature review, involved a focus group held for victim service providers in Washington, DC and 20 detailed one- to two-hour phone interviews conducted by the author of this chapter based on questions developed collaboratively with the support of non-profit and government agencies in the Washington, DC Victim Assistance Network (VAN). The project was supported with funding by the DC Office of Victim Services. The interviews were conducted with 20 VAN service providers, including executive directors of registered charities, lawyers, professional advocates (social workers), clinicians such as clinical social workers and therapists, two interpreters, a sexual assault nurse examiner, a director of disaster behavioural health services, a lieutenant fire chief, a police commander/language access coordinator, a manager for fire and emergency medical services and a domestic violence hotline counsellor.

Needs assessment highlights from the findings

Unless otherwise stated, the information discussed is taken from the *Healing Voices* surveys and focus groups, and quotations or information from the *Breaking Silence* interviews in this section are taken from Bancroft *et al.* (2016a).

About three-quarters of the respondents to the interpreter survey had at least 40 hours of formal training in interpreting (considered a minimum threshold for PSI training in the United States). Almost 40% had more than 10 years' experience as interpreters and the majority (92.2%) had completed a university degree while 29.5% held one or more graduate degrees. The majority of the providers surveyed (60.8%) worked often or primarily with survivors who needed interpreters of various languages (the providers named more than 50 languages). Nearly half (44%) worked with interpreters primarily in mental health services, one quarter (25%) in legal and court services and the remainder in medical services, social services, hotlines and other services.

A few survey and focus group highlights from the *Healing Voices* needs assessment are organised below under the rubrics of commonly accepted or discussed ethical principles for interpreters because this chapter is concerned with the ethical implications of the data. Note that these are only a few examples culled from a report of 74 pages (Bambarén-Call *et al.*, 2012). Also, it is important to note that various ethical codes for interpreters around the world have sharply divergent requirements related to such principles, canons or concepts as professionalism, cultural mediation, role boundaries and advocacy. A discussion of these issues exceeds the scope of this chapter; for an environmental scan of ethical requirements for interpreters around the world in six different specialisations of interpreting, see Bancroft (2005).

Accuracy

> [Interpreters] help me keep the client emotionally safe in the interview and help both myself and the client convey the information we mean, not just what we say. (Bancroft, 2005: 30)
>
> Not saying exactly what we as clinicians say is highly frustrating because we have a method that is vital to the therapeutic process. (Bancroft, 2005: 25)

Accuracy appeared to be one of the single greatest concerns that emerged, together with impartiality, in all phases of the needs assessment. Nearly three-quarters (73.8%) of interpreters surveyed said that they always interpreted in direct speech (first person), but only about half adopted the tone of voice of the speaker. Only 64.1% maintained the linguistic register of the provider and only 57.8% did so when interpreting for the patient or service user. Responses such as these leave open some serious questions about interpreter accuracy in TIS.

Providers, unfortunately, confirmed the concern. In many instances in the *Healing Voices* surveys and focus groups and also the *Breaking Silence* interviews and its focus group, providers recounted stories of interpreters who failed to be accurate or complete, such as one interpreter who refused to interpret a segment of a survivor's message, telling the therapist, 'You don't want to know' and others who could not interpret a message because they were crying. Yet, TII providers were adamant that they required accuracy of their interpreters because otherwise they could not do their work effectively. Many also wanted more: for example, they wanted interpreters to report when a lack of linguistic or conceptual equivalence caused a difficulty.

One clinical social worker interviewed for *Breaking Silence* reported the need for interpreters to mirror the survivor's language and not be 'victim-blaming or make them feel like they're being judged or watched. All these areas are so sensitive – it is very important to be very mindful of your word choice and the things you're saying'. The director of a domestic violence centre agreed, stating, 'Sometimes if an interpreter isn't well versed in the terms that they use, then the terms I would want them to use can cause problems. Like the term *survivor*, if they [interpret it as] the term *victim*. I am using very specific language, because in the criminal cases it's a legal term of art, so I have to make a distinction. If I call them one thing and [the interpreters] don't, that can be a bit of a challenge'. A Burmese refugee and interpreter suggested that accuracy is impaired by lack of impartiality: 'Some interpreters don't want to embarrass either the provider or the client. So they go soft on some of the things that come out. They don't want to say [it] the way it is'.

Certainly, providers did not want interpreters seeking clarification directly from the survivors. A sexual assault nurse examiner interviewed for *Breaking Silence* reported, 'I see interpreters really trying to clarify, and this is certainly difficult when you have patients either with limited understanding or psychiatric or mental disabilities, where interpreters try to clarify on their own as opposed to engaging the provider to help with clarification if the [survivor's] answer doesn't seem to make sense'. In another example from an interview for *Breaking Silence*, a sexual assault advocate reported:

> In situations of crisis, if the survivor hasn't had time to construct their own narrative... I feel like a lot of interpreters are helping out in the construction of the narrative [and sometimes it's conscious and sometimes it's not but] they are trying to make the story linear and understandable and therefore kind of constructing a narrative for that person.

Even in situations of danger, rather than accurately interpreting, the interpreter might choose to interfere. A hotline counsellor interviewed for *Breaking Silence* reported that she was urgently trying to get a domestic violence victim in active danger to phone the police, even as the abuser was banging violently on the door where the victim was locked up. Yet, the telephone interpreter instead spent three minutes asking the victim questions, even though the hotline counsellor kept interrupting to explain the danger.

Impartiality

> Mental health patients are sometimes all over the place, so it's hard to sequence things or make sense of them. Sometimes what they say is not what they really mean and it's difficult not to 'give advice' to the provider. If the provider doesn't get it then there's lots of intervention going and it could get confusing. I feel that establishing a good rapport with the provider really helps. – An interpreter (Bambarén-Call et al., 2012: 23)
>
> It's good that we all have compassion for each other, but the ability to separate oneself is very important. Otherwise the translation can be clouded and inaccurate. – Former interpreter, director of a domestic violence centre (Bancroft et al., 2016a)

When asked if they would give their opinion or advice to torture survivors, only 7% of interpreters surveyed said that they would provide advice, answer a survivor's question or provide other options. Yet, when asked the same question about service providers, nearly one third (31%) said that they would share their advice or opinion with the provider, which is usually considered an ethical violation.

The chief problems related to impartiality that providers reported in focus groups (apart from interpreters being emotionally affected, which is discussed below) were problems related to interpreters who knew the survivors, accepted gifts, gave rides to clients, passed judgment due to religious beliefs or had difficulty interpreting certain issues. For example, a male interpreter giggled while interpreting a woman's story of sexual violence, and many were so ill at ease when silence fell that they shuffled papers, moved their feet, cleared their throat or tried to get the provider's attention. Unlike TIC clinicians, the interpreters had not been trained to 'sit with silence' and found it uncomfortable.

Interviews for *Breaking Silence* confirmed all these examples, including the problems of men interpreting for female rape survivors. In addition, providers reported their concerns that interpreters who worked with lesbian, gay, bisexual or transgender (LGBT) trauma survivors too often displayed negative facial expressions and body language, particularly older interpreters, while other interpreters struggled with cultural issues related to prevalent norms in their local communities (such as elders advising women to stay with their abusers). Some interpreters in fact told abused women to stay with the husband or leave the husband, which greatly upset the providers. One provider reported that an Amharic interpreter deliberately added information to show that the woman had a history of several male partners with a tone of voice and body language suggesting he judged her for that history, which upset the provider.

Finally, in a *Breaking Silence* interview a disaster behavioural health specialist reported that he thought interpreters 'tend not to be prepared for their own emotional involvement and they are not necessarily prepared for the impact and how long it's going to stay with them after the event'.

Cultural mediation/cultural brokering (a disputed ethical topic)

Despite the fact that many and perhaps most codes of ethical conduct for interpreters do not condone cultural mediation (cf. Bancroft, 2005), cultural issues emerged repeatedly in the needs assessment for both programmes. For example, nearly half (49.6%) of the interpreters surveyed had experienced cultural conflicts in their interpreting work, but only about a third (32.6%) reported observing such conflicts in mental health settings.

Cultural issues were a cause of great concern in the interpreter focus groups as well. Here, interpreters often expressed frustration over cultural barriers: for example, cultural taboos can make it hard for interpreters to interpret certain questions about past sexual partners or sexual assault. The interpreters wanted some leeway to provide cultural input to get past cultural misunderstandings whether or not their ethical requirements permitted such action.

The interpreters also noted that body language and communication styles vary by culture and that providers often fail to see the need for certain kinds of pleasantries and conversation to establish rapport and build trust. Gender and age roles were another cultural concern (e.g. a young interpreter interpreting sensitive information like sexual violence for an elder, or men interpreting for female survivors and vice versa). Interpreters were very concerned about the lack of conceptual or linguistic equivalence for many terms or concepts emerging in TIS. (If the reader is bilingual, imagine the cultural–linguistic challenges of interpreting terms like 'flashback', post-traumatic stress disorder or 'feeling blue' into another language.)

Also, 65.1% of providers surveyed said that they had noticed cultural barriers during interpreted sessions, a much higher percentage than interpreters reported. They noted, for example, that some interpreters refused to interpret sexual content, while some survivors wanted only interpreters of the same gender for cultural or religious reasons. Yet, providers felt that at times they needed cultural guidance from the interpreters. A participant from Africa in *Healing Voices* was unable to engage in role plays describing sexual violence or abuse with a female American because, though he appeared young and modern, it felt culturally taboo or at least unendurably uncomfortable for him to engage in role plays of this kind with a woman.

Professionalism and role boundaries

Interpreters in the focus groups expressed a keen desire for providers to understand their role (e.g. not address remarks to interpreters during the sessions that providers didn't want interpreted) and to treat interpreters as a member of the care team. It can of course be difficult for interpreters to maintain their boundaries if a survivor gets angry, shouts or gets violent, and interpreters reported feeling the need for guidance from providers in such situations. Interpreters also felt that a post-session in such cases was critical to guide interpreters – even essential.

In all areas of need assessment, issues of professional boundaries emerged, including examples of interpreters interjecting with highly inappropriate comments to the provider such as, 'I think she is lying' or 'Is that the best you can do?' Too often, untrained or under-trained interpreters, as one provider reported, begin to take on themselves the responsibility of directing the session (Bambarén-Call, 2012: 34). The issue of role boundaries will be revisited below.

Vicarious trauma

A significant finding was the degree to which interpreters often suffer in this field. Nearly three-quarters (73%) of surveyed interpreters stated that they had been emotionally impacted by interpreting for survivors, a situation which self-evidently affects their impartiality. To some degree, they appeared to be reporting secondary trauma. In efforts to cope, the interpreters surveyed reported trying to remain calm (26%), crying during or outside the session (13%), processing their feelings through meditation, prayer or positive thinking (12%) or seeking counselling (5%).

Interpreters for *Breaking Silence* also wanted providers to be more sensitive to the need to provide them with breaks. Of particular note: more than half the surveyed providers (59.4%) reported having observed interpreters struggling emotionally with the content of the session, and nearly all the focus group providers reported the same.

VT in interpreters is discussed below. However, here are a few examples that emerged and cut across the various modalities of needs assessment, including published reports and articles (e.g. Lor, 2012). Interpreters reported getting dizzy, nauseated or fearful after sessions with survivors. They had nightmares or disturbed sleep. Their concentration was disrupted during interpreting. They had difficulty getting certain stories or images out of their head. After a session, they might shake or tremble. Most distressing of all was the degree to which a number of interpreters simply burned out.

The Development of Two Training Programmes for TII

Both the *Healing Voices* and *Breaking Silence* programmes were designed and implemented as non-language-specific programmes welcoming interpreters of all language pairs due to the urgent need for and the lack of language-specific resources. In particular, *Healing Voices* targets interpreting for refugees, a field that involves hundreds of languages.

Healing Voices was created by an all-volunteer national group of authors. Each chapter in its training manual corresponded to a half-day module. One author was assigned as 'lead' author for that chapter and recruited other authors to assist as needed. The first three chapters were written by clinicians who sought to inform the interpreters about trauma, torture and war trauma, how to manage their emotional responses and how to prevent VT. These authors, all torture treatment specialists, included a psychiatrist, a PhD licensed clinical social worker who is also a professor of social work and refugee mental health, and a PhD psychologist, with input from a licensed clinical social worker who is also a medical interpreter and interpreter trainer. Three of these authors have directed or worked with torture treatment programmes.

Breaking Silence was created by four contract authors, national interpreting specialists (including this author) with input from two trauma-informed therapists. It included a separate workbook and a victim services glossary for interpreters. These materials will all be made available in the public domain in 2016[1].

Based on the needs assessment, both programmes also required that candidates have prior basic training (at least 40 hours) in PSI. Candidates received advisories that the programme activities and materials contained potentially distressing content and that interpreters with prior histories of trauma might be affected. The curricula, role plays, activities, exercises and other training materials, including the training manual, focused on all the lessons learned from needs assessment, applying the expertise of the many authors and specialists who contributed to the creation of each programme. Both programmes include a large number of specific, helpful techniques reported by interpreters and providers in the needs assessment and in many cases by pilot participants during the pilot sessions. Finally, both programmes targeted spoken language interpreters primarily although, as mentioned earlier, *Breaking Silence* is also intended for sign language interpreters.

Teaching communicative autonomy and self-care

Of all the challenges that emerged, both in the planning and execution of the two programmes, the two greatest challenges proved to be (a) building an understanding in interpreters of the impact of trauma and the concomitant importance of supporting communicative autonomy for survivors; and (b) helping interpreters protect themselves from secondary trauma – *even during the training itself* (in the case of *Healing Voices*, as this problem had a smaller impact in *Breaking Silence* – perhaps because the refugee interpreting programme included even more intense and disturbing material).

While the reports on the two programmes offered here are informal, they are based on the experience of several trainers in addition to written comments by authors who observed the various modules; two oral feedback sessions with participants conducted after two *Healing Voices* pilots; informal phone interviews with three interpreters after they had completed *Breaking Silence* and the written programme evaluations for both programmes. Altogether *Healing Voices* has had five pilot sessions and *Breaking Silence* has had two so far.

Communicative autonomy

Tackling the first issue, communicative autonomy, proved especially challenging in training because both around the world and within the United States there has historically been little agreement about the role of the interpreter in PSI, and specifically the two ends of the continuum of the interpreter's role: restricting one's activities to interpreting vs. intervening during the session, often perceived by the interpreter as 'helping' the service user or promoting a beneficial outcome. The problem exposed in needs assessment had to be tackled on the ground.

If the concept of communicative autonomy for interpreters (Bancroft *et al.*, 2015: viii), mentioned earlier, is *the capacity to be in control of, and responsible for, one's own communication*, this concept is not well conveyed – as the *Healing Voices* first pilot showed – through lecture, slides and explanations. On the contrary: the interpreters needed to grasp the vital importance of survivor autonomy through a multimedia approach. There was some 'hit-and-miss' as each of the pilot trainers, who were all programme authors, found helpful teaching strategies.

Service providers in TIS are particularly sensitive to issues of power and control. However, few interpreters pause to consider that the interpreter holds real power over the message, including the power to retrigger trauma, because he/she *controls the message and the flow of communication*. What thus emerged as the single most valuable tool for both programmes proved to be heuristic activities and in particular demonstration role plays (by instructors working with each other and with volunteer students). These role plays were powerful because they dramatised ethical conflicts and challenges and showed the impact of trauma on survivors and/or interpreter decisions. Other critically effective tools that showed the interpreters how to adapt their professional ethics to TII 'on the ground' were:

- Realistic role plays for interpreters to practice in same-language triads (provider, survivor, interpreter), developed by or in collaboration with TIS service providers.

- Specific techniques for interpreting for trauma survivors (examples are discussed below).
- Practice in various relaxation techniques.
- Film vignettes showing survivors and their trauma.
- Case studies and real-life scenarios.
- Discussion.
- Hands-on heuristic activities.

These multi-pronged teaching strategies proved effective because trainers were seeking to change interpreter behaviours to promote the communicative autonomy of survivors and providers, which required 'buy-in' from the interpreters. Control has been taken away from victims of crime. One goal of TII providers is restoring the survivor's ability to impact the world. Thus, the interpreter who gets involved, gives advice or explains cultural issues out of an emotional desire to 'help out' is in fact taking control of that victim's life at a vulnerable moment. Telling the interpreter not to do so doesn't appear to work, as ample anecdotal evidence attests. Involving interpreters in heuristic activities designed to instil in them a deeper understanding of the issues at stake (including having interpreters play survivors in role plays) had more impact.

As a result, graduates of both programmes were motivated to avoid acting as a filter and instead support clear communication where all parties have the power and authority to make their own decisions without interference by the interpreter. In reality, not all graduates did so in the field after training; ideally, funding would have allowed a rigorous follow-up of programme graduates, but no funding was found. Anecdotally, the greatest resistance appears to be coming from older refugee interpreters and might be culturally rooted and/or rooted in long-standing habits.

Examples of areas of resistance that emerged during the pilots and afterwards included these: If you interpret for a survivor who breaks out weeping, why can't you touch or hug that survivor? Or offer a tissue? Or say words of encouragement? Why can't you stay alone with the survivor after the session to offer support or engage in casual conversation to build rapport and trust? How do you avoid crying if the survivor *and* the therapist are crying? If the survivor takes *your* hand, isn't it okay to squeeze their hand back and be supportive? Yet these are all acts that would not only potentially undermine the work of providers and impede recovery but also violate the interpreter's ethical requirements.

Alternatively, if you are listening to atrocities and find it impossible not to visualise them, how can you focus on interpreting accurately without crying or changing the message? Questions like these, raised from the data and supported during the pilot sessions, had to be answered by the development and refinement of helpful teaching techniques, resulting in two rich training curricula grounded in reality.

Examples of specific techniques taught in one or both programmes that helped interpreters to support communicative autonomy included:

- How to progressively and gently disengage if a survivor touches the interpreter (a technique developed by a psychiatrist, demonstrated in class, then practiced by participants in a role play).
- The importance of establishing a friendly introduction with a smile, a kind voice and a warm affect.
- Avoiding eye contact while interpreting to support the development of a relationship between the provider and survivor.
- How to avoid tears (strategies included deep breathing, visualisation, relaxation and other techniques that also help to prevent VT, discussed in the next section).
- Following cues at all times from the TIS provider.
- Intervening first with the provider before reporting an intervention to the client so that the provider could rephrase anything the interpreter stated that could inadvertently trigger or retraumatise the survivor if interpreted 'as is'.

Vicarious Trauma in Interpreters

Teaching interpreters to avoid developing VT proved to be one of the greatest challenges for both curricula. To address how the training programmes tackled the challenge, it is important to examine the problem of VT itself as it affects interpreters. First, it was not apparently recognised or observed prior to conducting these pilot sessions that interpreting traumatic content can be *more* stressful and traumatic for interpreters than for many service providers. The problem is a simple one. Each time an interpreter interprets traumatic content, he/she engages in the following process:

(1) The interpreter *listens* carefully, because active listening is essential to interpret accurately.
(2) The interpreter *extracts meaning* from the message, using a complex set of cognitive skills that require intense focus and higher-level reasoning.
(3) The interpreter *creates an equivalent conceptual meaning* in the target language, selecting among various possible options, which can be difficult across unrelated languages.
(4) The interpreter *delivers* the message into the target language, respecting the source-language register, tone and spirit.

If the interpreter is interpreting from notes, that process might even constitute a fifth step. In short, the interpreter is the only person present who will cognitively process the traumatic content at least four times. Furthermore, the interpreter is trained to perform this feat in first person, which can enhance the traumatic impact on the interpreter. Anecdotally, several therapists, including three clinician-authors of the *Healing Voices* training manual, have reported observing interpreters instinctively switch to third person at intense moments, presumably to protect themselves from the risk of secondary trauma.

If even babies as young as 18 hours old show distress when they hear another baby crying (McDonald & Messinger, 2011), imagine the impact that interpreting the graphic details of rape, torture or witnessing several family members killed could have on a sensitive interpreter. Language is a critical component of our experience: 'to imbue words with meaning requires a fusion between the sound of words and the shared meaning of the experience of action' (Gallese, 2007: 13).

What is striking about *Healing Voices* was the ability of authors and trainers to observe secondary trauma *as it happened during the training*. For example, the first morning of the first session, a psychiatrist author/trainer observed and reported that while another trainer taught about torture, a refugee participant from Africa exhibited clinical symptoms of dissociating, including glazed eyes and changes in body language.

Also, a documentary about rape as a weapon of war in Africa triggered in several interpreters – not refugee interpreters but women who had been sexually assaulted in the United States – traumatic reactions such as tears, intrusive memories, distress and the need to take an hour or two away from the session (although all participants returned), necessitating the active intervention of clinician trainers at times. By the fourth day of *Healing Voices*, typically in the afternoon after the aforementioned documentary was shown, a cathartic effect was observed that resulted in a powerful closing for the programme the next day.

Symptoms of VT

> You know the stories are really painful. It happened to me a few weeks ago, I heard something, my brain just could not take it. I came back and I talked with my friend who is working with me and cried then because it is hard.... I have another problem, I cannot wake up. I sleep very well and I just cannot wake up. These last few months when I started working so hard and I do not know, I am not taking therapy but I think I should.... I cry much more easily than before. (Refugee interpreter in Miller *et al.*, 2005: 35–36)

The terms secondary or vicarious trauma refer to the experience of trauma-related stress caused by working closely with trauma survivors and experiencing some of their symptoms (Stamm & Figley, 2009). As Harvey (2001, n.p.) reports, '[t]here is a cost to caring, particularly for those who have the capacity for compassion and empathy'.

Empathy is the ability to feel or imagine the emotional experience of someone else. For both providers and interpreters, however, empathy is a two-edged sword for the interpreter. On the one hand, being empathetic can enhance sensitivity and warmth in providers and accuracy and compassion in interpreters. On the other, it can also lead to VT. Interpreters, like trauma-informed service providers, need to control their empathy. Controlled empathy allows both service providers and interpreters to hear disturbing stories and show warmth without revealing inner distress.

> As the listener hears the revolting story, he or she begins to visualize it in the mind as if it is actually happening. The brain is struggling with another's upset. In this process, called controlled empathy, the helper has to rev up his or her internal resources to remain calm... the helper has to hold back because he or she needs to remain controlled. Imagine yourself setting a top spinning and then, needing to immediately interrupt its gyrations. It's like going against a force of nature. (Izzo & Miller, 2010: 11)

Certain 'red flags' or signs that suggest a service provider or interpreter might be experiencing VT include intrusive or distressing thoughts, anxiety, depression, insomnia and fears for one's own safety (e.g. fear of parking lots or dark places) or the safety of loved ones.

Vicarious resilience

Vicarious resilience is a new concept (Hernandez et al., 2010), the flip side of the coin of VT. Post-traumatic growth (PTG) involves positive changes in someone who has experienced trauma, such as a greater sense of strength, closer relationships and a new appreciation of life and/or spiritual growth. It is therefore delightful to note that PTG has even been documented in interpreters who work with trauma survivors (Splevins et al., 2010).

Overview of specialised techniques for preventing VT

Specific techniques developed for the *Healing Voices* and *Breaking Silence* programmes were divided into two categories: general wellness practices, which are important for all of us, and more specific techniques for use by interpreters. In *Breaking Silence*, such techniques were broken down into three categories for use or consideration before the encounter, during the encounter and after the encounter.

In both programmes, participants engaged in an exercise to write a wellness or self-care plan with specific and not general (vague) objectives. The *Healing Voices* plan focused on objectives that addressed specified behaviours (such as *walking*), performance criteria (such as walking *two days a week for 15 minutes*) and conditions (such as walking two days a week for 15 minutes *in the park*). The *Breaking Silence* self-care plan addressed SMART objectives, that is, objectives that are specific, measurable, appropriate action, realistic and time-bound. A wellness plan supports resilience, and often focuses on 'the big four' of health and wellness:

* Adequate sleep.
* Eating well.
* Exercise and activity.
* Relaxation (for example breathing exercises, meditation, yoga or prayer).

It was found in *Healing Voices* that the material itself was so intense because it focused heavily on torture and war trauma that relaxation exercises needed to be demonstrated and practised every day, not only during the self-care module (taught on the second day). Examples of such exercises led by clinician trainers included progressive relaxation, various breathing techniques, mindful eating and walking mediation.

Preventing or Reducing VT Before, During and After the Encounter

Examples of more specific techniques from *Breaking Silence* geared towards the interpreter encounter include the following.

Before the encounter

Preparing professionally to interpret for a trauma survivor can reduce surprise and stress during the encounter, enhance accuracy, help the interpreter to stay 'in role' and prevent or at least reduce potential VT. Such preparation could involve, for example, practicing interpreting emotionally sensitive terms and phrases with a partner (which took place during the programme) or facing a mirror; prearranging a potential 'interpreter distress signal' with the provider so that the provider can call for a break without the interpreter disrupting the session; setting boundaries, e.g. by carrying a special object to the appointment, or putting on an elastic band before the encounter that can be snapped to reground oneself when interpreting traumatic material (though not for sign language interpreters) or reciting a prayer or mantra before the session. In particular, interpreters were taught specific relaxation and breathing techniques to practice prior to such sessions to help reduce stress and potential VT.

During the encounter

Techniques taught to interpreters to help them during the encounter included grounding (bringing oneself back to the 'here and now'); breathing from the diaphragm (because stress often causes one to breathe from the throat, which can increase anxiety and strain the voice); strategies to help avoid visualising traumatic content; self-calming strategies such as switching briefly as needed from third to first person (from direct to indirect speech); and focusing on taking notes. Interpreters were also taught how to 'sit with silence' and appropriate ways to ask for a break and what to do during a break to be able to successfully return to the session.

After the encounter

Techniques for use after the encounter including asking for a debriefing with the provider, if feasible, engaging in self-care and consulting one's written wellness or self-care plan. Trainers emphasised the power and importance for distressed interpreters of seeking out their social supports. Interpreters discussed what could be shared about such sessions without violating confidentiality to reduce the emotional impact on interpreters: for example, they could share their feelings. Boundary rituals were suggested to help avoid intrusive thoughts after the encounter. Interpreters were also urged to consider taking the rest of the day off after a deeply distressing encounter and, if symptoms of VT emerged, consulting a therapist.

Conclusion: TII May Lead to 'Compassion Satisfaction'

This chapter examined the emerging specialisation of TII, with a particular focus on needs assessments conducted for two TII programmes and the development and delivery of those programmes. Interpreters from across the United States appeared to be very hungry and deeply grateful for this in-depth training. The sessions were all intense: indeed, *Healing Voices*, due to the particular arc of its curriculum, the focus on refugee interpreting and the involvement of seasoned clinicians, resulted in the most intense interpreter training sessions ever observed by this author. Yet, they culminated each time on a note of optimism and sometimes joy.

The work of interpreting for trauma survivors sounds sad, yet it often generates intense satisfaction. It can enrich the personal and professional lives of interpreters. Assuming adequate self-care, interpreters can even experience 'compassion satisfaction' – the happiness that comes from helping others. That feeling for interpreters is sometimes called 'interpreter's high' and it is the feeling that one has made a meaningful difference in the lives of others. With proper training, support and practice, trauma-informed interpreters can grow and thrive in this arena of service.

Notes

(1) These materials can be downloaded free of charge at http://ayuda.com/wp/get-help/language-services/resources/.

References

Bambarén-Call, A., Bancroft, M.A., Goodfriend-Koven, N., Hanscom, K., Kelly, N., Lewis, V., Roat, C., Robinson, L. and Rubio-Fitzpatrick, L. (2012) *Interpreting Compassion: A Needs Assessment Report on Interpreting for Survivors of Torture, War Trauma and Sexual Violence*. Columbia, MD: The Voice of Love. See www.voice-of-love.org (accessed 7 November 2016).

Bancroft, M. (2005) *The Interpreter's World Tour: An Environmental Scan of Standards of Practice for Interpreters*. Menlo Park, CA: California Endowment.

Bancroft, M.A., Beyaert García, S., Allen, K., Carriero-Contreras, G. and Socarrás-Estrada, D. (2015) *The Community Interpreter®: An International Textbook*. Columbia, MD: Culture and Language Press.

Bancroft, M.A., Bambarén-Call, A., Berthold, S.M., Chevalier, A., Goodfriend-Koven, N., Green, C., Hanscom, K., Kelly, N., Piwowarczyk, L., Roat, C. and Robinson, L. (in press) *Healing Voices: Interpreting for Survivors of Torture, War Trauma and Sexual Violence*. Toronto: MCIS.

Bancroft, M.A., Allen, K., Feuerle, L. and Green, C. (2016a) *Breaking Silence: Interpreting for Victim Services*. Washington, DC: Ayuda.

Bancroft, M.A., Allen, K., Feuerle, L. and Green, C. (2016b) *Breaking Silence: Interpreting for Victim Services – A Workbook of Role Plays and Exercises*. Washington, DC: Ayuda.

Burstow, B. (2003) Toward a radical understanding of trauma and trauma work. *Violence Against Women* 9, 1293–1317.

Elliott, D.E., Bjelajac, P., Fallot, R.D., Markoff, L.S. and Reed, B.G. (2005) Trauma-informed or trauma-denied: Principles and implementation of trauma-informed services for women. *Journal of Community Psychology* 33, 461–477.

Gallese, V. (2007) Mirror neurons and the social nature of language: The neural exploitation hypothesis. *Social Neuroscience* 2 (2), 1–17.

Harvey, M.A. (2001) The Hazards of Empathy: Vicarious Trauma of Interpreters for the Deaf. See http://www.michaelharvey-phd.com/pages/hazards.htm.

Harvey, M.R. (1996) An ecological view of psychological trauma and trauma recovery. *Journal of Traumatic Stress* 9, 3–23 (accessed 7 November 2016).

Herman, J. (1992, 1997, 2015) *Trauma and Recovery: The Aftermath of Violence—From Domestic Abuse to Political Terror*. New York: Basic Books.

Hodas, G.R. (2006) *Responding to Childhood Trauma: The Promise and Practice of Trauma Informed Care*. Philadelphia, PA: Pennsylvania Office of Mental Health and Substance Abuse Services. See http://www.echoparenting.org/wp-content/uploads/2012/05/promise_and_practice_of_ti_services_by_hodas.pdf (accessed 7 November 2016).

Hopper, E.K., Bassuk, E.L. and Olivet, J. (2010) Shelter from the storm: Trauma-informed care in homelessness services settings. *The Open Health Services and Policy Journal* 3, 80–100.

ISO (2014) *ISO 13611 Interpreting: Guidelines for Community Interpreting*. Geneva: International Organisation for Standardisation.

Izzo, E. and Miller, V.C. (2010) *Shock: Surviving and Overcoming Vicarious Trauma*. Scottsdale, AZ: HCI Press.

Ko, S.J., Ford, J.D., Kassam-Adams, N., Berkowitz, S.J., Wilson, C., Wong, M., Brymer, M.J. and Layne, C.M. (2008) Creating trauma-informed systems: Child welfare, education, first responders, health care, juvenile justice. *Professional Psychology: Research and Practice* 39 (4), 396–404.

Lor, M. (2012) Effects of client trauma on interpreters: An exploratory study of vicarious trauma. Master of Social Work Clinical Research Papers, Paper 53.

Macdonald, J.L. (2015) Vicarious trauma as applied to the professional sign language interpreter. *Montview Liberty University Journal of Undergraduate Research* 1 (1), Article 6. See http://digitalcommons.liberty.edu/montview/vol1/iss1/6 (accessed 7 November 2016).

McDonald, N.M. and Messinger, D.S. (2011) The development of empathy: How, when, and why. In A. Acerbi, J.A. Lombo and J.J. Sanguineti (eds) *Free Will, Emotions, and Moral Actions: Philosophy and Neuroscience in Dialogue* (pp. 330–360). IF-Press.

Miller, K.E., Martell, Z.L., Pazdirek, L., Caruth, M. and Lopez, D. (2005) The role of interpreters in psychotherapy with refugees: An exploratory study. *American Journal of Orthopsychiatry* 75, 27–39.

Morrissey, J.P., Jackson, E.W., Ellis, A.R., Amaro, H. and Brown, V.B. (2005) Twelve-month outcomes of trauma-informed interventions for women with co-occurring disorders. *Psychiatric Services* 56 (10), 1213–1222.

President's Interagency Task Force [United States] (2013) *Coordination, Collaboration, Capacity: Federal Strategic Action Plan on Services for Victims of Human Trafficking in the United States 2013–2017*. Washington, DC: US White House.

SAMHSA (2012) *SAMHSA's Working Definition of Trauma and Principles and Guidance for a Trauma-informed Approach* [Draft]. Rockville, MD: US Department of Health and Human Services, Substance Abuse and Mental Health Services Administration (SAMHSA).

Splevins, K.A., Cohen, K., Joseph, S., Murray, C. and Bowley, J. (2010) Vicarious posttraumatic growth among interpreters. *Qualitative Health Research* 22, 250–262.

Stamm, B.H. and Figley, C.R. (2009) Advances in the Theory of Compassion Satisfaction and Fatigue and its measurement with the ProQOL 5. International Society for Traumatic Stress Studies annual conference (November). Atlanta, GA.

Toledano Buendía, C. and Del Pozo Triviño, M. (eds) (2015) *Interpretación en contextos de violencia de género*. Valencia: Tirant Lo Blanch.

United Nations (1985) *Declaration of Basic Principles of Justice for Victims of Crime and Abuse of Power* A/RES/40/34. See http://www.un.org/documents/ga/res/40/a40r034.htm (accessed 7 November 2016).

United Nations (2015) *International Migration, 2015*. Migration Wall Chart. Geneva: UN Department of Economic and Social Affairs, Population Division. See http://www.un.org/en/development/desa/population/migration/publications/wallchart/docs/MigrationWallChart2015.pdf (accessed 7 November 2016).

van der Kolk, B. (2015) *The Body Keeps Score: Brain, Mind and Body in the Healing of Trauma*. New York: Penguin Books.

Young, M. and Stein, J. (2004) *The History of the Crime Victims' Movement in the United States: A Component of the Office for Victims of Crime Oral History Project*. Washington, DC: National Organisation for Victim Assistance.

Index

locals, recruitment of 16–18 *see also*
    autonomous vs heteronomous
    interpreting systems; casual/ ad-hoc
    interpreters
longitudinal studies, need for 59, 74–5, 91
Lor, M. 199, 209
low pay 26, 69, 72–4, 158
low status of professional interpreting
    26–7, 31, 70, 74–6, 126
Loyal, S. 43
loyalty 4–5, 6, 9–12, 14–15, 17–18
Lucero, M. 33–4
Lukes, S. 47

Macdonald, J.L. 199
Mack, G. 153
Maier, C. xvi, 31, 95, 107, 135, 140
Malinche 8
Malli, K. xv
Maniar, A. 69
manual/ mechanical task, interpreting as
    26–7, 31, 70, 126, 154, 179, 181, 190
Marks, J.H. 76
Marsh, R.M. 74
Martin, A. 35, 70, 76, 155, 182
Martin, J. 42
Martín Ruano, M.R. xv, 34, 41
Martinez Navarro, E. 96
Martínez-Gómez, A. 110, 111
Maryns, K. 180
Mason, I. 154
Masters, B. 13
May, T. 68
McCloskey, H.J. 97
McDonald, N.M. 214
McDonough, J. 32
McDowell, L. 137
McKay, C. 132
McLellan, D. xvii
McNeel, S.P. 93, 94
mediation role of interpreters 123,
    156–60, 173–4, 185–8 *see also*
    intercultural communication
medical interpreting
    –codes of conduct 33
    –impact on length of hospital stay
        70–1
    –as mediated communication 180
    –misdiagnosis 64, 79
    –in the Netherlands 66–8, 75–6, 77–8
    –within prisons 115
    –and reciprocity 77

Mendoza, R. 107–8
Messinger, D.S. 214
meta-ethics 85, 87, 93–6, 97, 98, 106–7
Meyer, B. 180
migrant and refugee community
    organisations (MRCOs) 47
migration *see also* refugees and asylum
    seekers
    –Belgium 158–60
    –interpreted asylum hearings in
        Warsaw 179–92
    –Italy 156–8
    –and the need to learn host country
        language 29, 64, 65–9
    –Poland 183–4
    –and the third sector 47–8
    –and third way politics 43–5
    –trauma-informed interpreting (TII)
        199
Mikado 72
Mikkelson, H. 28, 29
Miller, K.E. 214
Miller, V.C. 215
minority languages 26
minors 151–75
misrecognition 23–4, 25–30, 31
mistranslations 66, 190
Mitchell, D.E. 77
mixed economies of language support 48,
    50, 51–7, 59
mixed internal-external approaches to
    ethics 92–3
Mojica, E. 110, 111, 112, 114
monolingual norms 46
moral development 85–8
moral sentiments 135, 136–7, 143–5
morality 85, 109, 137 *see also* codes of
    ethics
Morgan, C. 28
Morrissey, J.P. 199
motivations for interpreters 16, 79, 217–18
Mouzelis, N. 42
Mulayim, S. 48
multicultural policy approaches 41, 43, 45
multicultural societies and recognition
    22–3
multilingual societies 42, 43, 46
Munday, J. xvi
Muscovites 11
mutual intelligibility 24

Nakane, I. 155, 191

For Product Safety Concerns and Information please contact our EU Authorised
Representative:

Easy Access System Europe

Mustamäe tee 50

10621 Tallinn

Estonia

gpsr.requests@easproject.com

www.ingramcontent.com/pod-product-compliance
Lightning Source LLC
Chambersburg PA
CBHW050420280326
41932CB00013BA/1932